IMAGES
of America

OKLAHOMA CITY'S MIDTOWN

On the Cover: Veazey's Drug, seen here on the east end of Midtown's iconic Plaza Court building at the intersection of Walker Avenue and Classen Drive, was a familiar sight across Oklahoma City. The combination of a drugstore and a soda fountain began as early as 1906 and expanded to 21 stores by the end of 1938. The chain continued until its demise in 1974. The Plaza Court building that housed them remained mostly vacant from the late 1980s until extensive renovations by forward-thinking developers were completed in 2010. It has since become one of Midtown's most recognized centerpieces. (Courtesy of the author and Typeworks.)

IMAGES
of America

OKLAHOMA CITY'S MIDTOWN

Bradley Wynn
Foreword by Dr. Bob L. Blackburn

ARCADIA
PUBLISHING

ISBN 978-1-7385-9437-8

Published by Arcadia Publishing
Charleston, South Carolina

Printed in the United States of America

Library of Congress Control Number: 2012950250

For all general information, please contact Arcadia Publishing:
Telephone 843-853-2070
Fax 843-853-0044
E-mail sales@arcadiapublishing.com
For customer service and orders:
Toll-Free 1-888-313-2665

Visit us on the Internet at www.arcadiapublishing.com

For the '89er spirit that built my hometown and gave rise to the great folks who live here.

To the Carmelite Sisters of St. Therese of Oklahoma, Franciscan Sisters of Mary, and the Sisters of Mercy, who allowed me into their home—I remain humbled by your sacrifice and dedication to our city and state.

Contents

Foreword

Today, the Midtown district of Oklahoma City is widely recognized as a high-energy neighborhood where historic preservation and inner city redevelopment are merging to create an attractive place to live, work, shop, and enjoy a vibrant urban experience. To understand this 21st-century transformation, the story must begin before there was a Midtown.

The first boundaries of Oklahoma City, established after the land run of April 22, 1889, extended from South Seventh Street to North Seventh Street and from the Santa Fe Railroad tracks on the east to Walker Avenue on the west. The area now known as the Midtown district was largely treeless prairie with a creek running north and south. A mile to the west and a mile to the south was the North Canadian River, and to the north and east would soon be farmland with small dairy operations.

The value of the land spiraled upward after 1898 with agricultural prosperity in the territory and the arrival of the Frisco Railroad that linked Oklahoma City with the markets in Kansas City, St. Louis, and Chicago. As the population surged to 10,000 by 1900 and 64,000 by 1910, the farmland northwest of town was swept up in that growth, first in 1902 when Anton Classen and John Shartel laid the first streetcar tracks north to Thirteenth Street, and then with the founding of three institutions around the edges of what would become Midtown.

The first urban pioneers to move northwest were the Sisters of St. Anthony, who decided in 1902 to build a new hospital out in the country at Northwest Ninth Street west of Walker Avenue. That same year, the Methodist Conference announced plans to build a new college and medical school at what would be Northwest Seventeenth Street and Classen Boulevard. They called the new institution Epworth College, later renamed Oklahoma City University. The third cornerstone marking the boundary of Midtown was Mercy Hospital, built south of Northwest Thirteenth Street between Dewey and Walker Avenues. By World War I, residential homes filled in most of the land between these institutions. Today, those neighborhoods are known as Heritage Hills, Mesta Park, and Gatewood.

As housing additions expanded to the north and west during the 1920s, the central commercial district grew steadily outward while retail businesses occasionally jumped to arterial intersections within residential neighborhoods. By 1923, Hudson Street was a mix of commercial buildings and apartments from Northwest Fourth Street to Northwest Tenth Street, including a new store called A.J. Kaiser Ice Cream at 1039 North Walker. To the north, at Northwest Twenty-third and Walker Avenue near the newly built Wilson Grade School, was a small commercial district with a cleaners, grocery store, drugstore, and barbershop. As this retail corridor expanded after World War II, it would be referred to as Up-Town.

The intersection at Northwest Tenth Street and Walker Avenue was even more attractive for commercial development because it was a crossroads for both streetcars and automobiles. With all of that traffic and the density of the population growing in surrounding neighborhoods, businessman John D. Thomas built Oklahoma City's first suburban shopping center on the north side of Tenth Street west of Walker Avenue. He called it Plaza Court.

Plaza Court was soon filled with a wide variety of shops and offices. One noteworthy occupant was WKY-Radio, owned by Edward King Gaylord, with studios open to the public for live performances from artists such as Bob Wills and his Texas Playboys. Another pioneering store in the Plaza Court was Crescent Market, a grocery store that would eventually move to a new suburban location farther north in Nichols Hills Plaza. The owners traced their history back to the land run of 1889.

Other new buildings soon lined the streets of Midtown. Part of the expanding medical complex between St. Anthony and Mercy hospitals was the Osler Building, which quickly competed with the Medical Arts Building on Broadway as the most prestigious address in town for medical offices. That trend would continue after World War II with the Pasteur Building, grocery stores, a Beverly's Chicken in the Rough restaurant, motels, and automobile dealerships.

By the 1960s, the balance of residential housing and commercial services in Midtown was changing the landscape. Suburban developments continued moving farther and farther from downtown, while the central business district suffered from aging buildings, urban renewal, and the flight of retail to shopping malls such as Penn Square, opened in 1960, and Shepherd Mall, opening in 1964. By 1969, when Oklahoma City adopted its first historic preservation ordinance to protect residential neighborhoods, the line was drawn in the sand at Thirteenth Street on the southern edge of Heritage Hills and Mesta Park. The aging houses of Midtown were either converted to rooming homes, abandoned, or demolished.

With declining residential density on three sides and the move of Mercy Hospital to the far north side of town in the 1970s, Midtown sank into a no-man's-land of underutilized buildings and vacant lots. City planners, who viewed the district as a place to get through, reconfigured streets as one-way speed corridors. One prominent city leader even suggested that the area be bulldozed and converted to an urban golf course. Fortunately, the urge and political support for urban renewal and its destructive forces remained downtown and to the east in what would become the new Health Sciences Center. Many of the historic structures of Midtown survived through neglect, while the borders of the district were secured by St. Anthony Hospital on the west, church row on the east, and Heritage Hills on the north.

The first efforts at redevelopment in Midtown came with the frenzied oil and gas boom of the late 1970s and early 1980s. Although most of the efforts were underfunded and unable to survive the economic crash that started in 1982, a few urban pioneers put down roots with businesses such as Kaiser's Ice Cream and Brown's Bakery. Then, as the city was emerging from economic stagnation, a flicker of hope followed the passage of funding for the Metropolitan Area Projects, better known as MAPS, and recovery from the tragic bombing of the Alfred P. Murrah Federal Building in 1995.

The transformation of the inner city gradually spread from the downtown business district and Bricktown to adjacent neighborhoods, including Auto Alley, the Arts District, the River, and Midtown. In 2006, the eyes of the community turned to Midtown when the investment group of Bob Howard, Mickey Clagg, and Chris Fleming restored and revitalized the iconic Plaza Court Building. Since that time, more than 20 buildings in the Midtown District have been restored, rehabilitated for adaptive reuse, or constructed.

Midtown, built at the crossroads of Oklahoma City, is once again a vital part of the urban experience.

—Dr. Bob L. Blackburn

ACKNOWLEDGMENTS

I am an urban archaeologist, and I love uncovering the stories of my hometown's past. For this book, I chose to delve into Oklahoma City's Midtown community. Midtown covers nearly 400 square acres, making it impossible to cover every aspect or include each photograph of its history in these limited pages. There is no doubt, upon the book's release, that a number of new images and stories will emerge that I will wish were included. I have strived to include what was made available at the time and the most significant and personal moments defining the area's rich and multilayered history.

The Midtown community is filled with amazing people and I appreciate each of them for helping me bring this book to fruition. I extend a special thank-you to those I consider Midtown's mentors and leaders, Greg Banta, Mickey Clagg, Chris Fleming, Randy Floyd, Bob Howard, Michael Smith, and many others who devoted much toward Midtown's development and future. I especially thank historian Dr. Bob Blackburn, the executive director of the Oklahoma History Center, for his support and contribution to this book and its foreword.

I extend a hearty thank-you to fellow historians William Hider, Larry "Buddy" Johnson, Steve Lackmeyer, Doug Loudenback, Catherine Montgomery, Beverly Mossman, Rachael Mossman, Terry Zinn, RetroMetroOKC.org, and OKCHistory.org.

A special thanks to Clancy's Grill, inside the Physicians and Surgeons building lobby at 1211 North Shartel Avenue, where owners Susan and Clancy allowed me to host meetings with Midtown folks in my "office" booth while researching, writing, and eating my fill of their amazing food.

For allowing me to share their photographs and memories, a heartfelt thank-you to the following: Cathy Ambler, William Boulton, Ramona Carey, Larry Chase, Nessa Chan, Sister Immaculata Commet, Robin Davison, Donald Ellis, Sarah Evans, Matt Goad, Malcolm Haney, Charles Harris, Garrett Johnston, Claudia Lovelace, Sammy Lovelace, Rebecca Morton, Daniel Opplinger, Cheryl Pernell, Sister Rose Power, Lynne Rostochil, Harrison Schroer, Jacquelyn Slater.

To my publisher and their amazing team, Maggie Bullwinkel, David Mandel, Jill Nunn, Amy Perryman, Mary Margaret Schley, Leigh Scott, and Winnie Timmons, thank you! Trust me—they had their hands full! To my cousin Robbin Davis for her support and input. To my "mom" Stella Davis and Faye "Nanny" Keller for their excitement and encouragement. Finally, to my wife and son—thank you for letting me out to play one more time.

Midtown's story continues. If you or someone you know, has more information or images about Midtown and its past, please contact author Bradley Wynn at PO Box 711, Oklahoma City, OK 73101-0711.

Introduction

When 200 million acres of unassigned land in the heart of what would become the future state of Oklahoma opened to settlement in 1889 an estimated 100,000 settlers surged to the designated borders in Indian Territory dubbed "Oklahoma country." According to the Homestead Act of 1862, signed by Abraham Lincoln, the title to 160-acre lots could be claimed by settlers who agreed to live on and improve the land for two years. In support of the Homestead Act, author Horace Greely touted, "Go west, young man, go west," and westward they came.

According to the Oklahoma Historical Society, "Prior to the land opening, the Southern Kansas Railway (later the Atchison, Topeka and Santa Fe Railway) built a line from the Kansas-Oklahoma border to Purcell, Indian Territory. At the North Canadian River, a watering stop along that line, known as Oklahoma Station, was established in February 1887. A post office at Oklahoma Station opened on December 30, 1887. The post office was renamed Oklahoma on December 18, 1888, and finally, Oklahoma City on July 1, 1923."

Using every mode of conveyance from horseback to wagons, buggies, bicycles, and racing sulkies, a surge of humanity arrived at the borders of what would become Canadian, Cleveland, Kingfisher, Logan, Oklahoma, and Payne Counties and impatiently waited for a signal that would announce the lands open to settlement at noon on Monday, April 22, 1889. Along the northern boundaries, 15 trains from Kansas waited while another 6 from Texas sat along the southern line, each jammed with passengers and possessions.

At Santa Fe Railroad's Oklahoma Station, which would become Oklahoma City, a southbound train arrived the night before filled with eager settlers and was met by four companies of United States infantry who arrived Saturday night by special car. The soldiers, under the command of Brig. Gen. Wesley Merritt, were sent from Missouri into the territory to maintain order in the absence of a governmental authority. The soldiers prevented anyone from disembarking and entering the new lands until the designated time, although a few managed to slink away into the night, becoming Oklahoma "Sooners." Prior to the arrival of soldier or settler, 320 acres of land was set aside for the formation of Oklahoma City, which was established under townsite legislation of the public domain, enacted in 1844. Much of this acreage was cleared by hand and control burned to prepare it for claim staking. All through Sunday night, train cars carried in tons of lumber, prefabricated buildings, household goods, personal belongings, and all other necessary materials to build a new town. It nearly overwhelmed the newly constructed depot, causing a scene far different from earlier in the day.

Before the controlled chaos began, Oklahoma Station was comprised of only the railroad depot, which was the home of the railway agent, post office building, a government building, a boarding house, and the offices of a stagecoach company in a former stockade. They were surrounded by a vast virgin landscape intersected by the North Canadian River, which flowed from the northwest to the southeast. According to eyewitness and author Irving Geff's, *First Eight Months of Oklahoma City*, printed in 1890, the riverbanks were covered by a wild collection of coffee bean, cottonwood, elm, hackberry, oak, and walnut trees. Away from the river, hundreds of acres were chiefly composed of white oaks. The expanse was teeming with a diverse assortment of wildlife that included badgers, bears, catamounts, deer, lynx, opossums, raccoons, squirrels, and wolves. The uplands were home to a large collection of chickens, quail, and turkeys. This serene landscape was the calm before the storm.

At high noon, a bugle call sounded over the horizon as soldiers stationed wide distances apart fired their carbine pistols, rifles, or cannon, initiating the most unusual and unique moment world history ever recorded. The sound from so many people racing into the vast unknown was a clamor that historians have failed to describe adequately over time. Within that surge of settlement came those who would literally carve and shape what would become Oklahoma City.

By that evening, Oklahoma City had become a city of tents. Within 25 days, nearly 1,700 permanent structures stood along a grid of new streets. Within 10 years the city's population increased from 4,151 to 10,037 and with a healthy agricultural income the commercial areas of Oklahoma City experienced a huge growth. Demand for new housing prompted further expansion northward through new plats past Northwest Seventh Street to Northwest Thirteenth Street, thereby giving birth to Midtown.

Like so much of Oklahoma City, Midtown was bustling with entrepreneurs and new families out of which came new businesses and the need for new housing. Education also became key to the advancement and development of Oklahoma City. Institutes took shape and became Emerson and Washington schools. Within a few short years, Oklahoma City established Central High School, the first public-funded high school in the state, with nearly 2,000 students.

The sprawl would include the establishment of an extensive Midtown health care network that included St. Anthony Hospital (the first in Oklahoma), Oklahoma General (Mercy Hospital), Wesley Hospital, and numerous physician offices and laboratories housed in places like the Osler Medical and Pasteur buildings. Commercial development included the two-story iconic Plaza Court building—home to KOCY, WKY, Veazey's Pharmacy, and Crescent Market (Oklahoma City's first grocery store), to name only a few.

Three orders of Catholic sisters worked side by side in caring for the citizens surrounding them, which included the Sisters of St. Francis and the Sisters of Mercy, whose orders established St. Anthony and Mercy Hospitals. The third was the Carmelite Sisters of St. Therese of the Infant Jesus, whose focus centered on education and whose efforts established Oklahoma's first kindergarten and later the Villa Theresa Catholic School.

The need for hotels and residential space soared and brought forth the Marion Hotel—one of Oklahoma City's oldest commercial structures still standing—and the Rockwall, Palo Alto, Hadden Hall, and Mayfair apartments. Midtown residents became deeply rooted in their faiths as well, as Church Row along Robinson Avenue would attest. It is here and among a small scattering of churches throughout Midtown that every Christian denomination was represented, as well as a synagogue along Broadway Circle. As a result, Midtown residents are surrounded by a well-rounded legacy of community spirit, which is especially evident in current efforts to renovate and revitalize the districts within it, insuring that generations to come will have a ringside seat to the wonders yet to unfold.

One

A Run for the Future

The birth of Midtown is a direct result of Oklahoma City's own birth and unprecedented growth. The opening of unassigned lands on April 22, 1889, had no match of its kind anywhere in the world or in the historic annals of man. It was unique only to Oklahoma, and such an event on such a scale has never been duplicated or exceeded since.

In less than a month after its founding, Oklahoma City had established itself as a rival to surrounding towns and a contender to becoming the future state's capital city, a very hot and contentious battle. It was this drive that broke the new city free of its growing pains and allowed entrepreneurs and bold innovators to establish a firm foothold toward the future. Within just 10 years, their efforts would transform the cityscape into a thriving community complete with the first streetcar and interurban rail system, advanced medical care facilities, universities, and much more.

One visionary was an attorney from Chicago named Anton Classen, who arrived with the land rush and, through his appointment to the US Land Office by President McKinley, realized the value and potential the new city offered in the West. With his investment and vision for a future metropolis rivaling larger cities eastward, Classen inspired and drew forth many other visionaries, who in turn would also invest their wealth, knowledge, and business savvy into transforming the former tent city into what would become one of the most modern and beloved cities in America today.

Classen first set aside land for public use and parks, planted trees, and eventually established what would become Heritage Hills. With the aid of businessman John W. Shartel, they laid the tracks that established the city streetcar and interurban lines, removing the barrier of distance from employment, shopping, and education. This further enhanced Midtown's own development. In less than 25 years, Oklahoma City would become the state's capital, build its first of many skyscrapers, and give rise to a community located midway between the downtown core and the drive of urban expansion in the north.

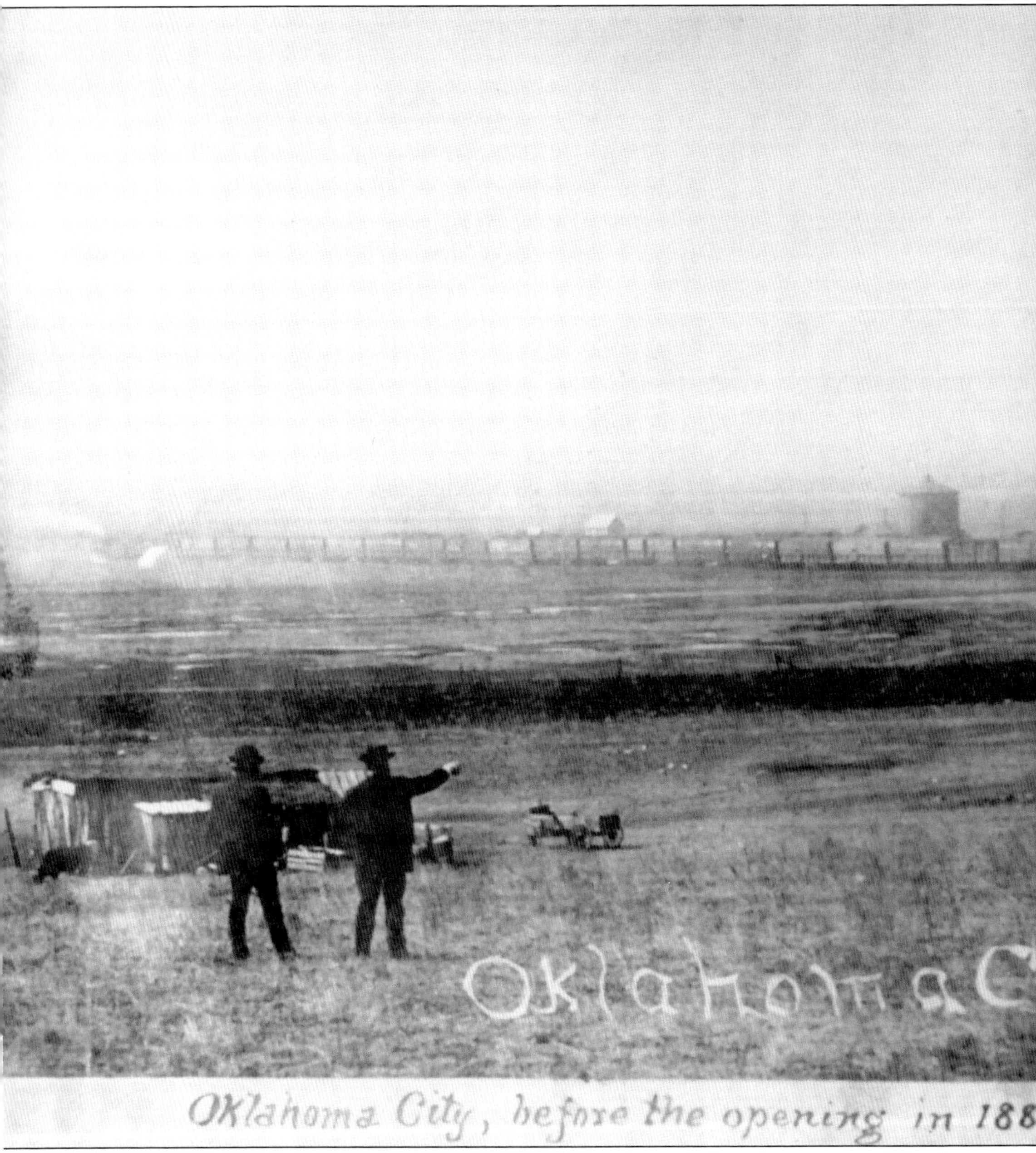

Oklahoma Station is pictured here approximately two hours before the unassigned lands were opened to settlement. Two men stand on land that became Brick Town and faces what will eventually become downtown Oklahoma City 100 years later. Numerous trains came into the station for days leading up to the opening to deliver prefabricated buildings, lumber, household goods, and other goods and tools necessary for a new beginning. In many cases, people tried to disembark from the trains in attempts to stake a claim early, but soldiers from the Missouri 5th

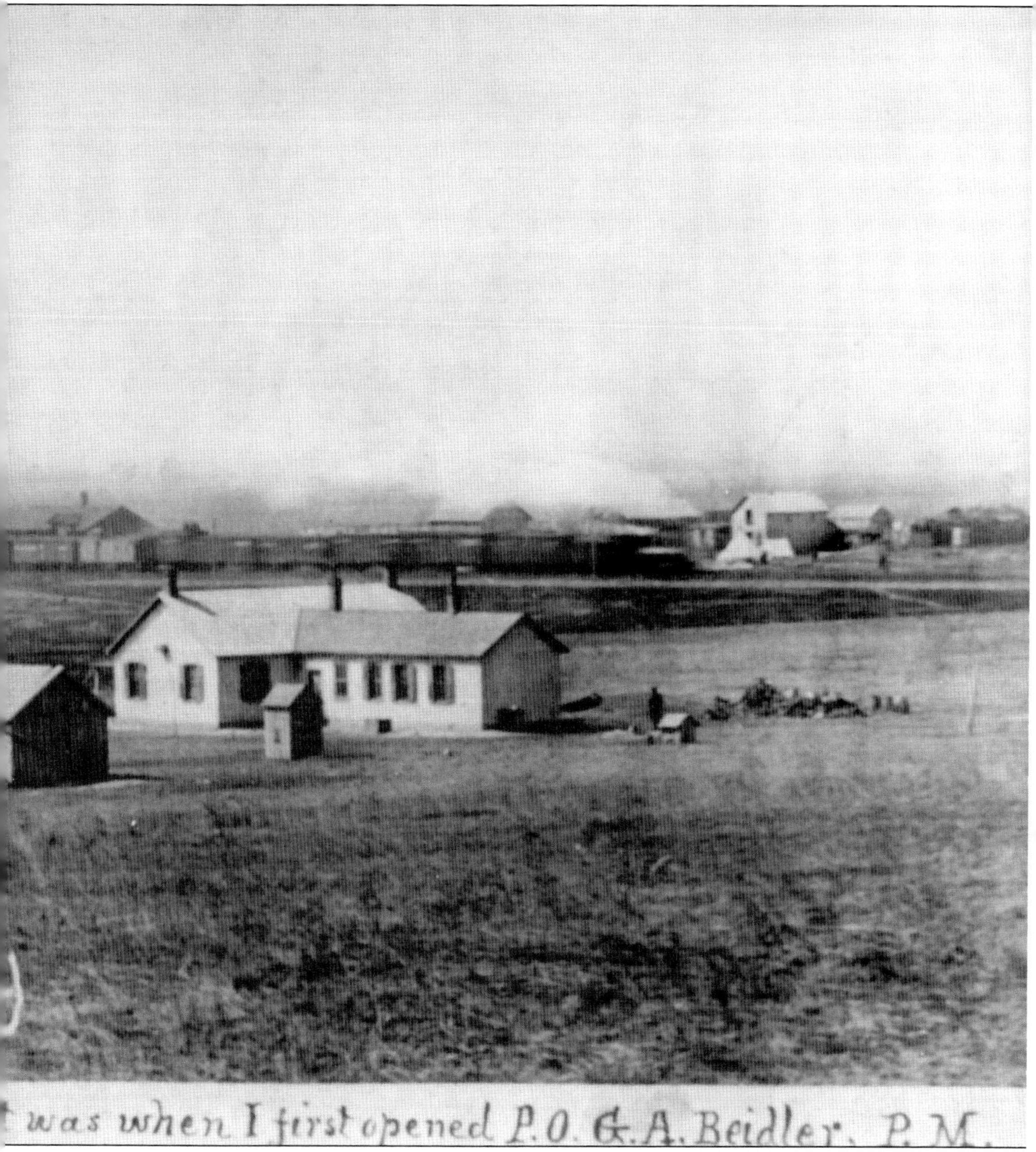

Calvary, under the command of Brigadier General Merritt arrived days before to prevent such occurrences and to keep the peace after the land rush. However, some managed to sneak into the territory, illegally claiming lands. These men and women were referred to as Sooners; hence, Oklahoma's nicknamed the "Sooner State." (Courtesy of Oklahoma City Central High Collection and RetroMetroOKC.org.)

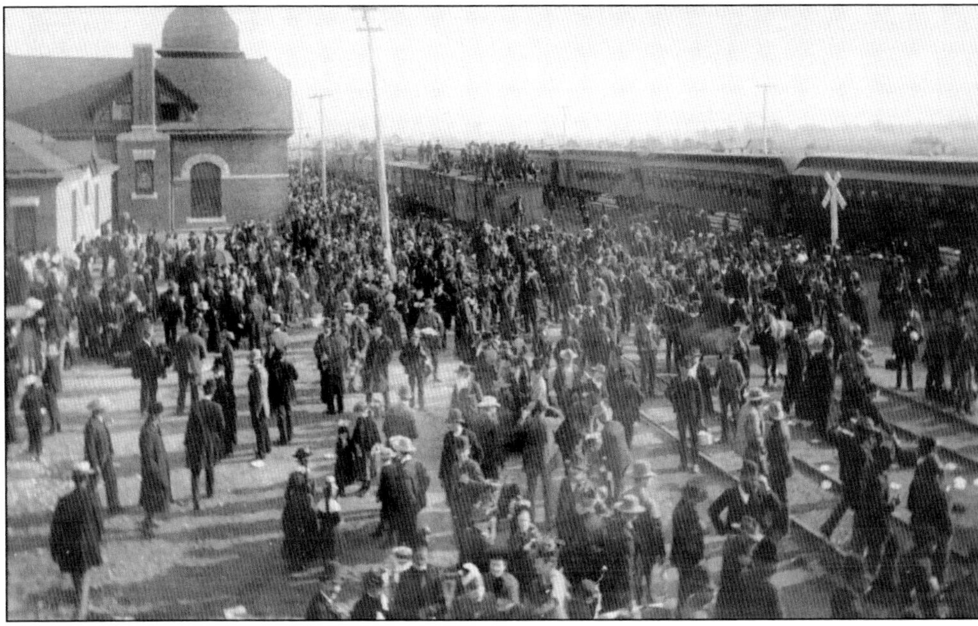

Settlers, like those pictured here, gathered along the territorial borders on numerous trains backed up end-to-end or in large bands of wagons to wait for the assigned time they would be allowed to enter the future state of Oklahoma and claim land promised by the Homestead Act. The image above captures trains backed up at Arkansas City, Kansas, depots. The image below is of a 3.5-mile-long "Boomer" train of 4,000 covered wagons crossing the Salt Fork of the Arkansas River, approximately 40 miles south of the Kansas border via a railroad bridge. Both images were taken on the morning of April 22, 1889. (Both, courtesy of the Oklahoma Historical Society.)

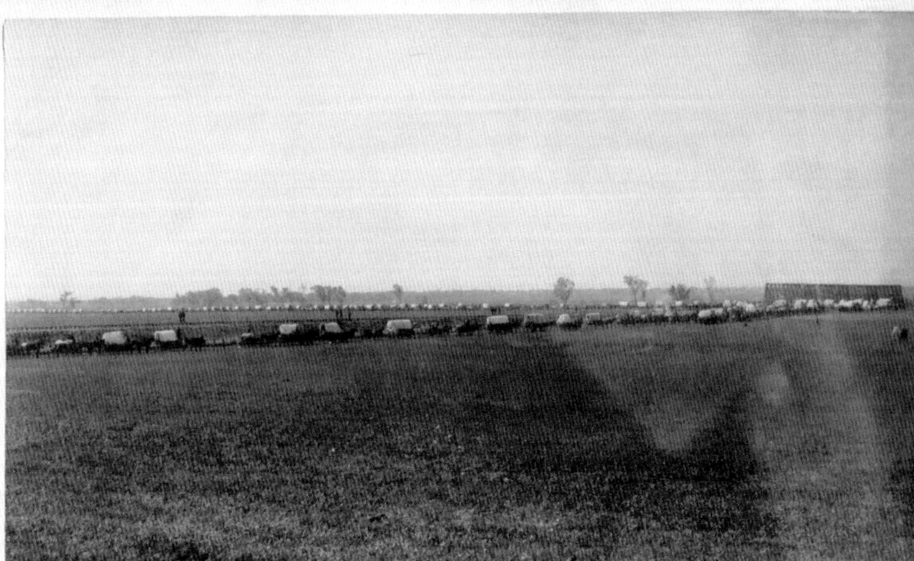

4,000 Wagons crossing Salt Fork River on R. R. Bridge.
Photographed By
W. S. Prettyman, Arkansas City, Kas.

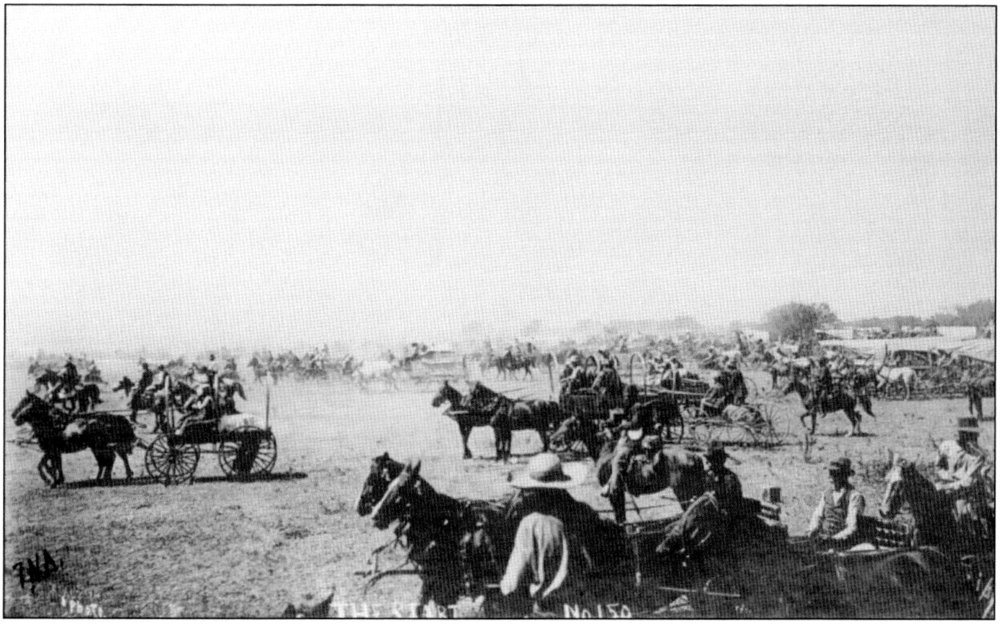

After the signal opening the unassigned lands, a massive wave of men, women, and children swarmed into the territory on every conveyance possible, as seen in the image above. In Oklahoma City, lots were claimed by enterprising folk who leapt from numerous train cars along Santa Fe's railroad tracks. The trains that brought them also bore prefabricated buildings and materials needed to build a new city. (Courtesy of the Oklahoma Historical Society.)

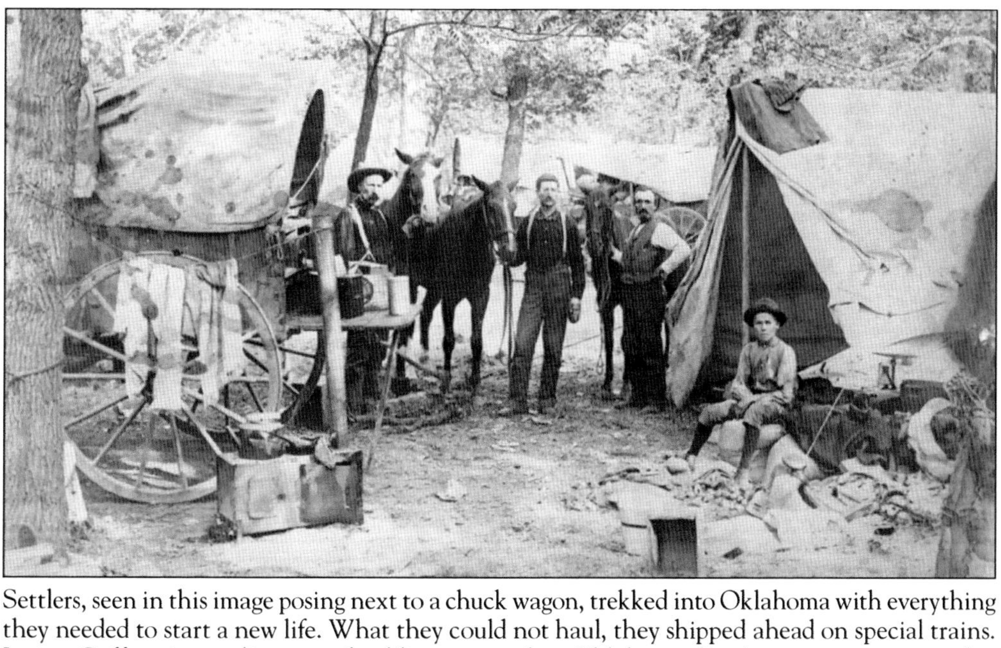

Settlers, seen in this image posing next to a chuck wagon, trekked into Oklahoma with everything they needed to start a new life. What they could not haul, they shipped ahead on special trains. Irving Geffs, a journalist turned soldier assigned to Oklahoma City's contingent, wrote his eyewitness account titled *The First Eight Months of Oklahoma City*, under the pen name of "Bunky." (Courtesy of the Oklahoma Historical Society.)

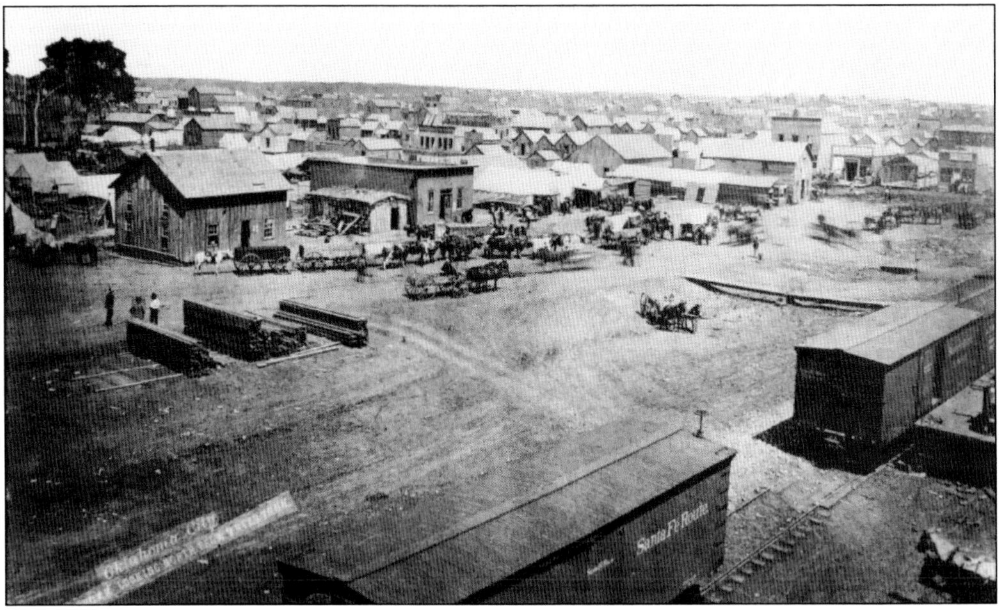

When Oklahoma City's newest residents settled down that first night, a man named Joe searched for his missing mule. Around 10:00 p.m., another settler found the animal and bellowed, "Oh Joe, here's your mule!" Because the night was so quiet, his call was heard at a long distance. It was repeated by each of the 10,000 new settlers, one after the other. The image above is of Oklahoma City 25 days later. (Courtesy of the Oklahoma Historical Society.)

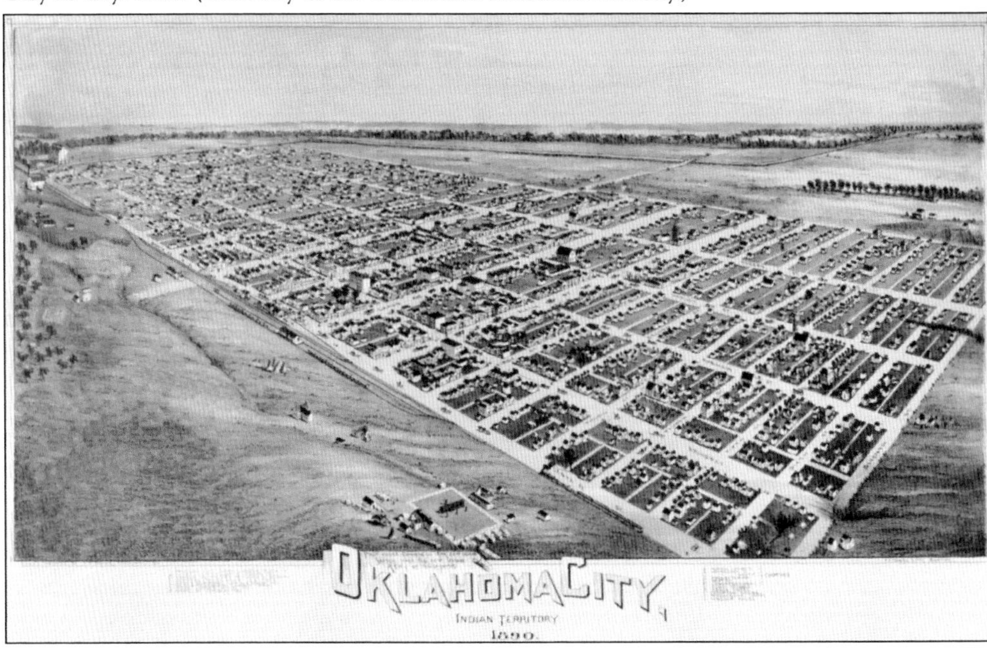

This bird's-eye view is an early map of Oklahoma City produced by T.M. Fowler in 1890. The city boundaries eventually grew beyond farms and homesteads when the Metropolitan Railway Company, renamed later to Oklahoma City Railway Company, installed light rail lines. The company was operated by business leaders and early city advocates Anton Classen and John W. Shartel. (Courtesy of the Oklahoma Historical Society.)

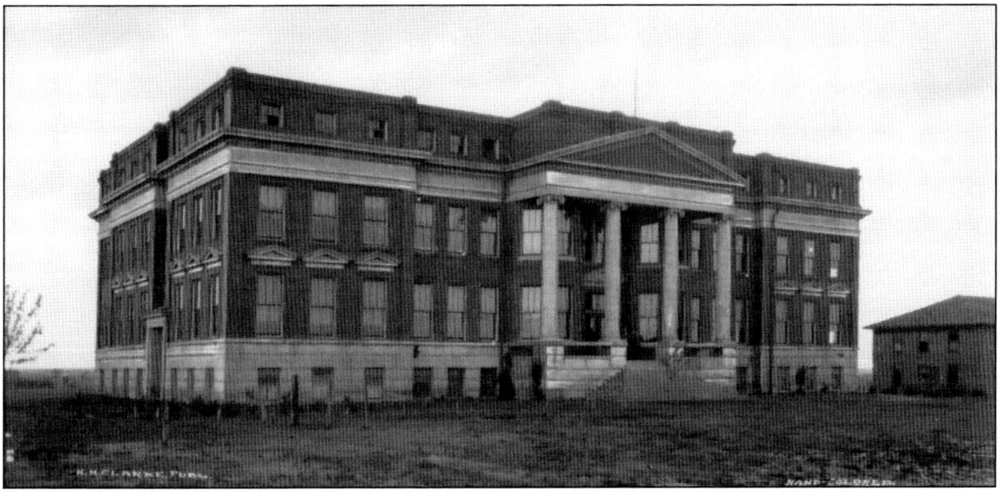

In the fall of 1901, Anton Classen, Charles Colcord, J.B. Zeigler, Margaret McKinley, and John W. Shartel acquired 360 acres from McKinley Avenue to Walker Avenue, bordered by Northwest Sixteenth and Twenty-third Streets to form the University Development Company. Fifty-two of the acres were given to the creation of Epworth University, the state's first college and precursor to Oklahoma City University. Surrounding acres were sold as lots to benefit the university and begin expansion of Oklahoma City. The cornerstone was laid April 1, 1903, and the main building, as seen above with the adjacent two-story Girl's Hall, featured 32 rooms, steam heat, baths, electric lighting, and a large dining hall. Below, Epworth is seen in the background of the University Station Line stop, an interurban trolley system. The building remains standing today behind the Classen School of Advanced Studies, named in honor of Anton Classen. (Both, courtesy of the Oklahoma Historical Society.)

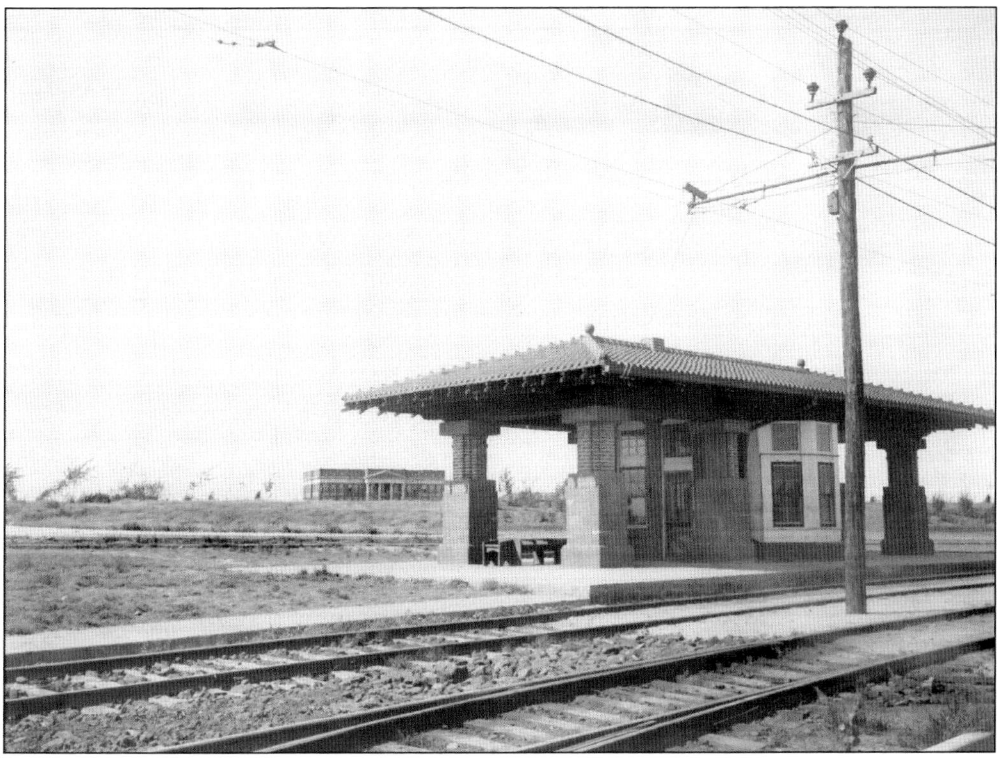

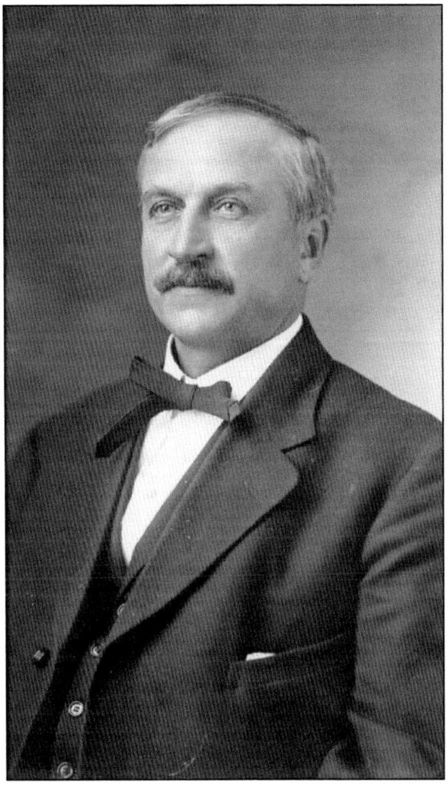

Pres. William McKinley appointed Anton Classen, an attorney from Chicago, as a receiver in the US Land Office after making his run into Oklahoma City in 1889. Realizing how important city development was, Classen speculated in land—including a farm north of Northwest Thirteenth Street. He transformed parcels of it into public parks and planted numerous trees. The area developed into Highland Park Addition, later renamed Heritage Hills. He joined forces with businessman John W. Shartel (pictured below) in establishing the Oklahoma City Railway Company. Together they laid a mass-transit system that became a catalyst for Oklahoma City's urban sprawl. As a member of the city's German community, Classen helped establish the University of Oklahoma, Oklahoma City University, and the First German Methodist Church at Northwest Eighth Street and Lee Avenue in addition to becoming a prominent developer and philanthropist for Oklahoma City. (Both, courtesy of the Oklahoma Historical Society.)

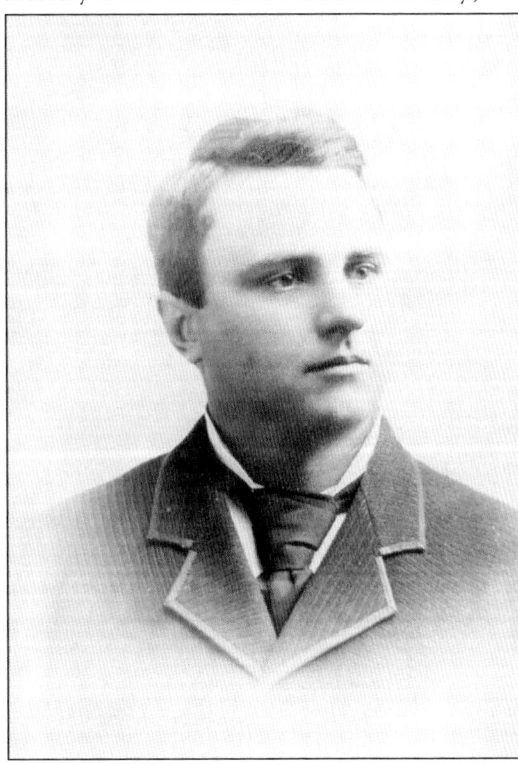

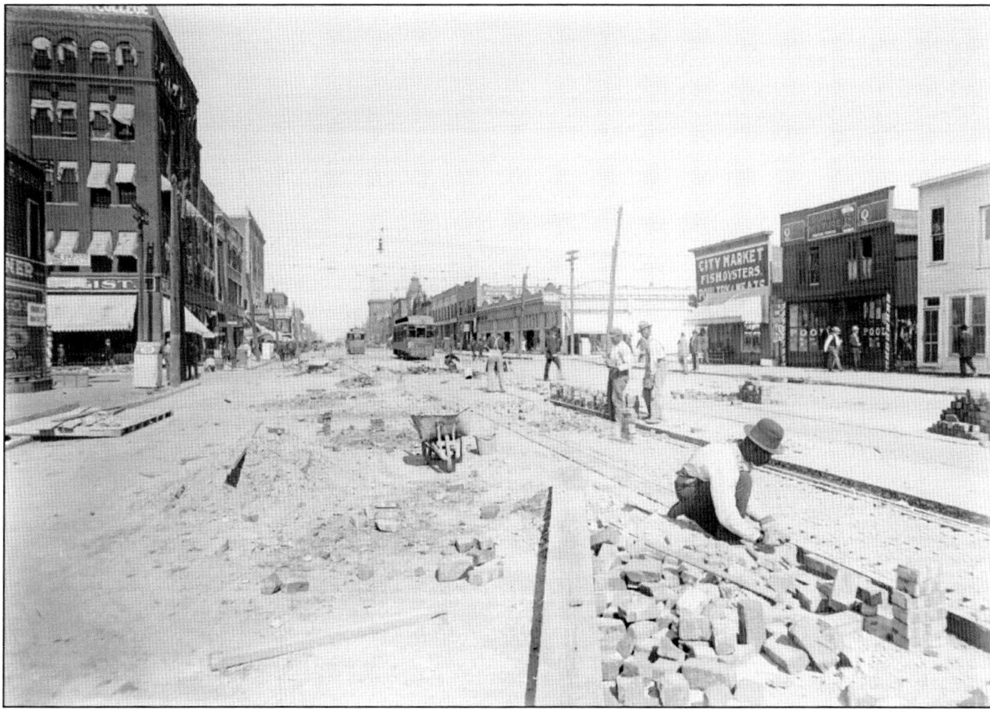

The Oklahoma Railway Company installed and operated streetcar lines across the cityscape, as seen here, enabling faster urban growth. The company expanded operations to include El Reno, Guthrie, and Norman. As World War II approached, the company shifted from rail to bus service. The Company gradually ceased rail operations, selling its rail lines to the Santa Fe and Rock Island companies around 1947. (Courtesy of the Oklahoma Historical Society.)

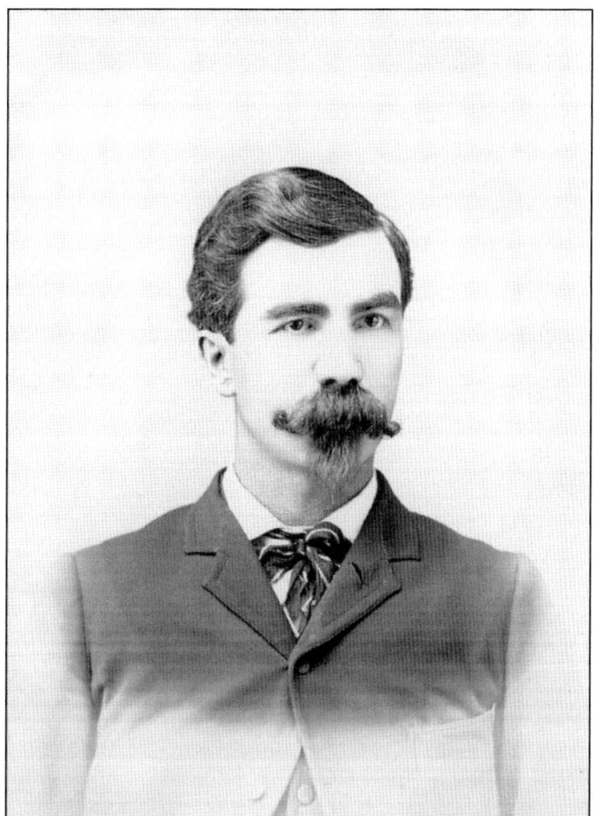

Frank M. Gault, an '89er, sold his cornfield to the Sisters of Francis, through Thomas O'Keefe in February 1899. A 25-bed facility was built there, becoming Oklahoma's first hospital on November 23, 1899. Gault became a lawman and after retirement became president of the State Board of Agriculture, threatening to shoot any employee stealing from the state under his watch. (Courtesy of the Oklahoma Historical Society.)

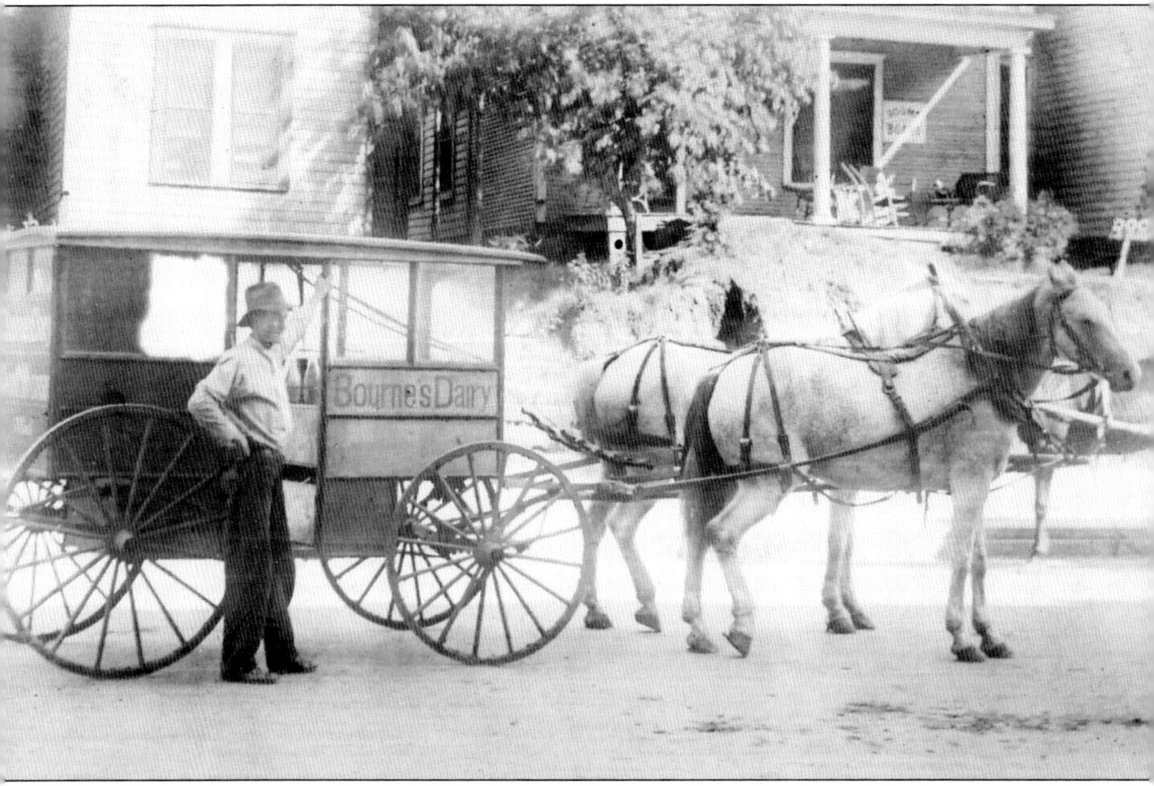

This Bourne's Dairy wagon is driven by Bert Bourne and his team of horses, Whitey and Spec in 1912. The Dairy was established by Elias Whitfield Bourne's family, arriving in a covered wagon driving three cows, on April 22, 1889. Their claim would become Northwest Thirteenth and Broadway Avenue and today encompasses the eastern portion of the Midtown district. The dairy migrated north to Northwest Fifty-eighth Street and Eastern Avenue, as the city expanded encompassing where the Western Heritage Center and Cowboy Hall of Fame stand today. Bert described how his well-trained team turned the wagon around themselves as he walked to the front door at the end of their route. The dairy was forced to utilize trucks for deliveries for safety reasons by 1915. It was milking around 200 cows by the 1920s. The family sold the dairy in 1944 and all operations ceased. The original farm building near Northwest Fifty-eighth still stands, across from the Remington racetrack and behind the Family Dollar store as of this writing. (Courtesy of the Oklahoma Historical Society.)

Two

Laying the Foundation

Midtown's long-term endurance and success through the ups and downs posed to it through the decades is a direct result of its roots, the people and places that secured a foothold in a mix of residential and commercial properties. It is reflected in the diversity of the businesses and made strong by its educational institutions. Extended residential and job opportunities kept the people who built and maintained Midtown within the community that everything revolved around.

Education was tantamount to the city's future, and construction of the state's only high school of its caliber in the Midtown area made a huge social impact. The high school was a massive structure, easily recognized, and offered the latest in advanced courses with the newest technology and styles. The latter is represented by ornate details that included tile, stone, and woodwork.

The introduction of rail service kept locals and their spending within the community. The addition of the state's, and possibly the nation's, first shopping center—in the guise of the Plaza Court building—provided a much needed retail space. Oklahoma's earliest and most trusted market, the Crescent Market, was the most notable diver of this economy. This was also the first time in Oklahoma City that the design of a building was driven by the frequent use of the automobile.

The addition to residential housing and hotel accommodations, the neighborhood's population increased along with light rail service through the area. The same service was also used to transport tons of equipment and building materials to construct the infrastructure and new buildings rising up across Midtown like the Osler Medical building, Mid-Continent Life building, and the continued expansion of St. Anthony Hospital.

Midtown was quickly growing to provide nearly every necessary service, including food, health, work, living, and play. Midtown was laying the foundation upon which it would grow in the years ahead.

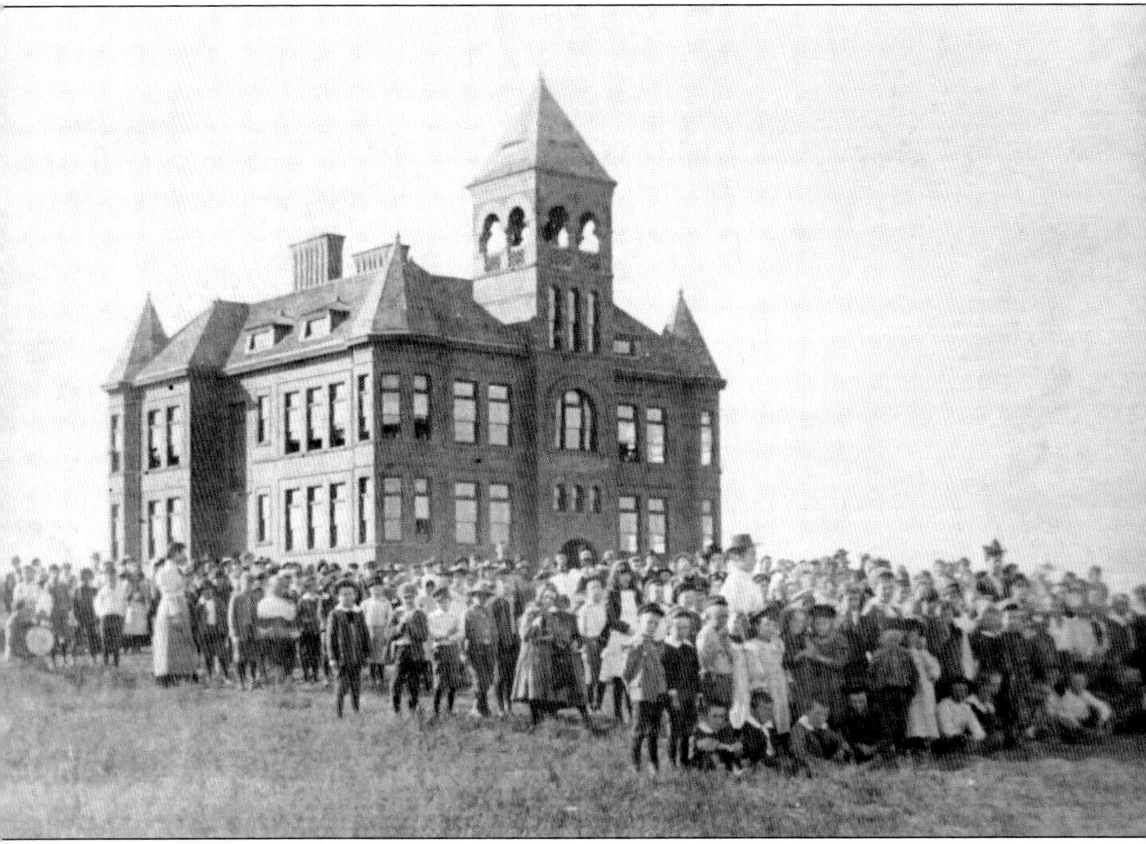

Oklahoma City's education system began with the Emerson and Washington schools as early as 1889. Emerson is pictured above shortly after opening. These were considered private schools as they received no public funding and had no legal authority to do so. The newly opened unassigned lands and formation of Oklahoma City made public education possible, and the first public high school, heralded as a major cultural achievement for the city, opened in 1892. That first class was held at 319 West California Avenue in a one-story storefront building. The first instructor, Mary D. Couch, was 22 years old and recently married. She may have introduced her class to advanced studies. (Courtesy of the Oklahoma Historical Society.)

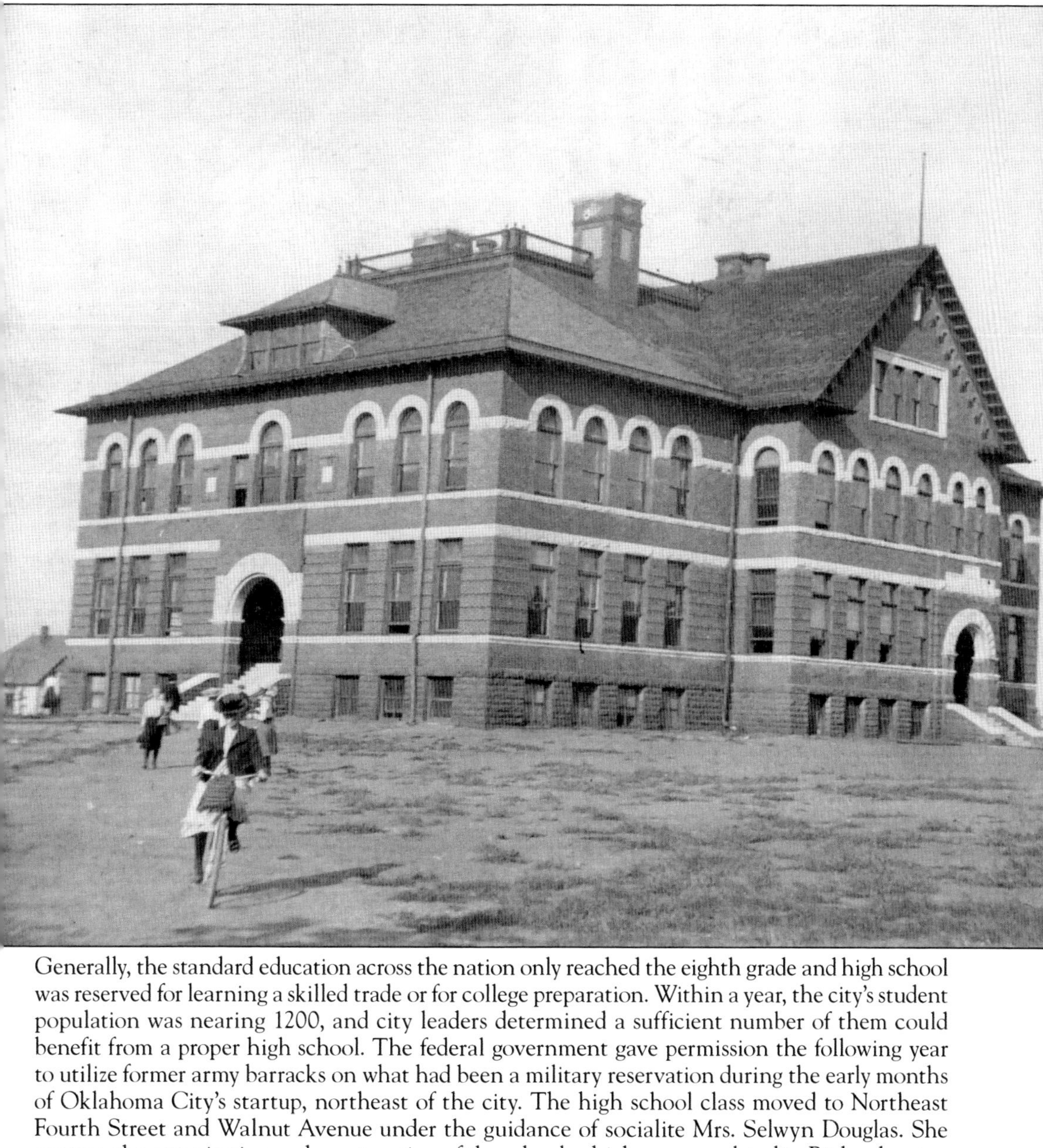

Generally, the standard education across the nation only reached the eighth grade and high school was reserved for learning a skilled trade or for college preparation. Within a year, the city's student population was nearing 1200, and city leaders determined a sufficient number of them could benefit from a proper high school. The federal government gave permission the following year to utilize former army barracks on what had been a military reservation during the early months of Oklahoma City's startup, northeast of the city. The high school class moved to Northeast Fourth Street and Walnut Avenue under the guidance of socialite Mrs. Selwyn Douglas. She oversaw the organization and construction of the school, which was completed in Richardsonian Romanesque style (see above image) and was unofficially called Irving High School sometime in between 1893–1894. (Courtesy of the Oklahoma Historical Society.)

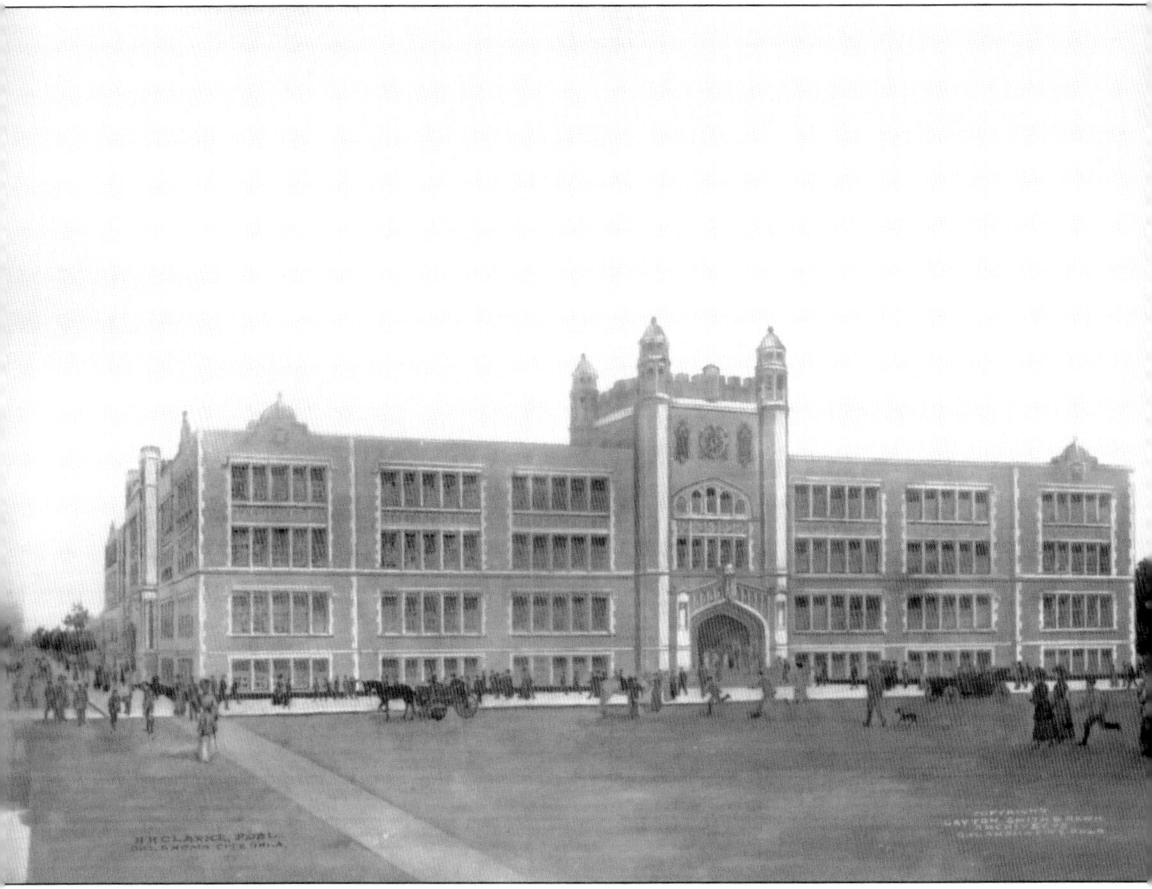

Unfortunately, a fire during the third year forced the students to gather at 119 Northwest Third Street in a Methodist Church, which would eventually become St. Luke's. Classes were not able to resume at Irving until about the following year. A population and building boom in Oklahoma City occurred 1909–1910, inspiring a permanent home for the Oklahoma City high school. Local architects Solomon Layton, Hawk, and Smith designed an impressive Collegiate Gothic–styled multistory building along the southern end of Church Row, at 801 North Robinson Avenue. Eventually the lands surrounding the school on Military Hill were given over to homesteading, although Irving would remain a public school into the 1950s. At some point a new building was erected, most likely in the 1930s. Classes began in the new Oklahoma City High School September 11, 1910 according to official records. However, alumni reports show classes started in 1909, while the school was still under construction so the 1910 graduating class could hold ceremonies in the new building. (Courtesy of the Oklahoma Historical Society.)

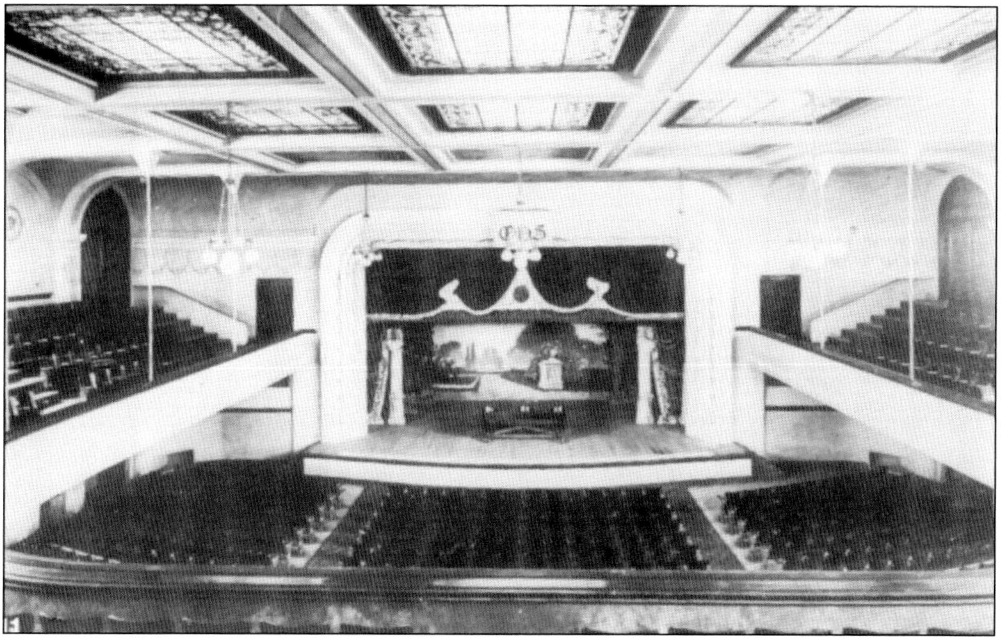

The new high school offered numerous features that enabled its students to receive a complete education. Among them were an auditorium as seen in an early image above and below after a later remodel. It featured a two-tiered gymnasium, swimming pool, and specially equipped classrooms for such courses as home economics and shop. With the addition of Classen Junior High in 1919 to the west and a proposed new high school in Capital Hill to the south, Oklahoma City High School's name was changed to Central High School in 1926. However, its students and alumni continued referring to it as Central for some time in the school's newsletter *Sooner Spirit* and in city newspapers. (Both, courtesy of the Oklahoma Historical Society.)

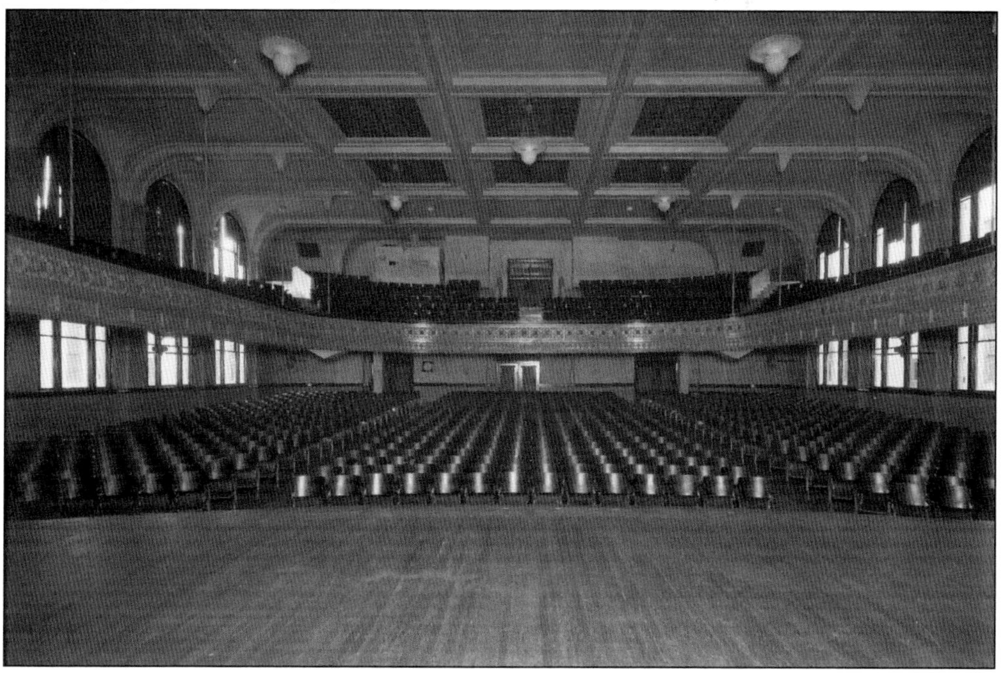

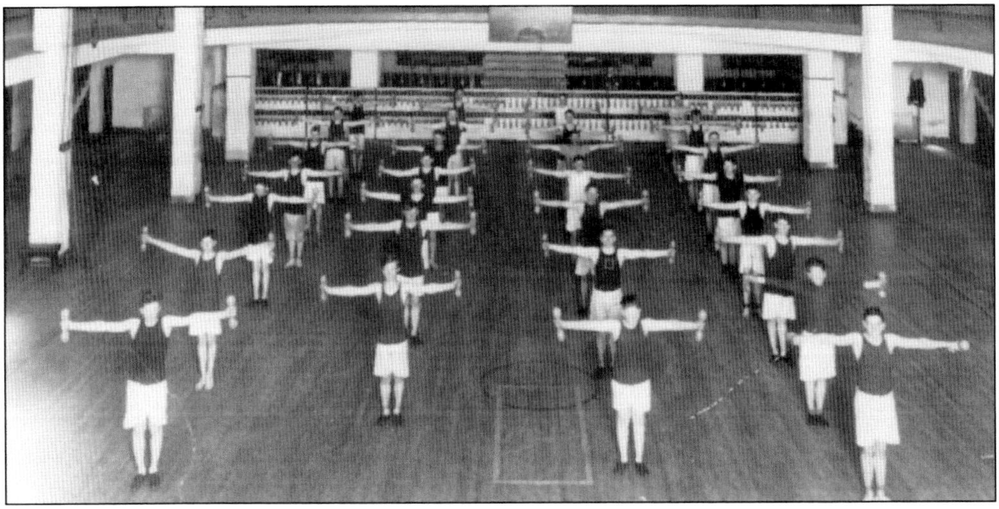

Central High School operated up until the mid-1950s, when urban sprawl presented a decline in student enrollment. The school ceased operating as a high school around 1968 when it was reclassified as a junior high. The property was sold by the school board to the Southwestern Bell Corporation in 1981, which remodeled the former institution into its new offices, Bell Central. A museum of school artifacts and a portion of the interior were preserved near the old principal's office. Today, the property is being renovated to accommodate the Oklahoma City University law program so that once more higher learning will fill the walls of this unique Midtown landmark. In the image above, students are vigorously exercising in Central High School's advanced gymnasium. Below is a view inside one of Central's elaborate school hallways across from its auditoriums. (Both, courtesy of the Oklahoma Historical Society.)

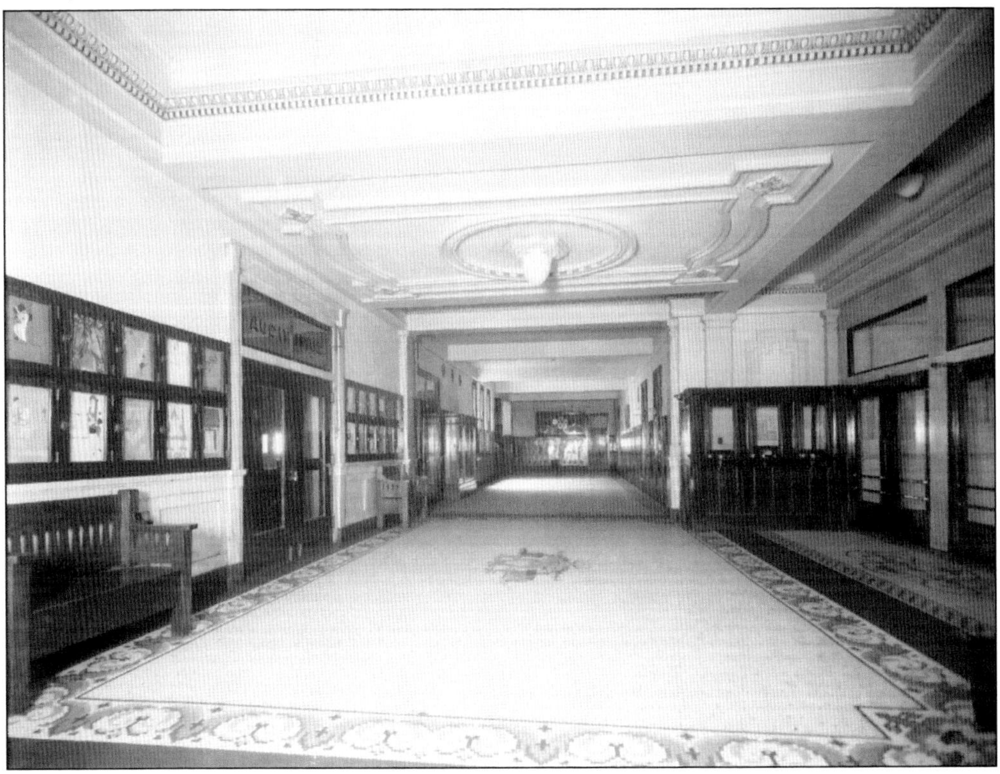

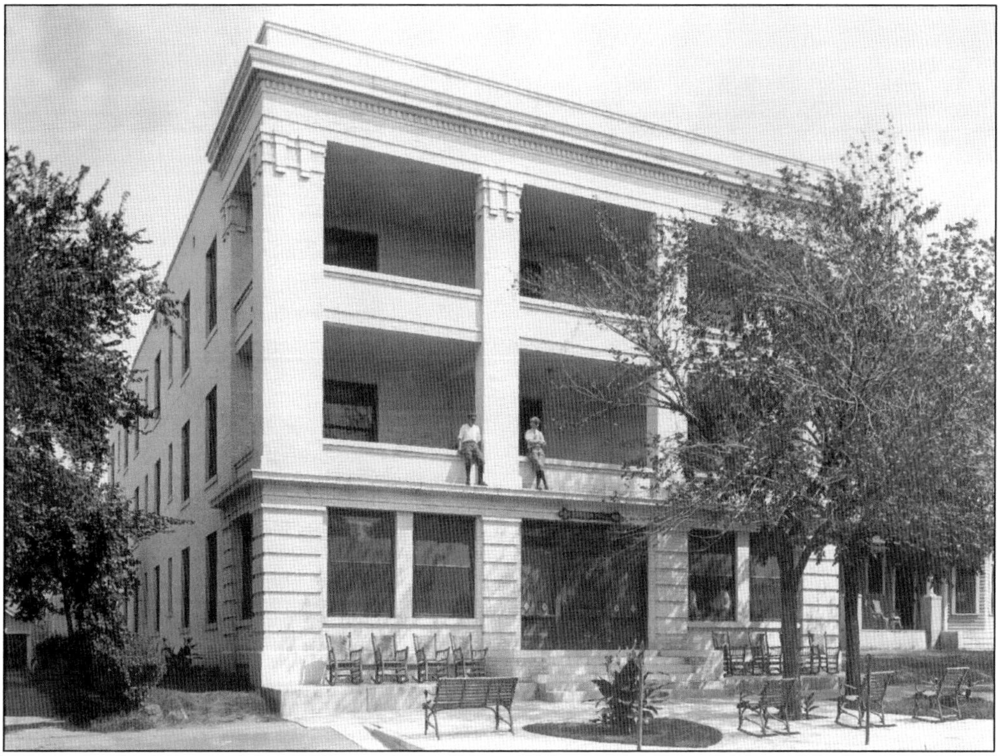

Constructed around 1910 at 215 Northwest Tenth Street, Hadden Hall offered furnished apartments until the early to mid-1920s, when it was converted to a hotel. The above image depicts two daring lads on Hadden's second story ledge in 1912. Below the converted Hadden Hall Hotel receives guests. The sign at left advertises rooms equipped with General Electric refrigerators. The longest resident at Hadden Hall was Helen Ferris in apartment six, who rented the room after being hired as an English teacher at nearby Central High School around 1912. She resided there until her death in 1951. She was the first female elected as vice-principal and was highly loved by the students and community. Her funeral was held in the school's auditorium. The building also served as home to Traveler's Aid but stood vacant through much of the 1990s until it was acquired and renovated into 18 luxury apartments in 2011. (Both, courtesy of Donald Ellis.)

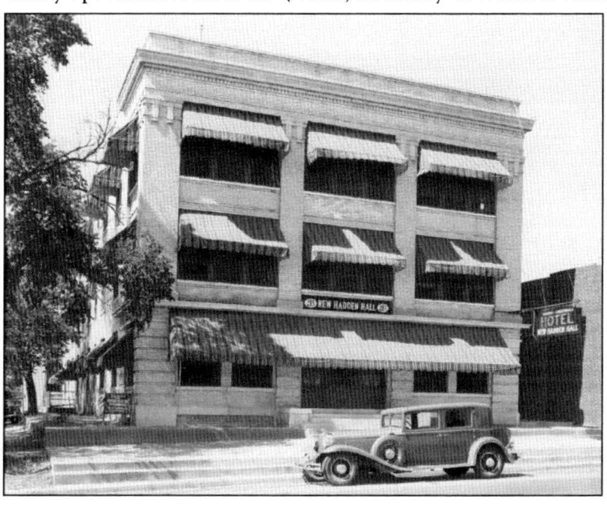

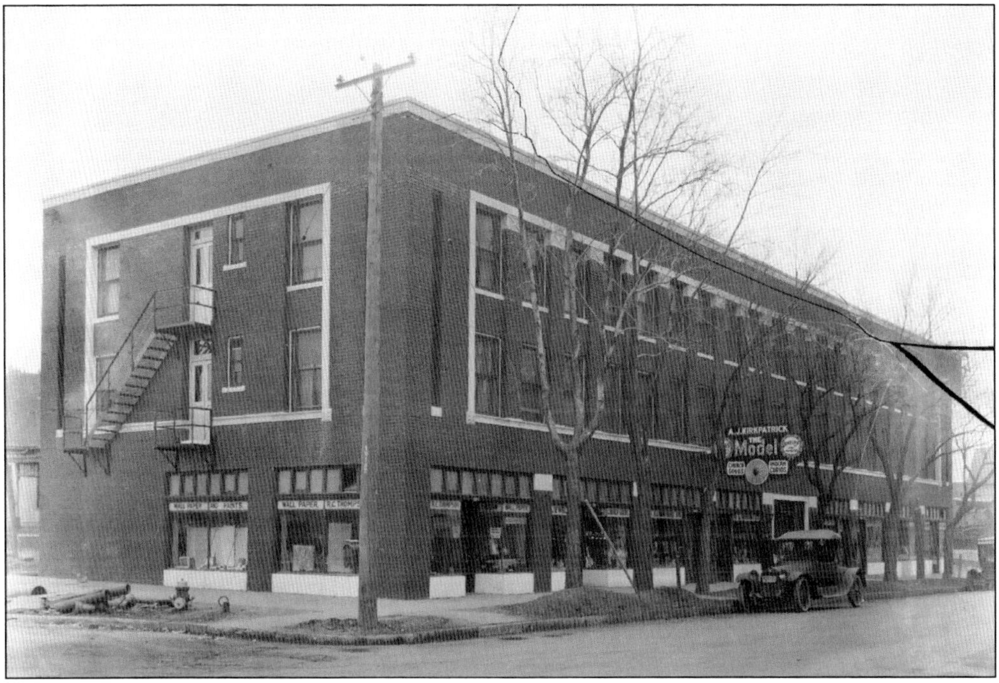

A.J. Kirkpatrick ordered this European-themed, 45-room building designed by Monot & Reid and constructed by W.S. Bellows in November 1922 at Northwest Sixth and Robinson Avenue. The Kirkpatrick Hotel, built with fireproof brick, featured amenities that included the spacious Green Room Café dining room, a telephone in every room, steam heating, servants, and a complimentary newspaper at guests' doors daily—for just $5 a week. The Kirkpatrick became an apartment building over the decades but was destroyed by a massive shock wave from a Ryder truck bomb detonated by domestic terrorists Timothy McVeigh and Terry Nichols in front of the Alfred P. Murrah Federal Building at 9:02am of April 19, 1995. The residents and businesses, which included a pizza and hot dog restaurant, salon, karate studio, and loan company, were immediately displaced. The building was condemned and razed nearly one year later on April 10, 1996. (Both, courtesy of the Oklahoma Historical Society.)

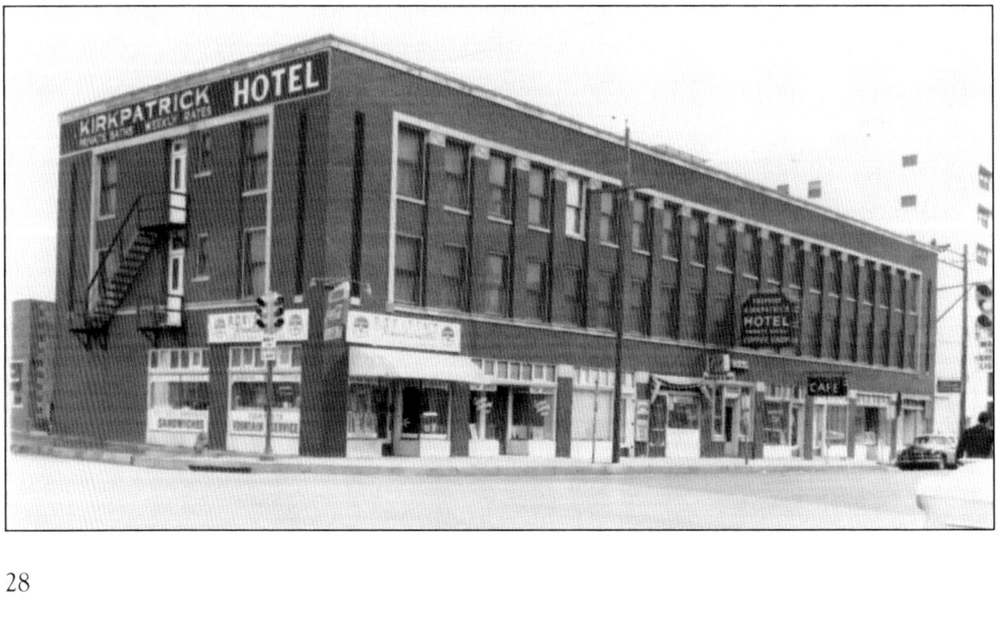

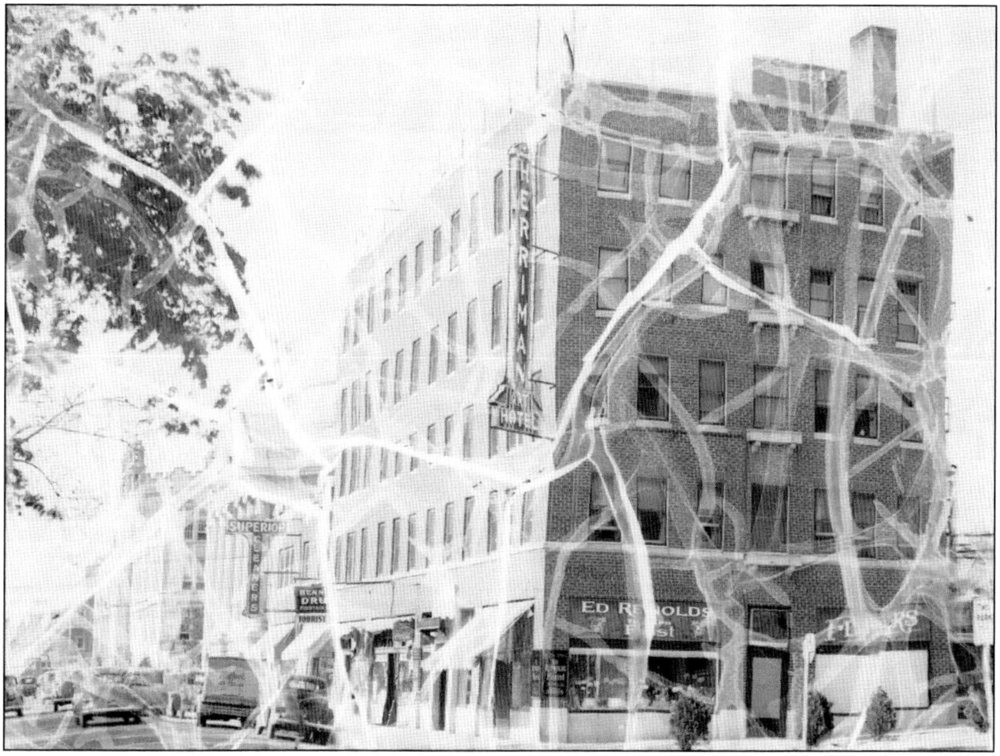

David B. "Uncle" Herriman and his wife, Nellie, built the five-story Herriman around 1923. It became the first apartment hotel built in Oklahoma City at 923 North Robinson Avenue. Herriman arrived in the 1893 run on Pawnee, Oklahoma, and relocated to Oklahoma City around 1915. He and Nellie operated several hotels until his death 28 years later. Herriman was a Mason and an avid sports shooter, and he served as founder and president of the Oklahoma State Sportsmen's Association. The Herriman was sold to the Lourette Investment Company's Mrs. John Hale, an oil woman, and her husband for $250,000 in 1928. Five additional floors were announced but never realized. They operated about 40 rooms with retail on the ground floor. Today, it is used as an office building. In the image below, the Bish building (left) opened in 1925 for Bish Photography & Framing Co. Unfortunately, these images were water damaged at some point. (Both, courtesy of the Oklahoma Historical Society.)

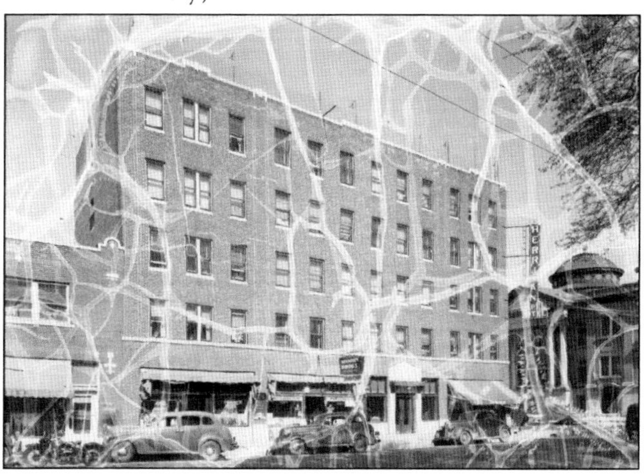

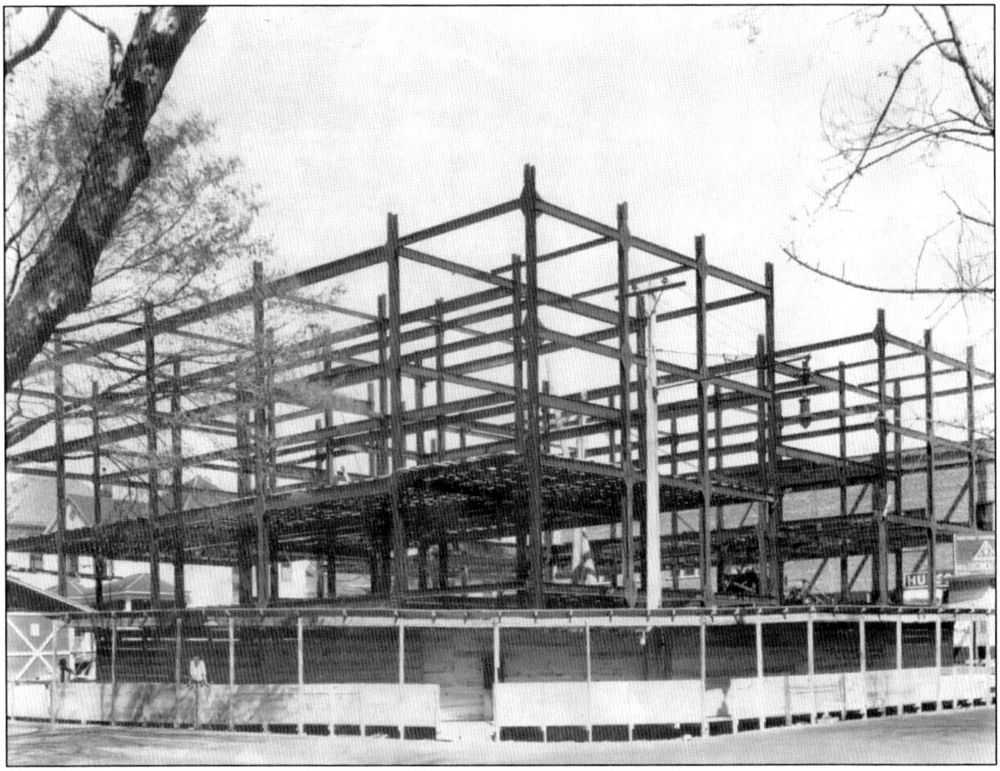

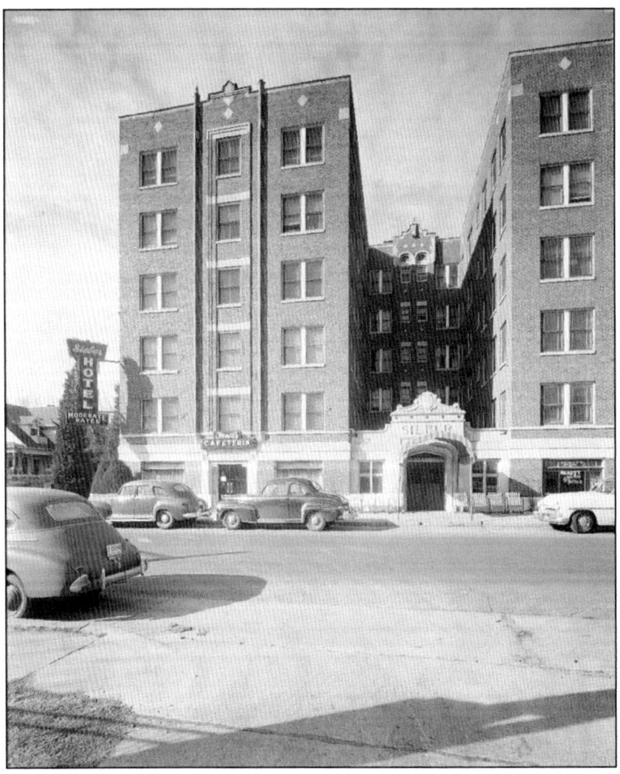

The steel lattice work of one of Oklahoma City's earliest hotel apartments rises at 1305 North Hudson in this photograph taken on March 15, 1928. The Sieber Hotel was built by Swiss immigrant Robert G. Sieber with his wife, Nora. However, Robert was also a noted purveyor of fine meats and sausages in a four-state area. and the six-story hotel was preceded by a two-story grocery building in 1924, as seen in the c. 1950 image on the top of the following page. The Sieber family lived upstairs, while the first floor consisted of a butcher shop and grocery. Income from the store eventually led to construction of the hotel. (Both, courtesy of the Oklahoma City Metropolitan Library System and the Oklahoma Historical Society.)

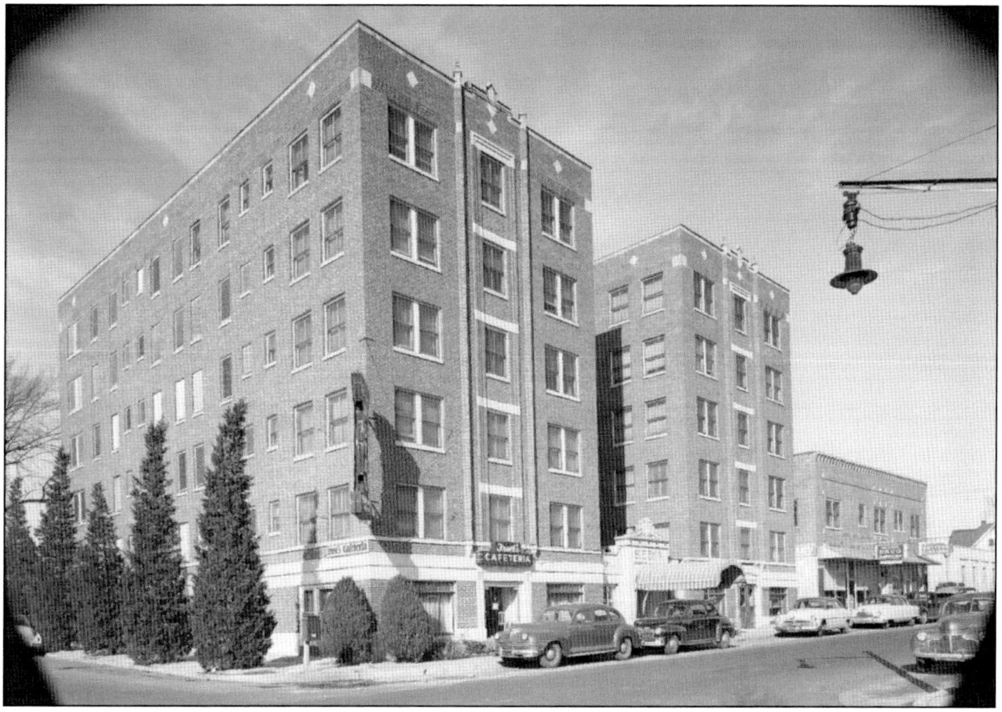

Due to the hotel's close proximity to the area's surrounding hospitals, the Sieber was mostly booked year round both as a hotel and apartments. When opened, there were over 80 rooms, a drugstore, beauty shop, restaurant, and bar. The image below shows the Sieber's café. In the distance is an early Sinclair full-service gas station. As economic woes struck the surrounding neighborhood in the 1970s and 1980s, the hotel folded and the last resident departed in 1983. The structure remained vacant for almost 25 years but was acquired and restored back to its former glory by a private group of investors that included Marva Ellard, Mike Meye, Ray McMinn, and Joanie Elder. The grandparents of the latter two owned the hotel from the 1930s to the 1950s. Both buildings were listed in the National Register of Historic Places in 2006. (Both, courtesy of the Oklahoma Historical Society and the Western History Collections, University of Oklahoma.)

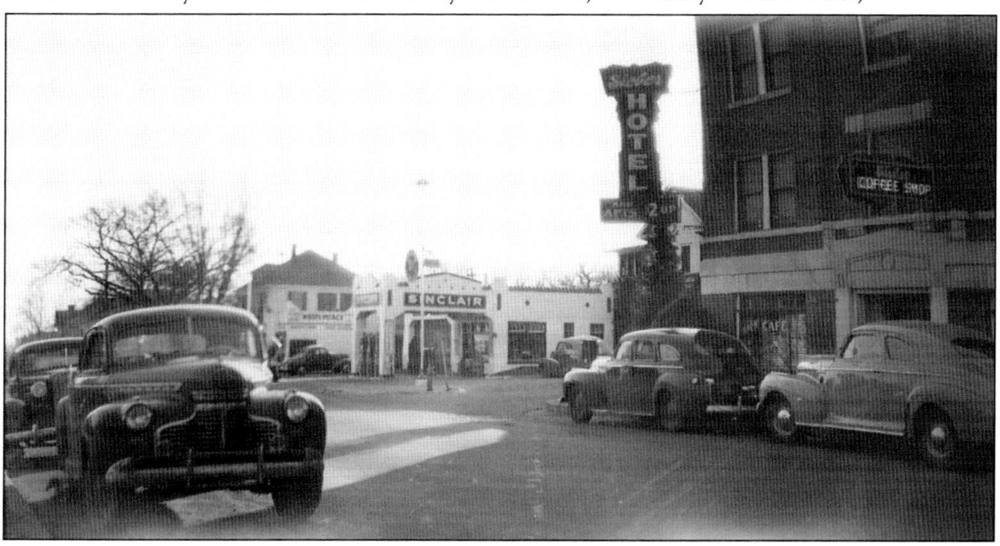

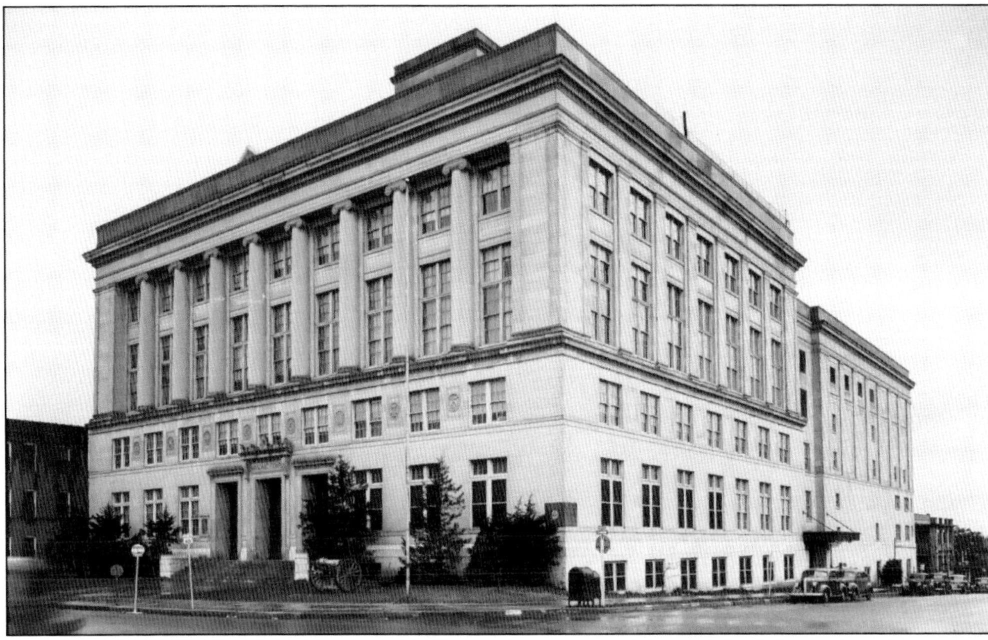

The neoclassical India Shrine Masonic Temple, built at 621 North Robinson Avenue opened in April 1941. It was constructed when 16 lodges pooled their resources to create a temple accommodating all lodge activities. The temple was completed in 1923 for approximately $1.3 million, but conditions from the Great Depression forced them to relocate 10 years later. The building stood empty until purchased at auction by Home State Life Insurance Company for $201,000 in December 1945. The Journal Record Publishing Company acquired the building in 1977 but was forced to relocate after the structure was significantly damaged in the Alfred P. Murrah Federal Building bombing across the street, April 19, 1995. Today, the building serves as home to the Oklahoma City National Memorial Museum and the National Memorial Institute for the Prevention of Terrorism. The image below was water damaged at some point, unfortunately. (Both, courtesy of the Oklahoma Historical Society.)

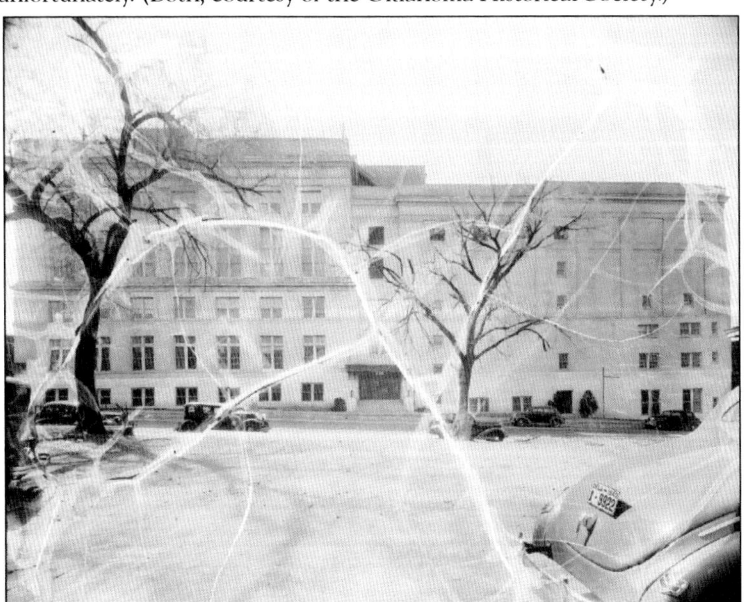

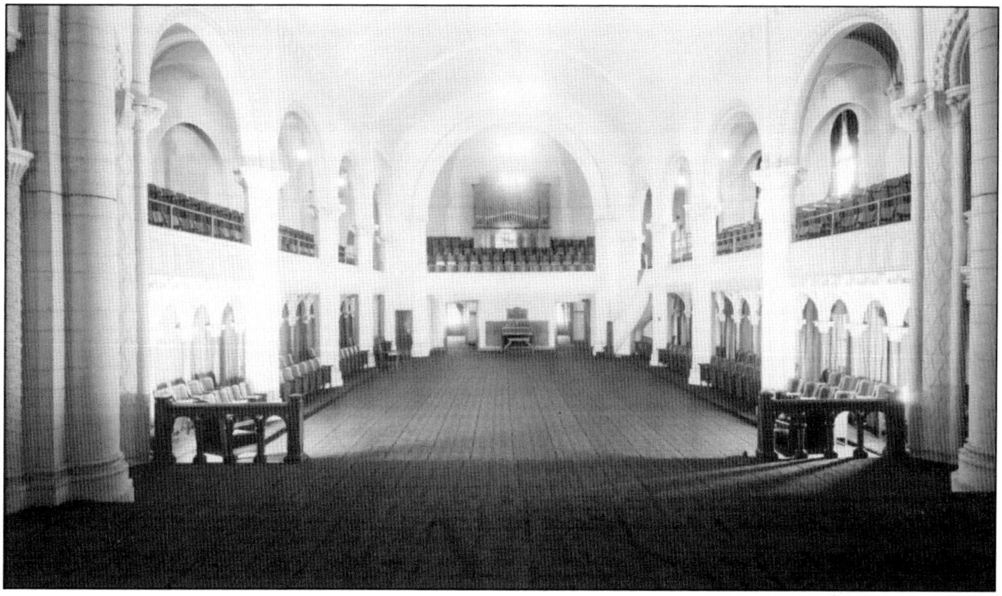

Above is the Altar Commandry, or Council Room chamber, built in what appears to be a Byzantine style. The building was elaborately constructed and ornately decorated in Egyptian, Greek, and Roman styles. When the building was acquired by Joe Morris of the Home State Life Insurance Company, most of the ornamentation was removed for remodeling into office space. Below is an image of Harding Hall, which was later converted into a fifth-floor newsreel cinema. Around 1930, Warner Brothers acquired the auditorium seen on the following page, renamed it Warner Auditorium, and moved its entrance to 210 Northwest Sixth Street, as seen above. The Home Insurance Company bought the space and changed the name to the Home State Auditorium during the World War II years and leased it to RKO, where newsreels were screened throughout the war. The cinema closed in 1951. (Both, courtesy of the Oklahoma Historical Society.)

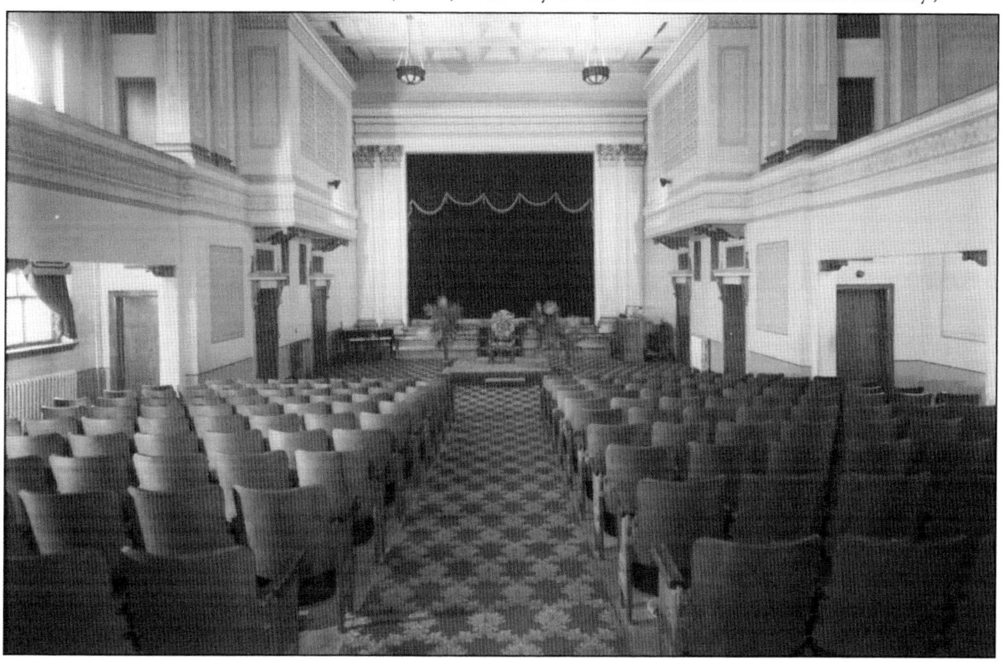

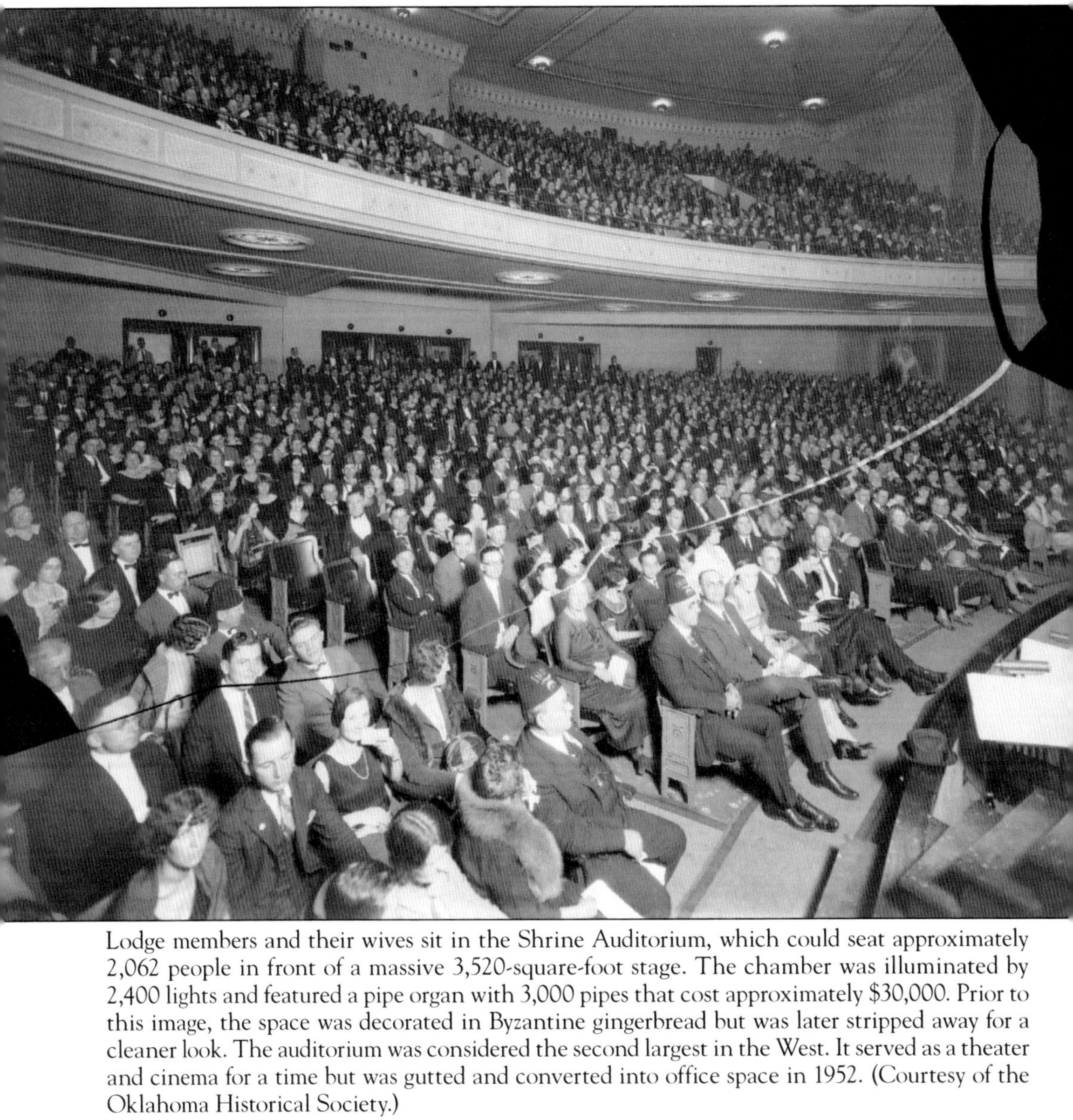

Lodge members and their wives sit in the Shrine Auditorium, which could seat approximately 2,062 people in front of a massive 3,520-square-foot stage. The chamber was illuminated by 2,400 lights and featured a pipe organ with 3,000 pipes that cost approximately $30,000. Prior to this image, the space was decorated in Byzantine gingerbread but was later stripped away for a cleaner look. The auditorium was considered the second largest in the West. It served as a theater and cinema for a time but was gutted and converted into office space in 1952. (Courtesy of the Oklahoma Historical Society.)

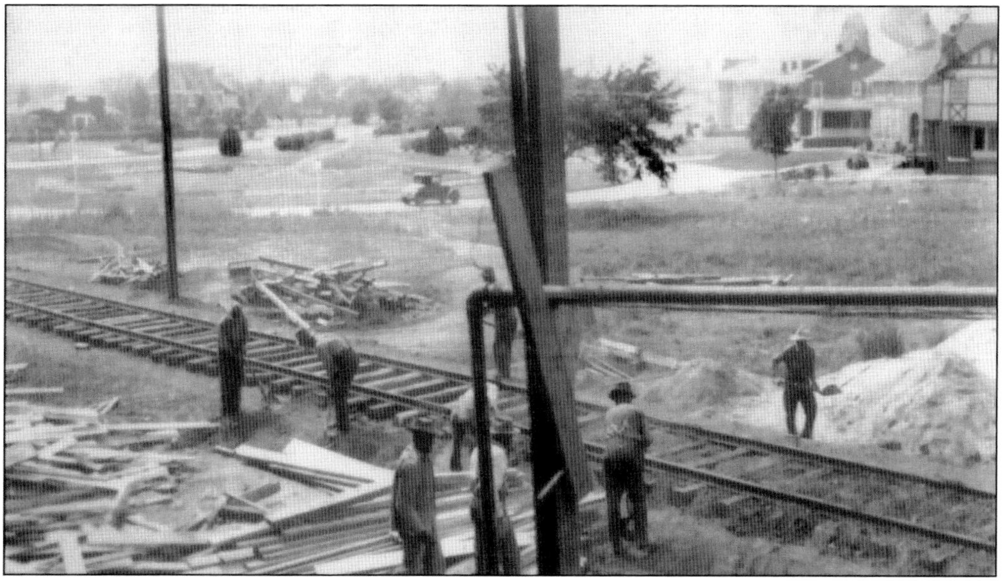

Just on the edge of Midtown, at 1400 Classen Boulevard, is a unique structure surrounded by historic neighborhoods. It is the former massive four-story home of Mid-Continent Life Insurance Company. The first shovel of dirt was turned by Mid-Continent president R.T. Stuart in a morning ceremony on May 10, 1926, and immediately put under construction by J.H. Fredrickson and company contractors. At the time, the surrounding neighborhoods were not as developed. This allowed a railroad spur to be brought directly into the site, as pictured above on July 21, 1926, as finishing touches are being made on the rail spur. The Mesta Park addition is in the background. The image below shows a work car on the spur. (Both, courtesy of the George Pickens Oklahoma Heritage Museum.)

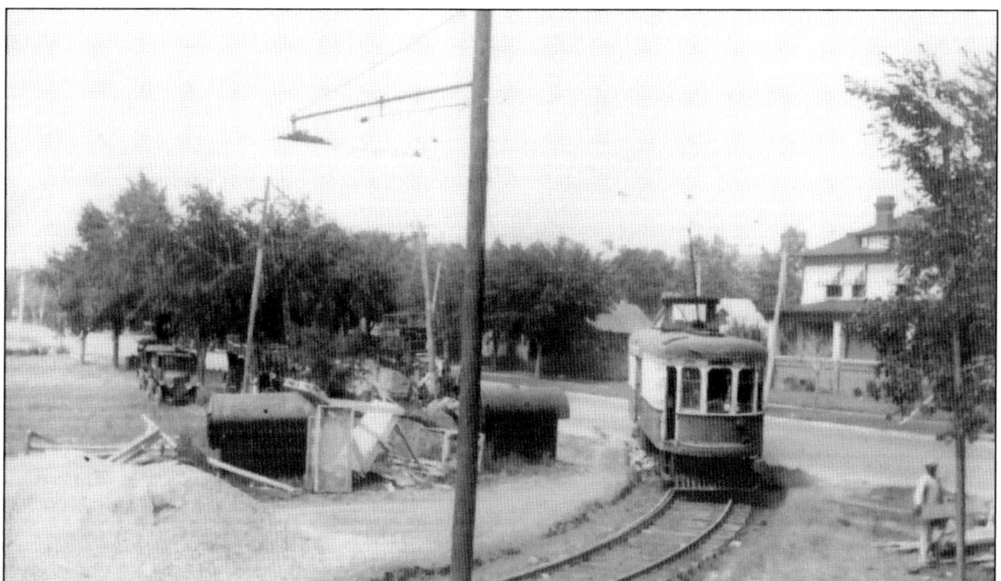

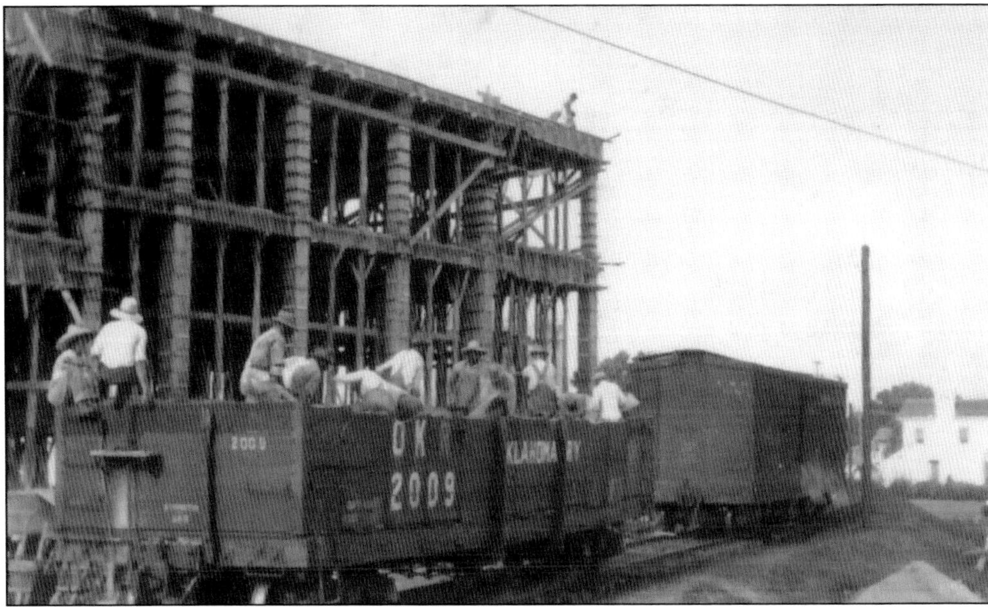

The new Mid-Continent building was constructed with a diverse list of materials, all of which were hauled in via rail service. The materials count was enormous and included 1,620 tons of sand, 2,182 tons of crushed gravel, 2,990 barrels of cement, 128 tons of structural-grade steel bars, 150,000 feet of lumber, 61 kegs of nails, 26,300 pieces of hollow terra-cotta building tiles, and 6,776 pieces of white stone for the exterior. The image above, taken July 22, 1926, shows two cars being unloaded by workmen. The image below was taken July 21, 1926, and shows construction progressing quickly. Many of the building materials are scattered about the base of the building. (Both, courtesy of the George Pickens Oklahoma Heritage Museum.)

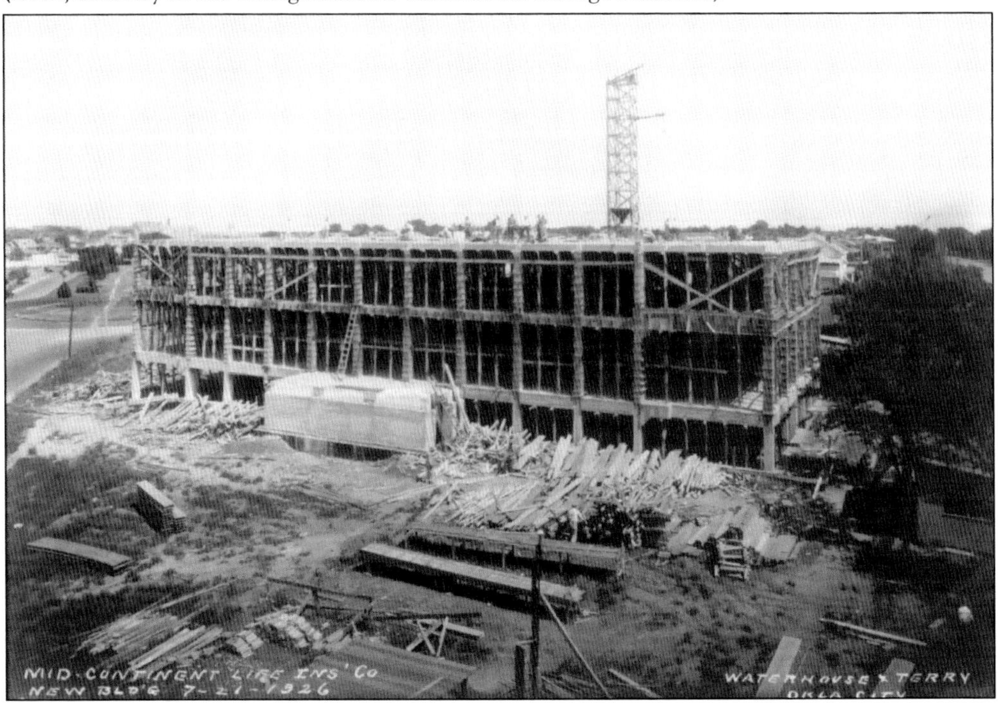

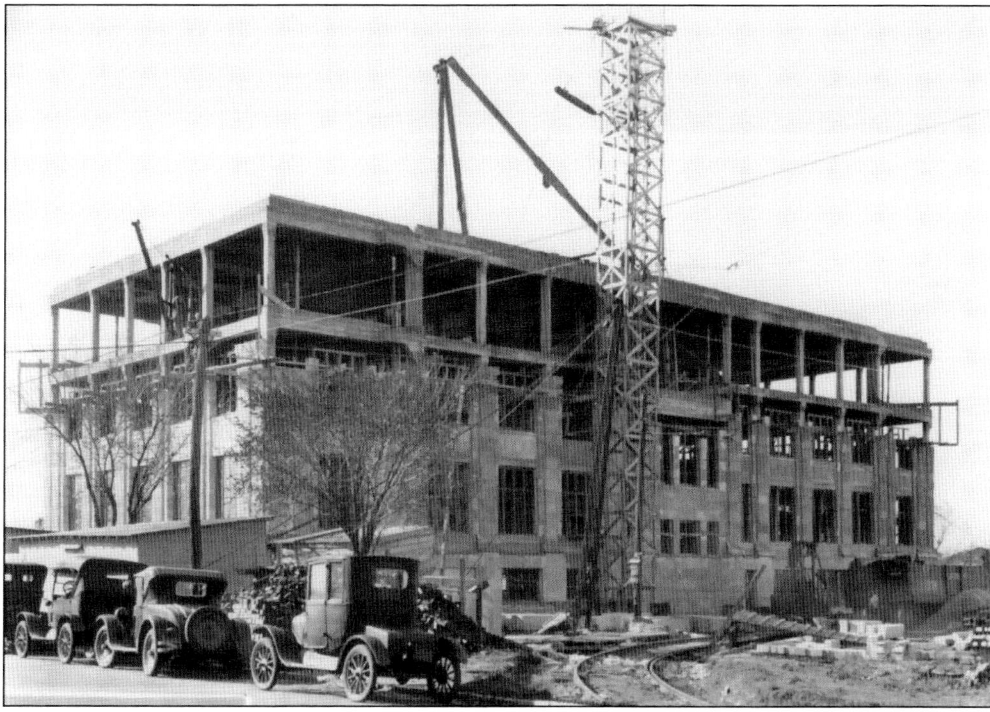

Above, the outer walls are going up on November 17, 1926, while below the building is nearly complete on March 2, 1927. The 125 exterior Browne windows were built with steel, while the interior consisted of 3,200 mahogany wood panels, solid bronze hardware on all doors featuring the Mid-Continent logo cast into every knob, and ornamental cast plasterwork. The president's desk was an experiment from the laboratories of Stow-Davis Engineering. The fine desk was completely submerged in water during a three-day convention of the Office Equipment Society to showcase its waterproof glue and acid-proof wood finish. The same firm furnished the rest of the building. Mid-Continent served the public from this space until the early 2000s. Today, the space is occupied by the Gaylord Pickens Oklahoma Heritage Museum, an award-winning tech savvy collection of Oklahoma heritage and oral histories. (Both, courtesy of the George Pickens Oklahoma Heritage Museum.)

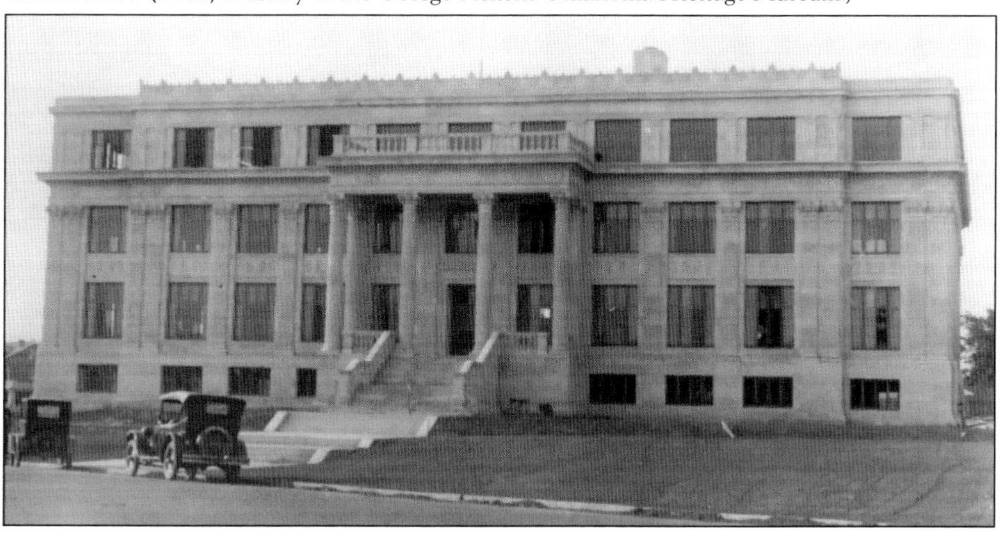

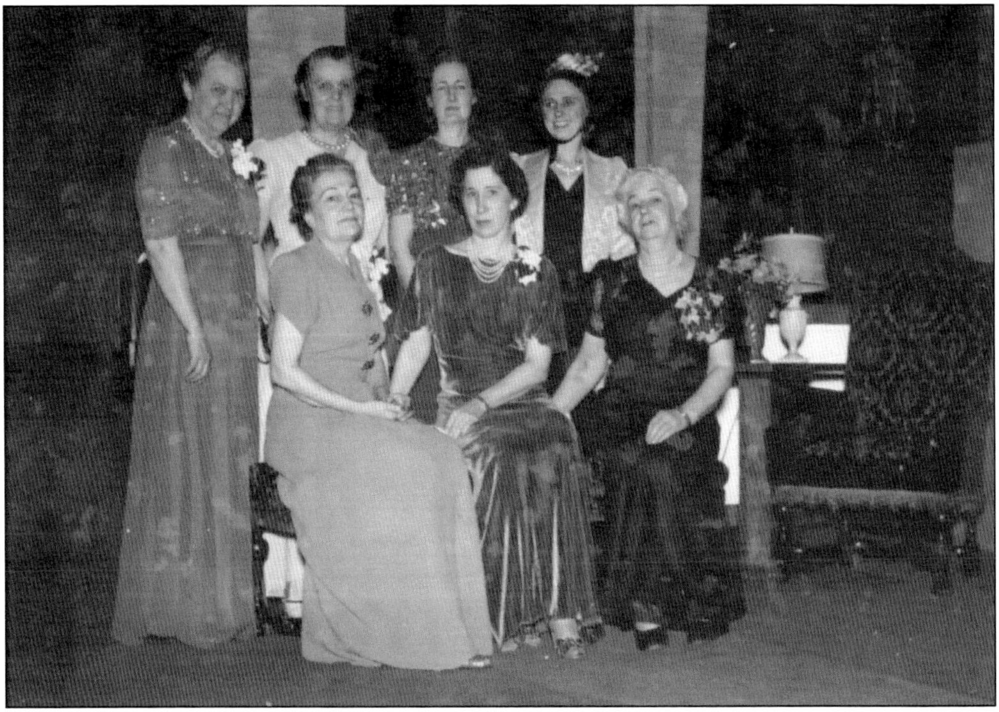

The Rosalie Pollock Private School at 424 West Twelfth Street operated from 1924 until Pollock's death in May 1953. She offered "Education through motivation. Individual development through the recognition of individual differences." Pollock was a member of the First Presbyterian Church and president of the Oklahoma City American Association of University Women. She is seated at far right in this 1941 photograph above. (Courtesy of the Oklahoma Historical Society.)

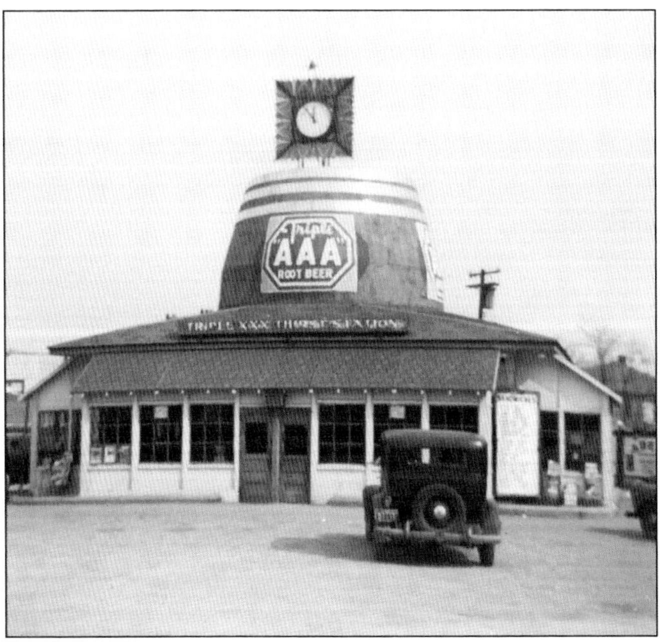

AAA Root Beer, an Oklahoma City company providing extracts and syrups to soft drink distributors, operated this thirst station restaurant at Northwest Thirteenth Street and Broadway Avenue. Albert Rochau and D.G. Carpenter, who produced over 20 flavors made with natural ingredients, founded the brand in 1937. Although it closed in 1974, Bricktown Candy Company owner Justin Thomas, who again bottles AAA in Oklahoma City, revived the brand in 2010. (Courtesy of the Western History Collections, University of Oklahoma.)

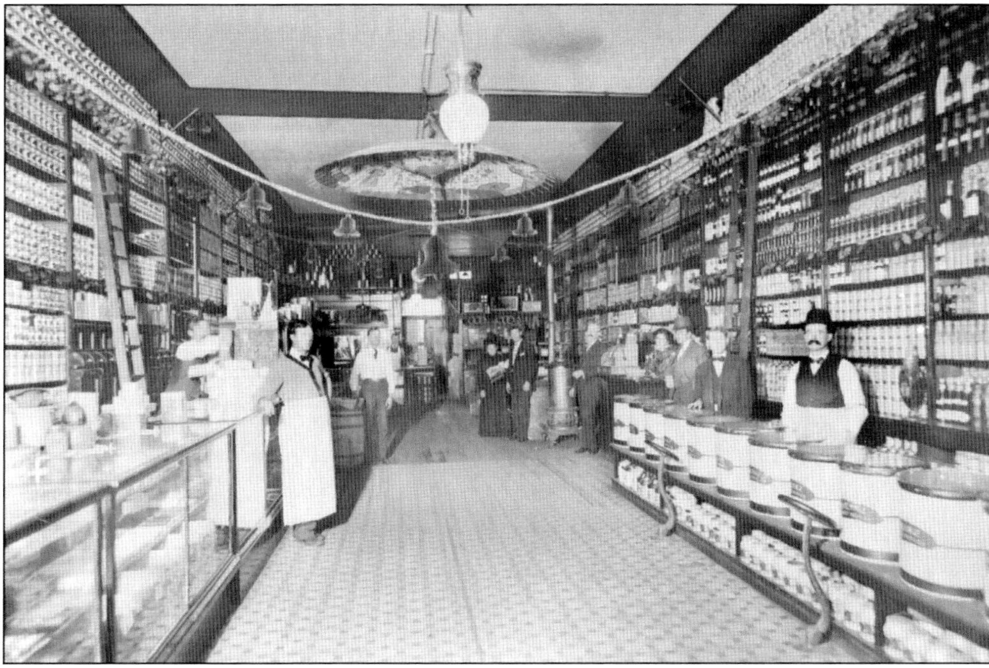

The interior images above and below were taken of the 207 West Main Street Crescent Market store around 1910. On May 22, 1926, the Oklahoman reported that Crescent Market grocery store owner John D. Thomas had purchased a large triangular lot bordered by Walker and Classen Drives for the purpose of building a new store. The lot was considered one of the most expensive locations north of Main Street and sold for an estimated $60,000 through the G.A. Nichols Company. Under the auspices of the Plaza Investment Company, created by Thomas, advertisements announced that the new multistory building would feature parking for over 100 cars and would be "Oklahoma City's most convenient shopping center." (Both, courtesy of the Tom Walbert collection.)

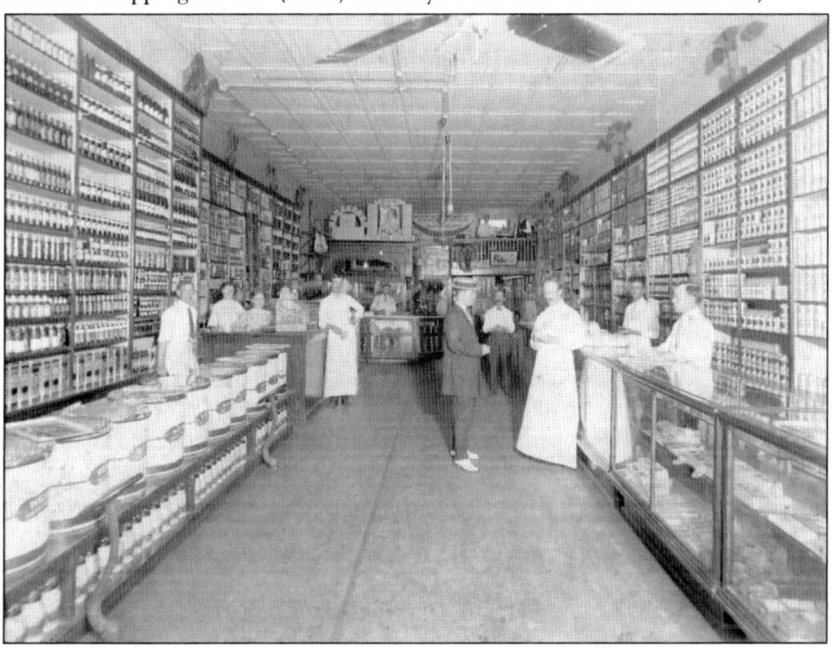

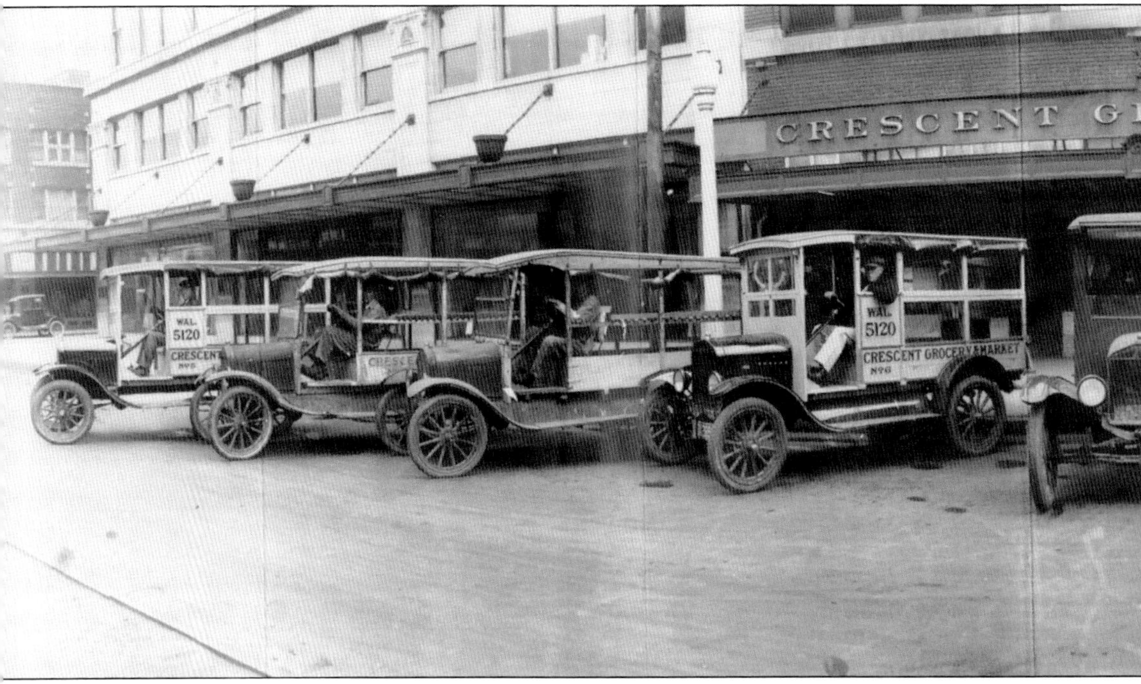

Here, a fleet of Crescent Market delivery trucks is parked outside their Main Street store in 1914. John L. Wyatt started the grocery from the back of a covered wagon during the land rush of April 22, 1889. He sold the store to Simmons and Forsberg Grocers in 1895. John Lloyd, business partner and uncle to John Thomas, purchased it in 1906 and renamed it Crescent Grocery. According to Thomas, "Pickle barrels stood in a row down the center and a big stove with benches and chairs

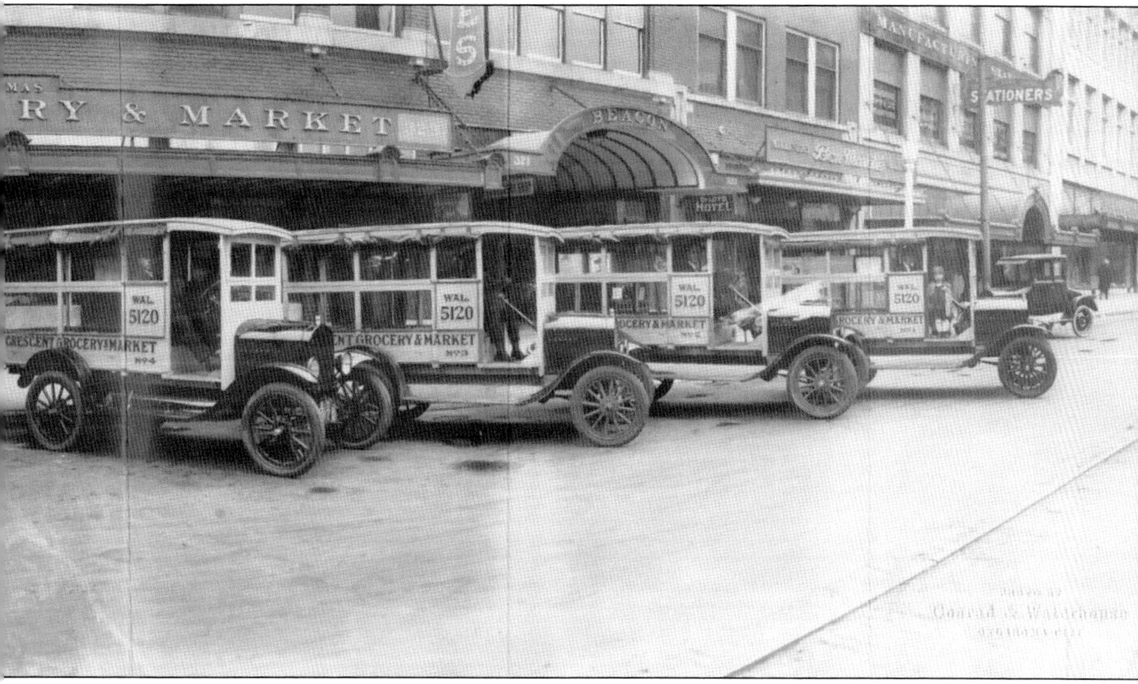

around it made the store the town's loafing place. I got rid of the barrels, took out the stove and put a covering on the floor." Furthermore, the entire cigar stock was given away. In 1909, he relocated to 323 West Main Street and added a meat market but moved again in 1917. (Courtesy of the Tom Walbert collection.)

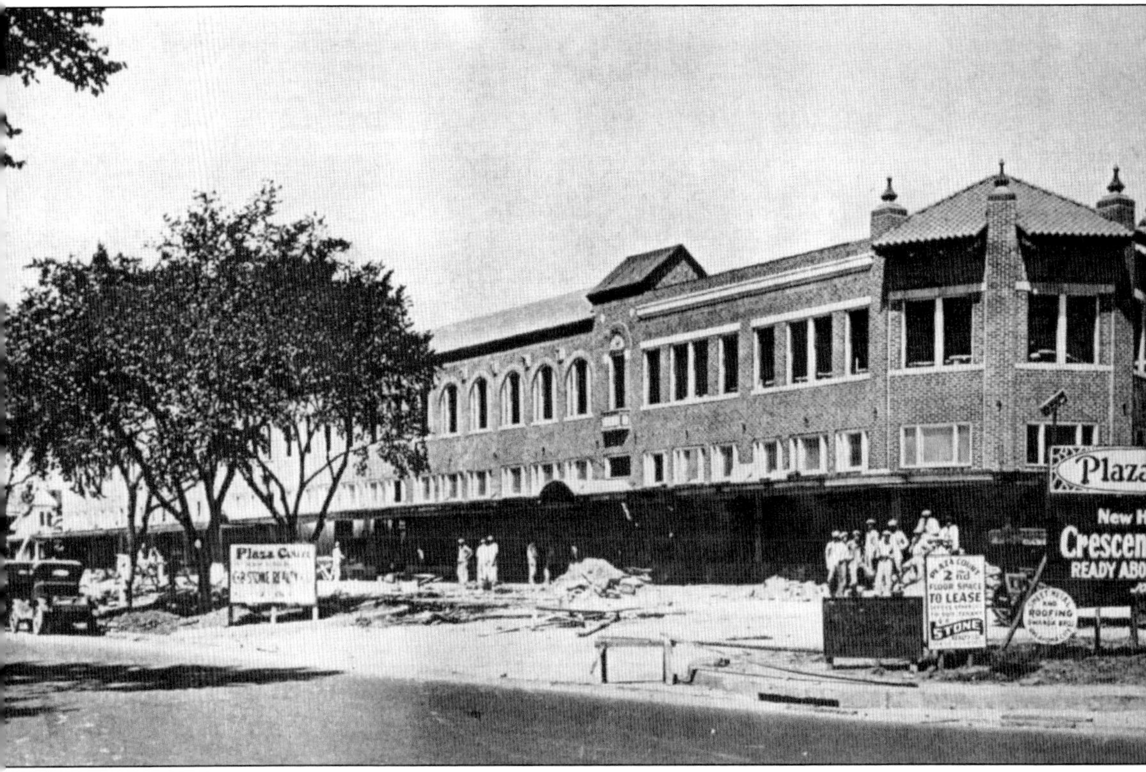

The above image captures Plaza Court under construction. The need for an expansion of Crescent Market became evident within a year of the purchase. Their downtown store had become cramped due to growing prosperity and very limited parking. The new store would feature much-needed additional amenities, including more stockroom space. Filling stations, drugstores, hospitals, medical offices, and a large residential population surrounded the triangular property giving it every advantage to succeed. Designed by Hawk and Parr—one of the city's best firms—at an estimated cost of $200,000, construction of Plaza Court began the fall of 1926 and was completed in 1927 at Northwest Tenth Street and Walker Avenue. (Courtesy of Chris Fleming.)

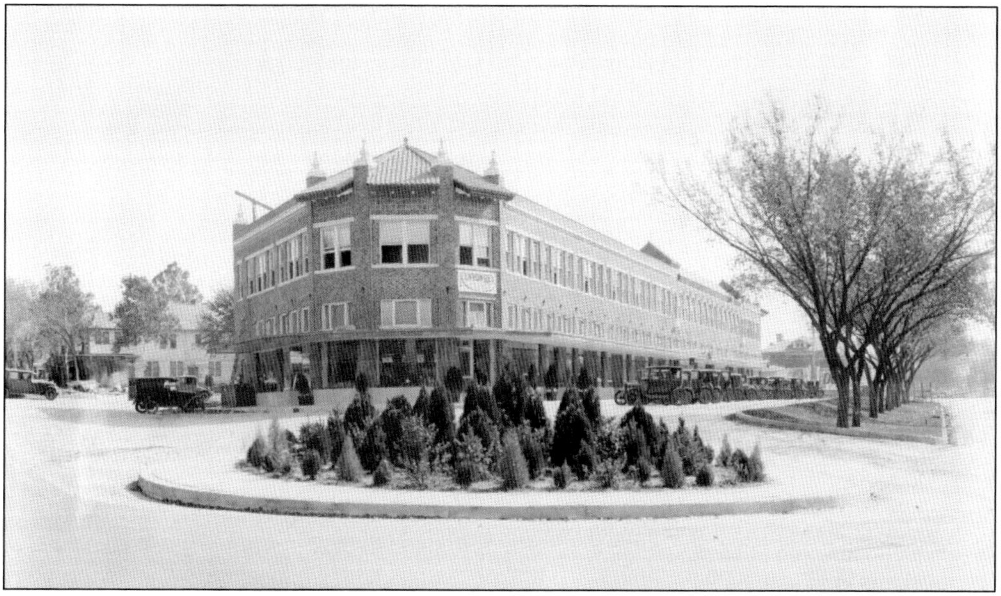

Above and below, Plaza Court's west and east ends are captured shortly after construction was completed. The design featured Spanish influences, and the name reflected this. "Plaza" means marketplace, and "court" referenced that the building would cater to automobiles rather than streetcars. When Plaza Court opened in 1927, it was considered the first shopping center in Oklahoma and possibly nationwide. Its development was a farsighted response to surrounding urban conditions as the family automobile began decreasing the dependence of shoppers on streetcars and population growth increased. From 1925–1930, the population in Oklahoma City increased from 91,295 to 182,845 due to the oil boom. Plaza Court further offered parking amenities to automobiles with free parking and eventually upper-deck parking in later years. (Both, courtesy of Chris Fleming.)

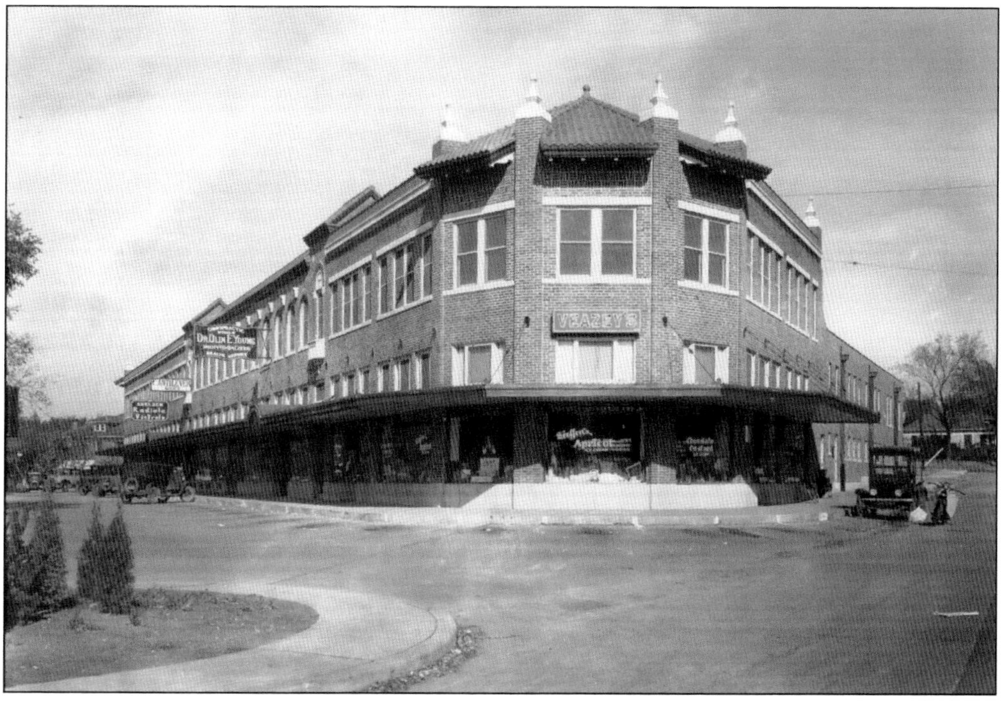

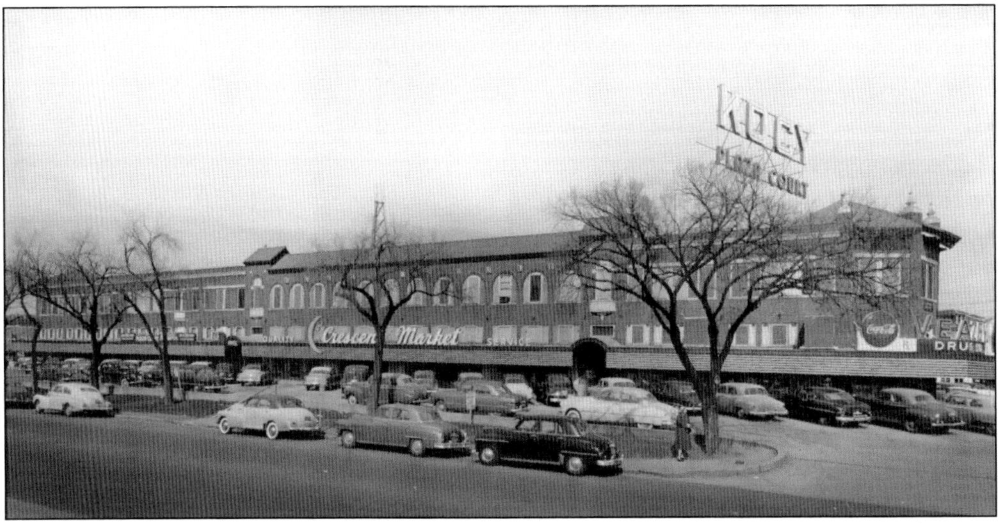

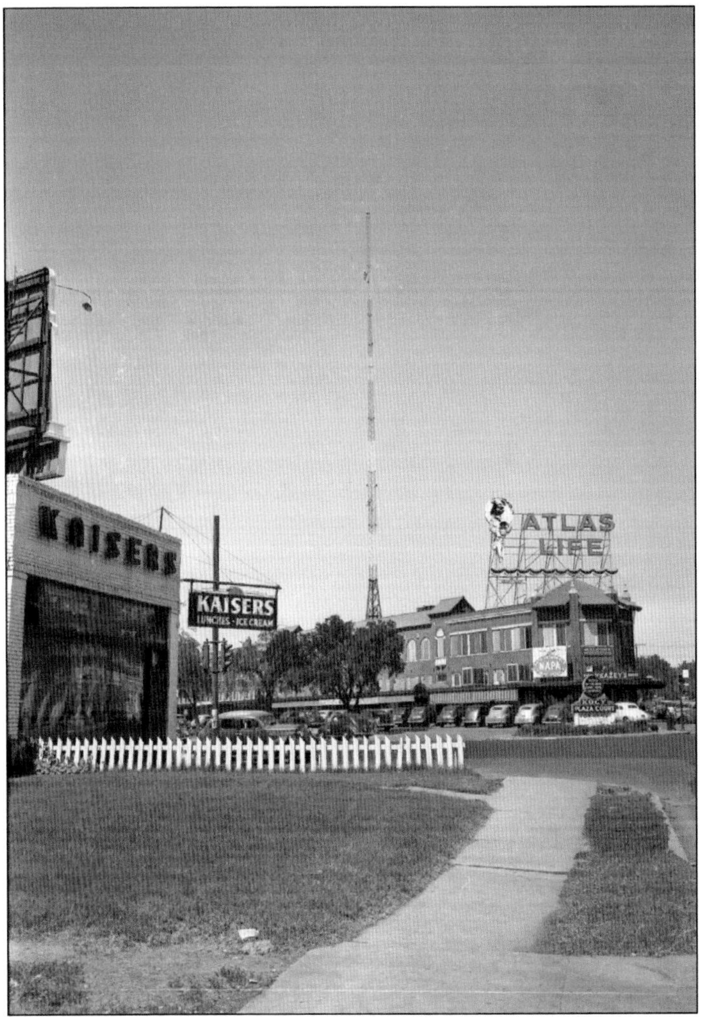

Plaza Court hosted KOCY Radio in the 1950s, one of the first rock-and-roll 24-hour stations in the country. WKY Radio, Oklahoma's first radio station and among the first to be established west of the Mississippi River, was among the many unique tenants in Plaza Court. Dr. John Roddy, a resident for several years, is believed to be the first doctor in Oklahoma to administer insulin to a diabetic patient. Crescent Market was bought into by Art L. Pemberton in 1942, and he relocated the store to Nichols Hill Plaza in 1968. Parking was expanded after rooftop access was added to Plaza Court sometime in the 1950s. At left, Plaza Court is captured as it hosts tenant Atlas Life. Kaiser's Ice Cream, another famous Midtown icon is in the foreground. (Both, courtesy of the Tom Walbert collection and the Oklahoma Historical Society.)

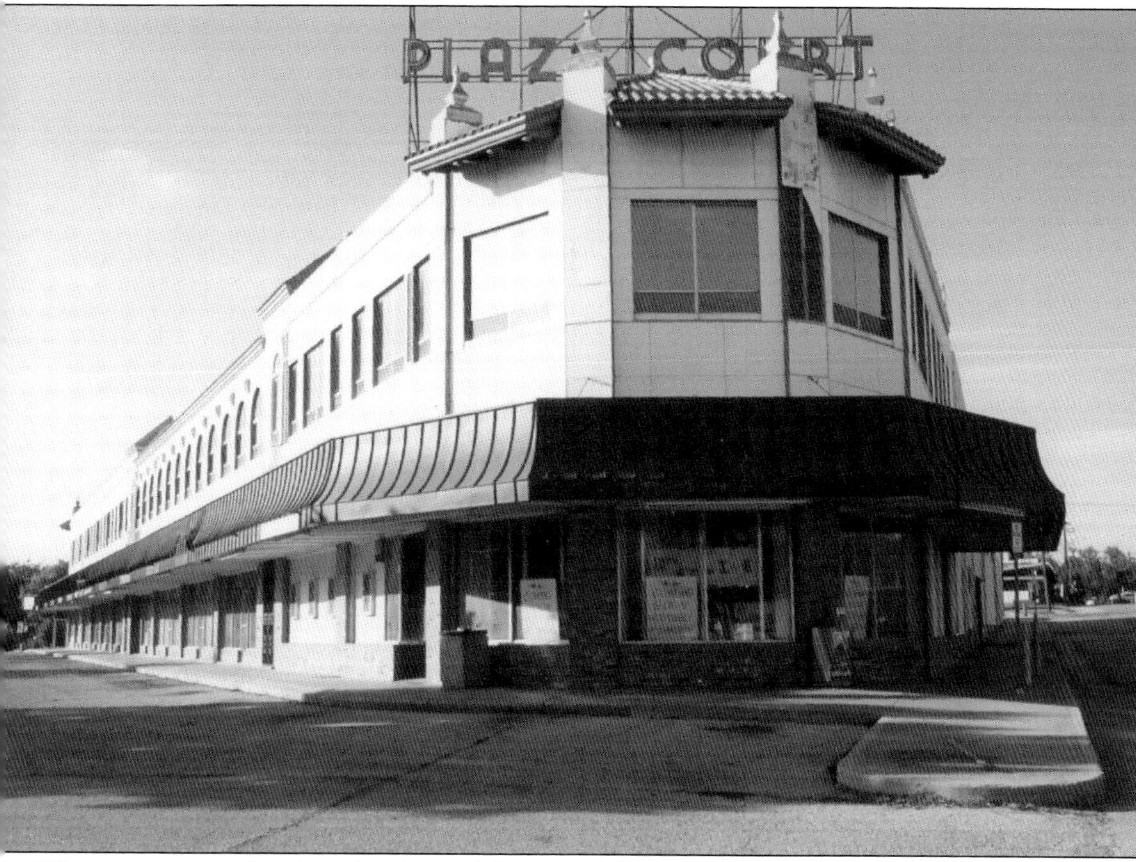

The property was placed on the National Register of Historic Places in 1980, became vacant for sometime later, and remained that way for a while. It was acquired for $900,000 by Corsair Coughran in 2005 from the Oklahoma Investment Group and later by Midtown Renaissance developers, who have successfully restored and revived the use of the property. It now includes a YMCA gym on the second story. On the lower level is James E. McNellie's Public House, which occupies what was once Veazy's Drug Store. Prairie Thunder Bakery and Irma's Burgers are also among the new tenants, to name a few. The image above shows Plaza Court in disrepair sometime in the 1980s. (Courtesy of Chris Fleming.)

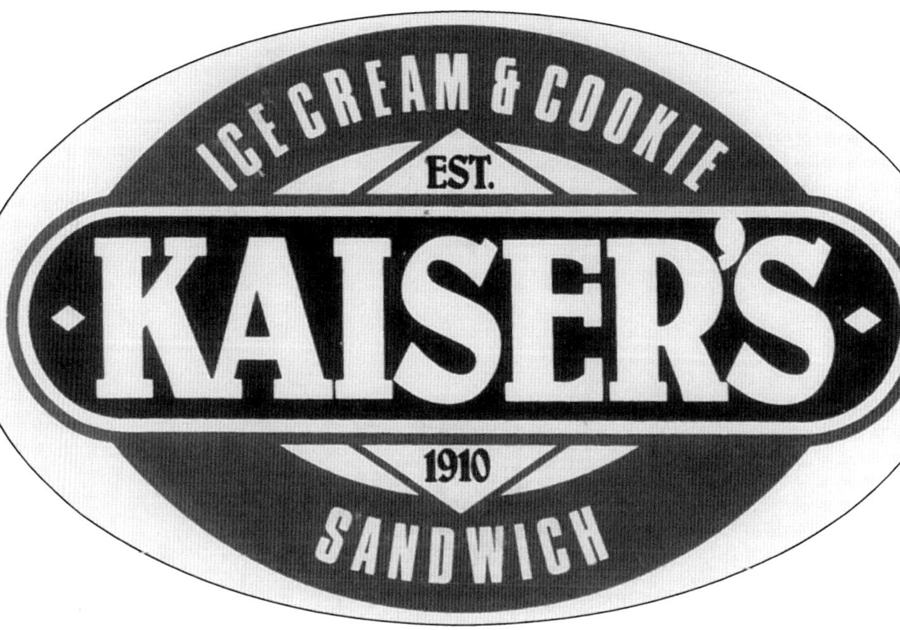

Anthony J. Kaiser, coming from a Swiss family background, arrived in Oklahoma City in 1909 with 50¢ and a three-quart ice cream freezer. Kaiser purchased a bankrupt confectionary and ice cream parlor a few blocks from St. Anthony Hospital. In 1919, he relocated to 1039 North Walker Avenue, where the business has remained for the past 94 years. The parlor is noted for its exotic hand-cranked freezer ice creams, ices, punches, and frozen puddings that are sold across a mahogany and glass bar with a vintage soda fountain. The modest building is surrounded with large windows topped by stained glass imported from Italy. The ceilings are ornate pressed iron panels, trimmed with engraved molding. These windows were once protected by roll-down canvas awnings. Above is Kaiser's logo, and below is a menu from the 1930s. Today, Kaiser's is owned and operated by the Good Egg Company. (Both, courtesy of the Good Egg Company.)

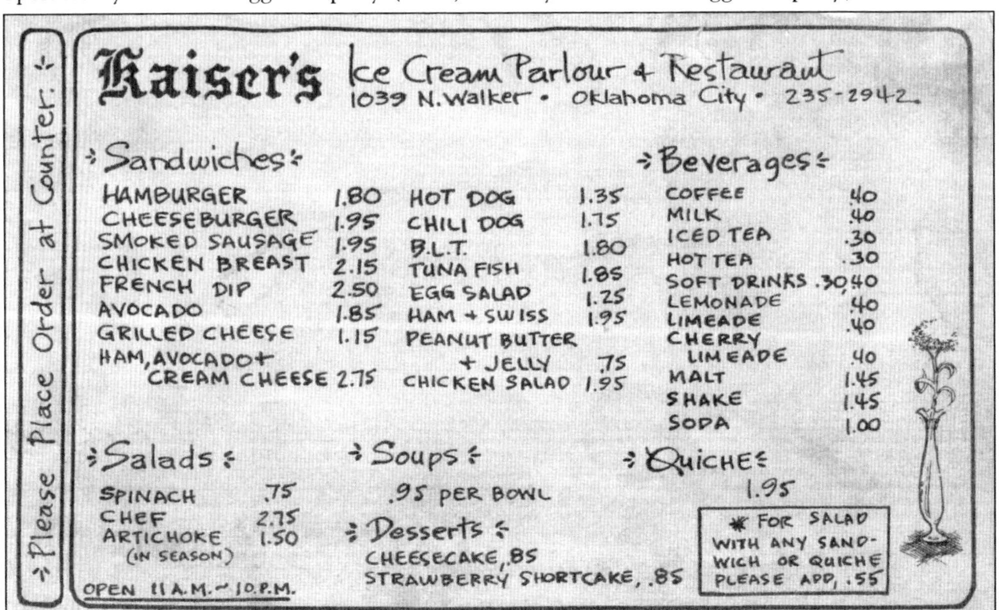

Please Place Order at Counter.

Kaiser's Ice Cream Parlour + Restaurant
1039 N. Walker • Oklahoma City • 235-2942

Sandwiches

HAMBURGER	1.80	HOT DOG	1.35
CHEESEBURGER	1.95	CHILI DOG	1.75
SMOKED SAUSAGE	1.95	B.L.T.	1.80
CHICKEN BREAST	2.15	TUNA FISH	1.85
FRENCH DIP	2.50	EGG SALAD	1.25
AVOCADO	1.85	HAM + SWISS	1.95
GRILLED CHEESE	1.15	PEANUT BUTTER + JELLY	.75
HAM, AVOCADO + CREAM CHEESE	2.75	CHICKEN SALAD	1.95

Beverages

COFFEE	.40
MILK	.40
ICED TEA	.30
HOT TEA	.30
SOFT DRINKS	.30, .40
LEMONADE	.40
LIMEADE	.40
CHERRY LIMEADE	.40
MALT	1.45
SHAKE	1.45
SODA	1.00

Salads

SPINACH	.75
CHEF	2.75
ARTICHOKE (IN SEASON)	1.50

Soups
.95 PER BOWL

Quiche
1.95

Desserts
CHEESECAKE .85
STRAWBERRY SHORTCAKE .85

* FOR SALAD WITH ANY SANDWICH OR QUICHE PLEASE ADD .55

OPEN 11 A.M. – 10 P.M.

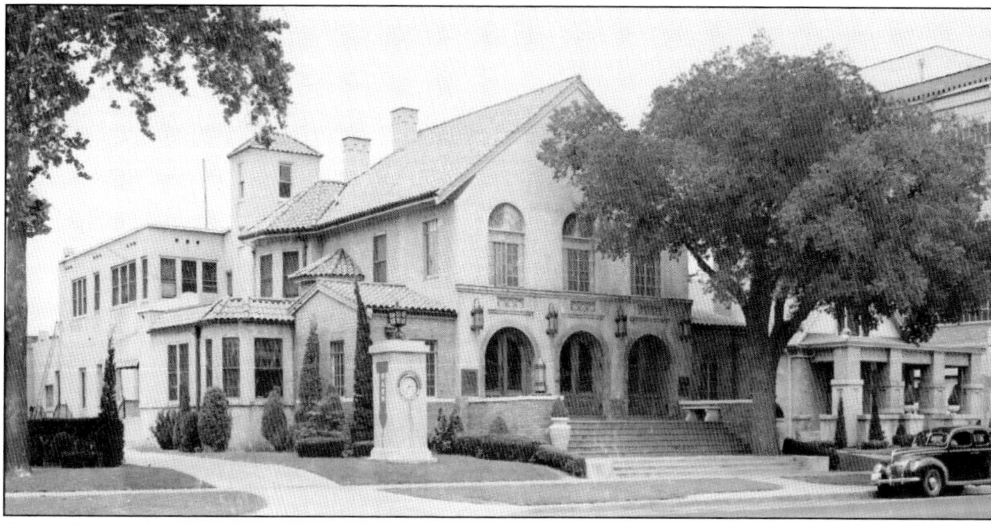

Formed in 1916, the Hahn Funeral Home was among Oklahoma City's earliest. Ed and Chester Hahn opened the new funeral home (above) at 119 Northwest Tenth Street across the street from the Marion Hotel and situated near Church Row in 1920. Hahn merged with Cook Funeral Company in the mid-1940s. After the owners' deaths, daughter Lelia Hahn continued the service until she merged with Street & Draper in 1967 and relocated to 6006 Northwest Grand Boulevard. Street & Draper had operated since before statehood, beginning as the Street & Harper Furniture and Undertaking Company in 1891, evolving into Street & Draper at the turn of the 20th century. The home provided Elvis Presley's casket after his death in 1977. The image below depicts the Hahns' elaborate chapel and pipe organ in 1944. The Hahn-Cook/Street & Draper Funeral Home continues today from 6600 Broadway Extension in Oklahoma City. (Both, courtesy of the Oklahoma Historical Society.)

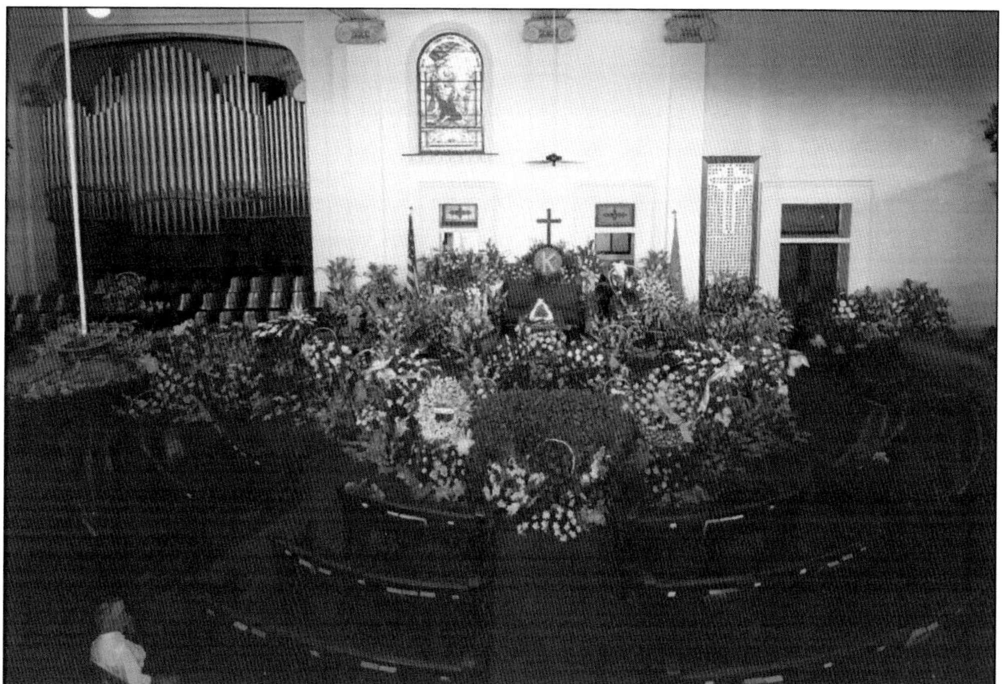

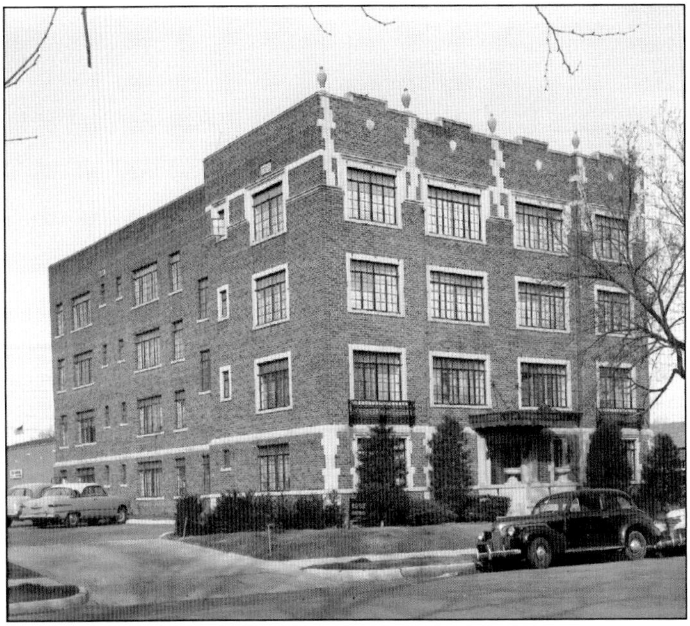

The "brick box" styled Mayfair Apartments, designed by George F. Swisher, at 1315 Broadway Place offered a range of amenities that included full-tiled baths, kitchens, refrigeration, and thick Wilton-brand carpeting. Mayfair management promoted the property with the following statement: "The charming exterior architecture, alluring cozy lobby, wide stately halls, and atmosphere combine to lend the air of an exclusive club." (Courtesy of the Oklahoma Historical Society.)

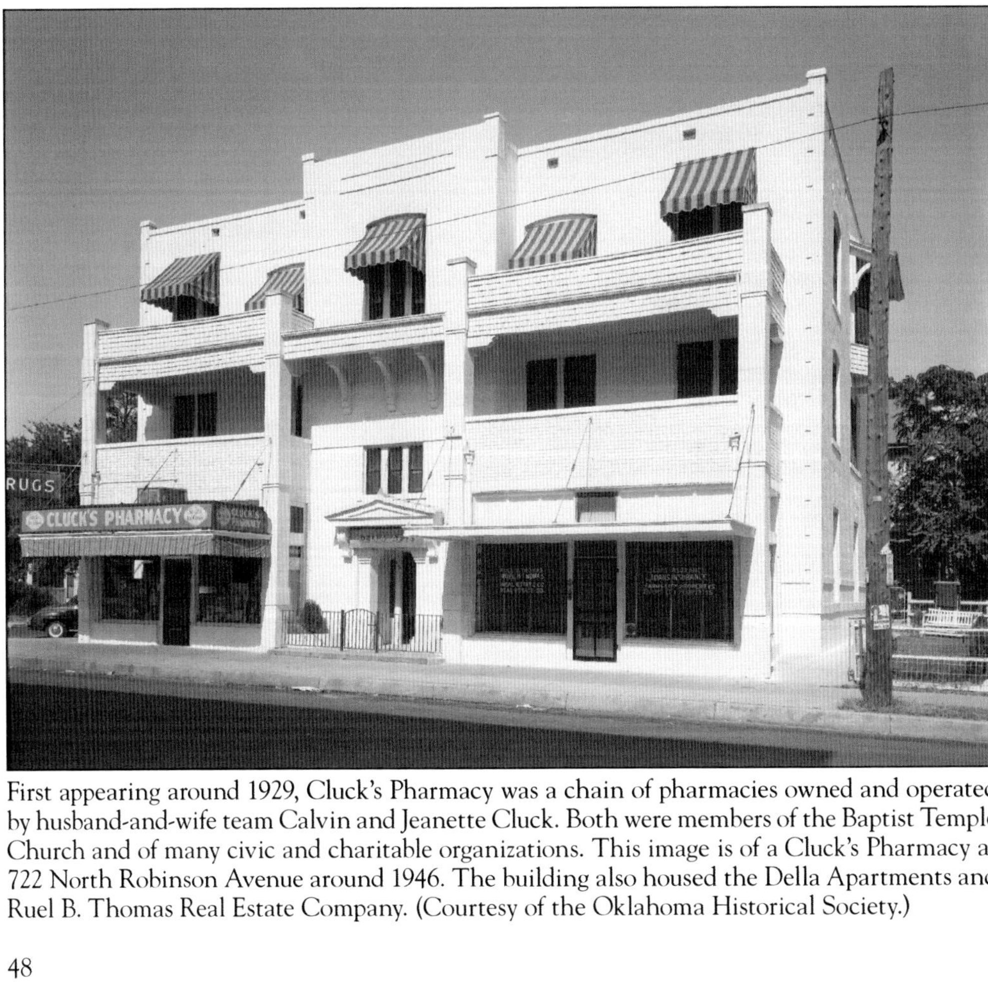

First appearing around 1929, Cluck's Pharmacy was a chain of pharmacies owned and operated by husband-and-wife team Calvin and Jeanette Cluck. Both were members of the Baptist Temple Church and of many civic and charitable organizations. This image is of a Cluck's Pharmacy at 722 North Robinson Avenue around 1946. The building also housed the Della Apartments and Ruel B. Thomas Real Estate Company. (Courtesy of the Oklahoma Historical Society.)

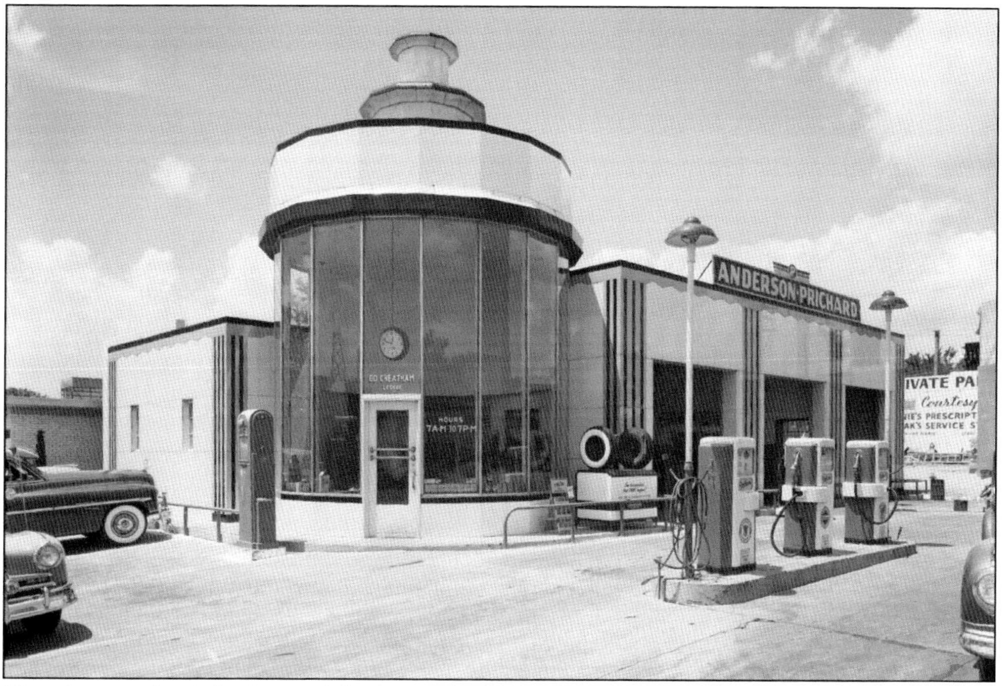

The gleam and polish of one of Anderson-Prichard's unique styled filling stations at 1201 North Walker Avenue is captured in these images from May 17, 1950. The station is the only design of its kind, and its most prominent feature is the glass-walled waiting area, which resembles an early gravity fuel pump. Steve Anderson and Alexander Pritchard, an attorney from Mississippi, pooled their resources to start the Anderson-Prichard Oil Company in 1917. In 1920, the men had acquired hundreds of oil-producing acres, which by 1924 led to an annual profit of over $10 million. The firm operated from the seventh floor of the Colcord building, Oklahoma City's first skyscraper. Like so many other oil and gas companies, Anderson-Prichard appears to have become a victim of the 1980s bust. The restored structure has hosted Stella, a modern Italian cuisine restaurant offering elegant dining, in Midtown since 2010. (Both, courtesy of the Oklahoma Historical Society.)

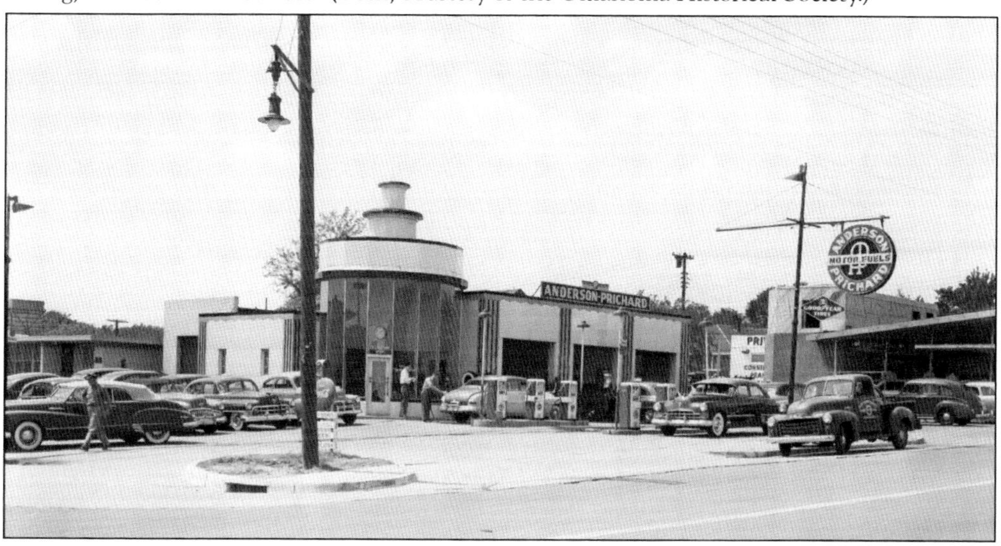

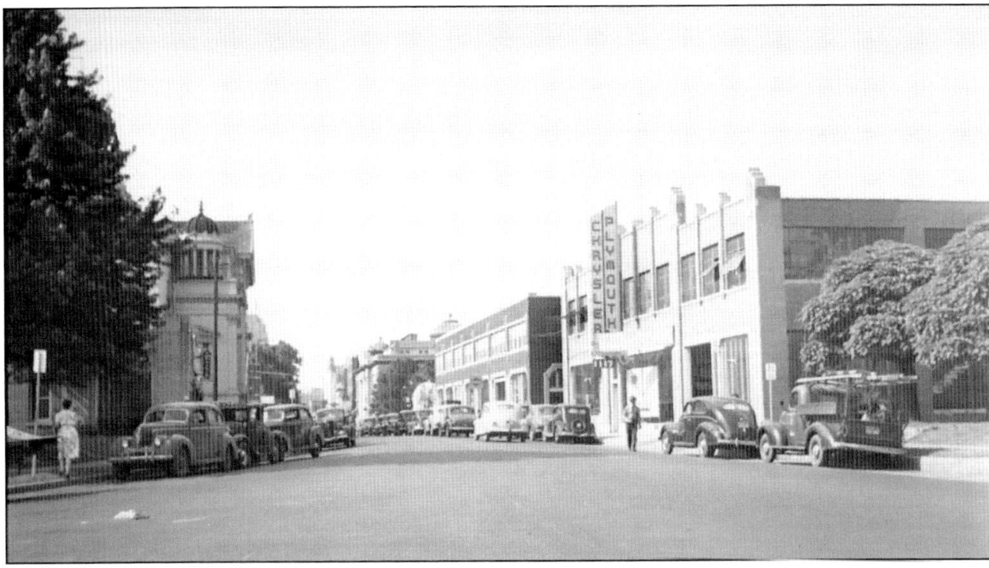

This 1940s view looking south toward Northwest Tenth Street along Robinson Avenue shows First Christian Church on the left and the Guardian and Packard buildings along the right with the First Presbyterian Church spires in the distance. Beyond the First Presbyterian is Central High School. The majority of structures in this photograph still stand, and most have been repurposed for new businesses and residential space. The image below captures the same scene during a 1950s snow-covered traffic jam. (Both, courtesy of the Western History Collections, University of Oklahoma.)

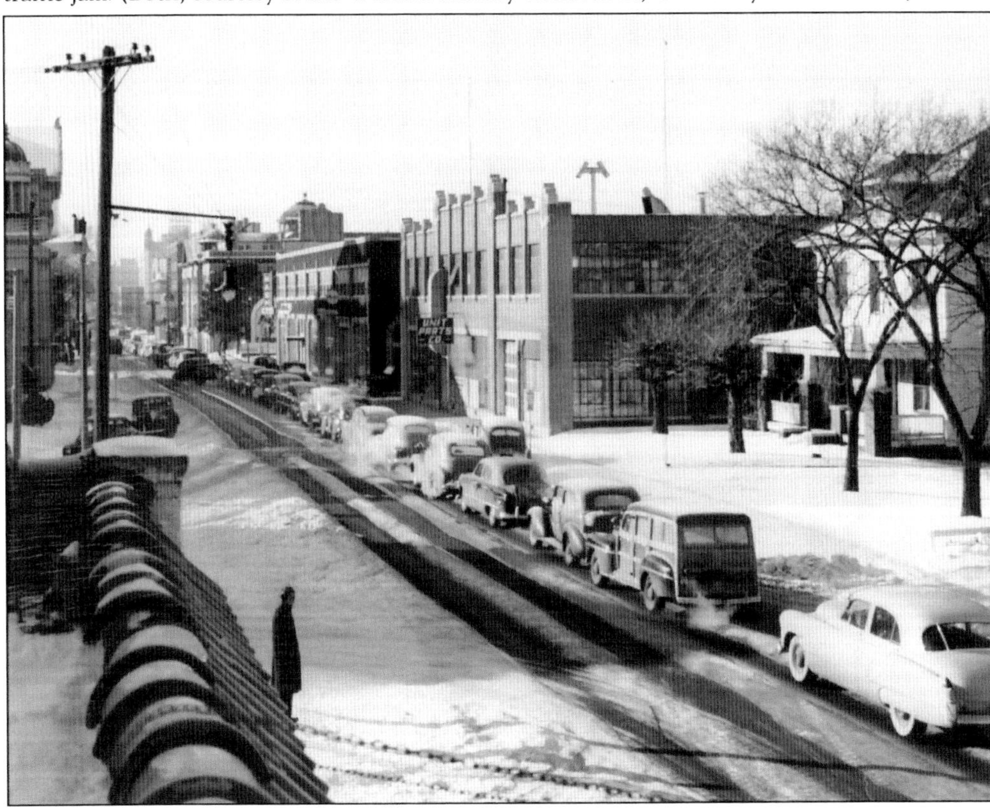

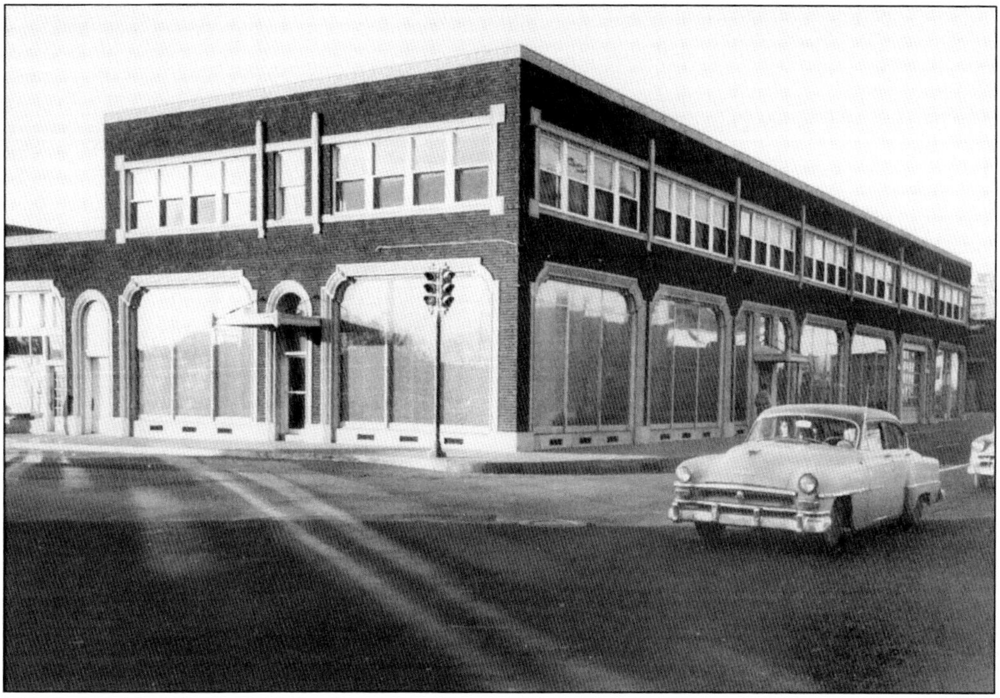

The Packard building at 201 Northwest Tenth Street began life when it was constructed by J.A. Eisele for his Packard dealership, which first opened at 123 West Third Street in March 1926. Expansion led to a temporary move in 1926 to 913–915 North Broadway and again to 800 North Broadway in 1927. The new dealership on Robinson Avenue opened on May 5, 1928. According to newspapers of the time, Eisele built additional space as an annex north of the dealership at 1117 North Robinson Avenue, which was used as the service department. United Parts occupied this space in 1947, and the Packard dealership folded completely by the mid-1950s. The image above shows the Packard building on the corner of Northwest Tenth Street and Robinson Avenue around this time. Below, the space is nearly vacant, with the exception of a bar next door. (Both, courtesy of Chris Fleming.)

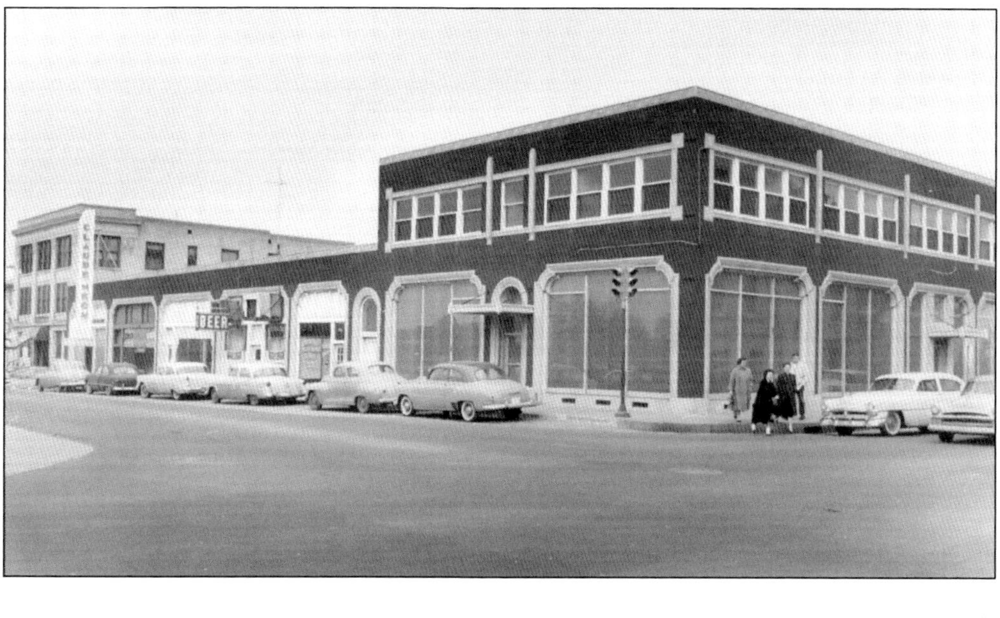

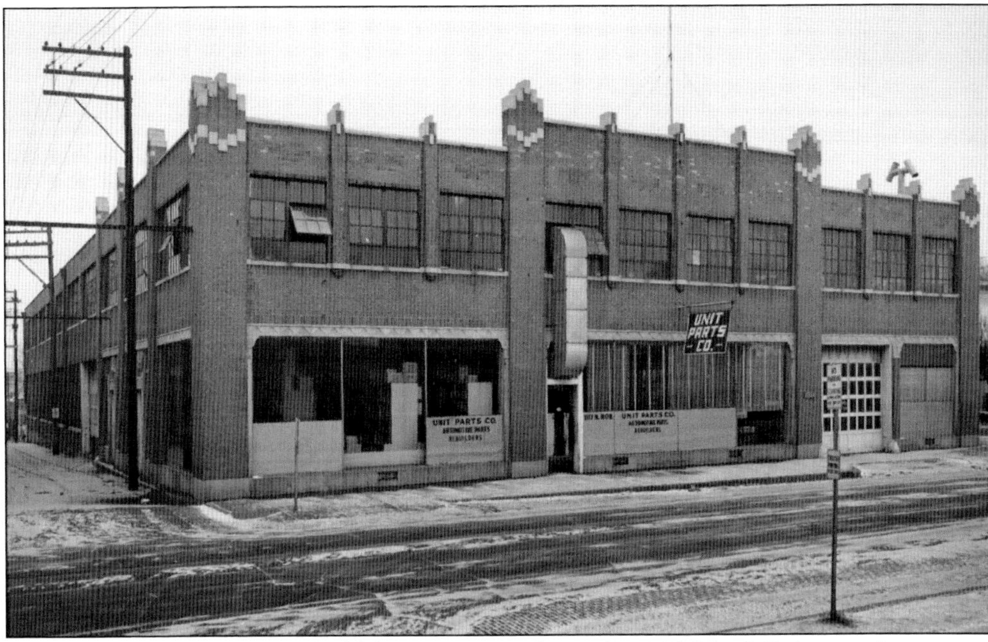

The United Parts Company of Oklahoma City was located at 1117 North Robinson Avenue and was considered America's largest and finest equipped automotive parts rebuilding factory. Started by John William "Bill" Boulton in 1937 with only two employees, the company's high standard of workmanship increased the volume of business for United to $5 million annually and increased its workforce to 107 by 1947. Seen above is the plant and offices of United Parts. Below is its family of owners. From left to right are Don C. Boulton, who attended the Oklahoma Military Academy; J.W. Boulton Sr.; James Boulton, sales manager; John Boulton Jr.; C.B. Boulton, uncle and vice president. The photograph was taken in between United and the Packard building to the south on Park Avenue. (Both, courtesy of the William Boulton Collection.)

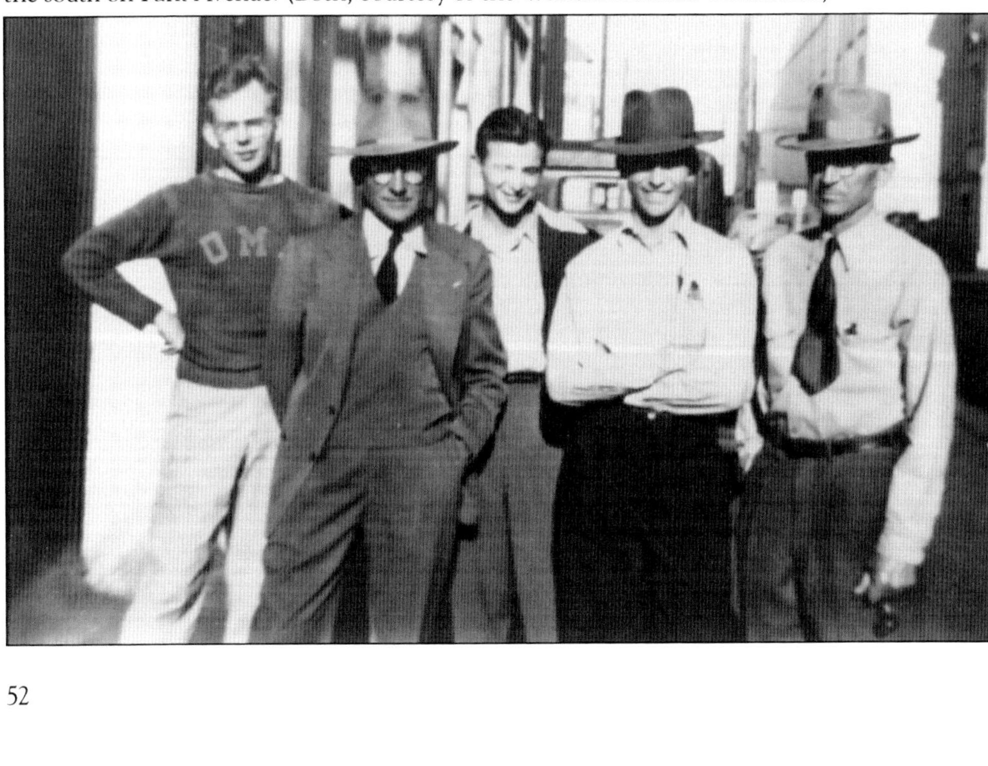

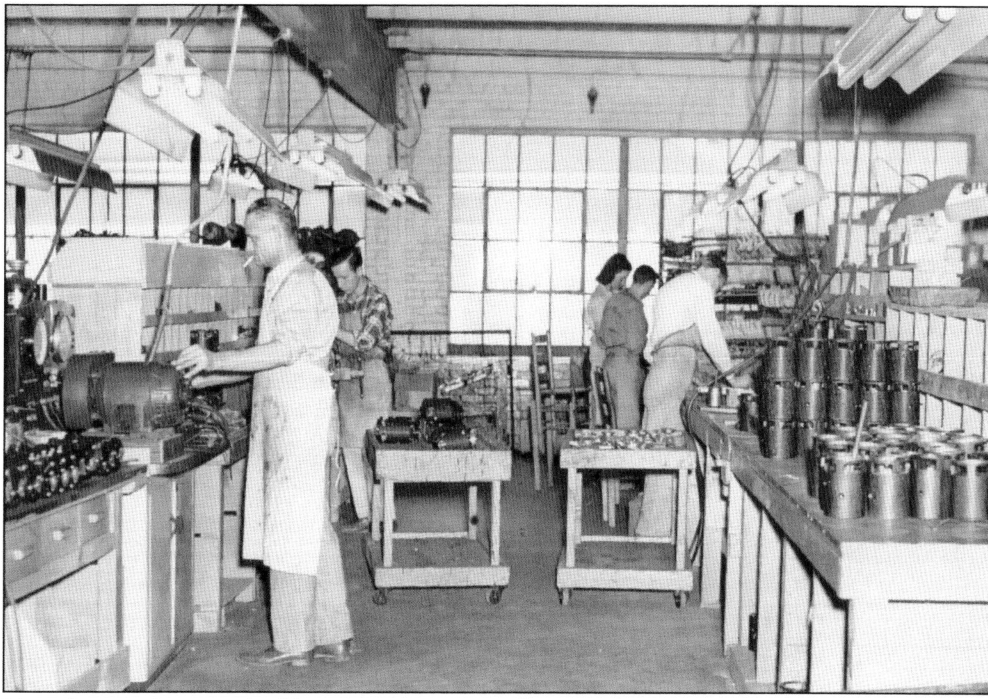

United's specialty was rebuilding generators, as Ford engines had an unusual means of distributing electricity. In the image above, Leo Lichtenstein (at left with the cigarette) works testing generators after assembly. According to Bill Boulton, Leo was a hard worker and had a heavy German accent. He eventually became shop foreman and remained with the company for a long time. Below, an unidentified woman works at winding coils for the generators. Women were an integral part of the workforce and took on the same roles as their male counterparts. (Both, courtesy of the William Boulton Collection.)

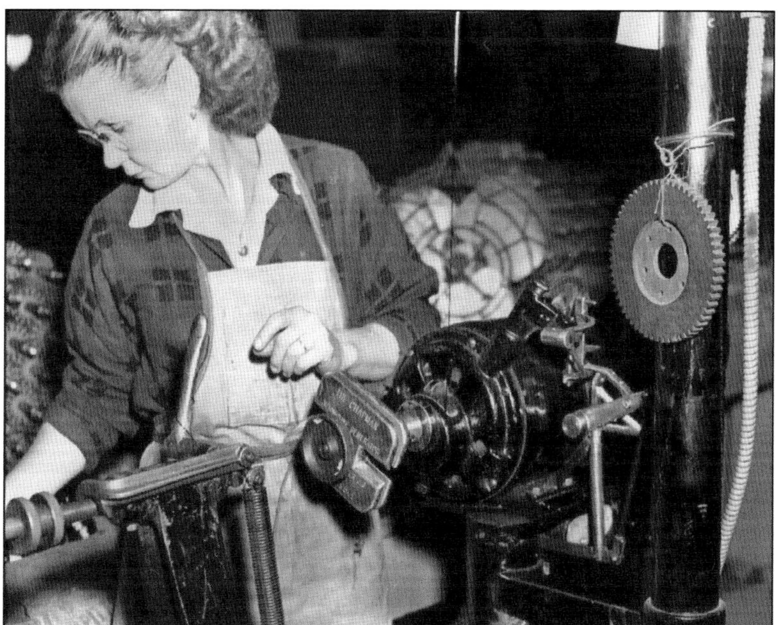

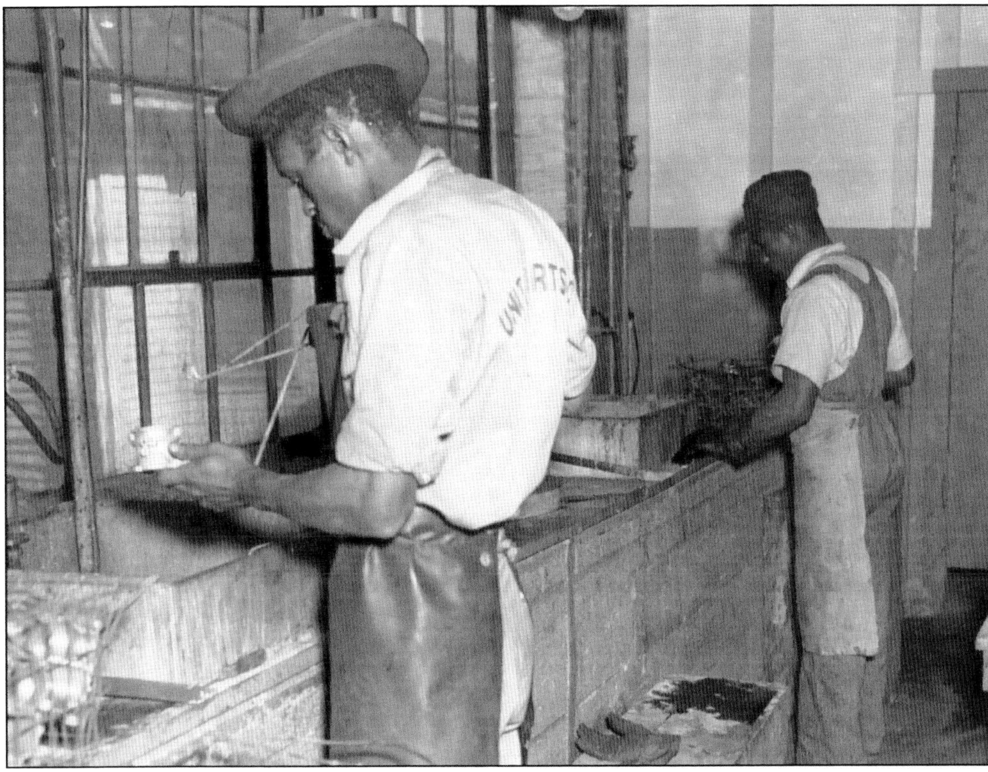

According to owner Bill Boulton, among his most prized employees was Dewey Derrington, pictured here in the fedora. The carburetors United rebuilt were cast from pot metals. Each one was dipped and cleaned in an acid bath of nitric, sulfuric, and hydrochloric acids. It was an evil brew that Dewey handled every day—never getting burned—earning him the title "neoprene man." (Courtesy of the William Boulton Collection.)

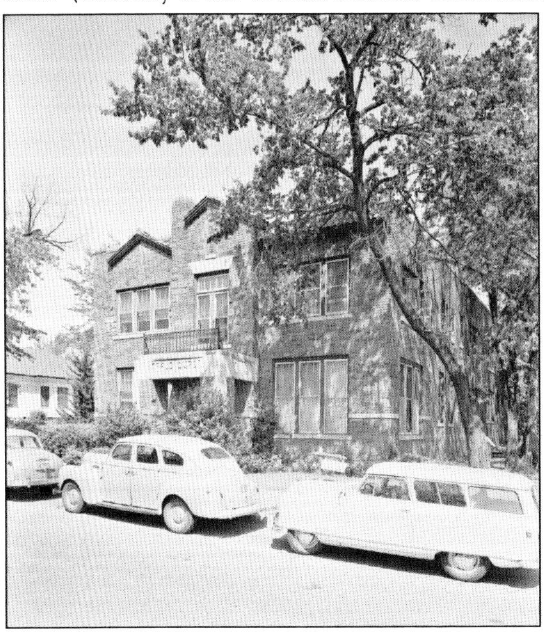

Opening in 1930, the Palo Duro apartments at 409 Northwest Eleventh Street offered full maid service, all bills paid, and air-conditioned furnished apartments. The living spaces stood vacant and boarded up through the 1990s until they were remodeled and offered to mentally ill residents through programs reintegrating them into society in 1995. Today, they have been completely remodeled. (Courtesy of the Oklahoma Historical Society.)

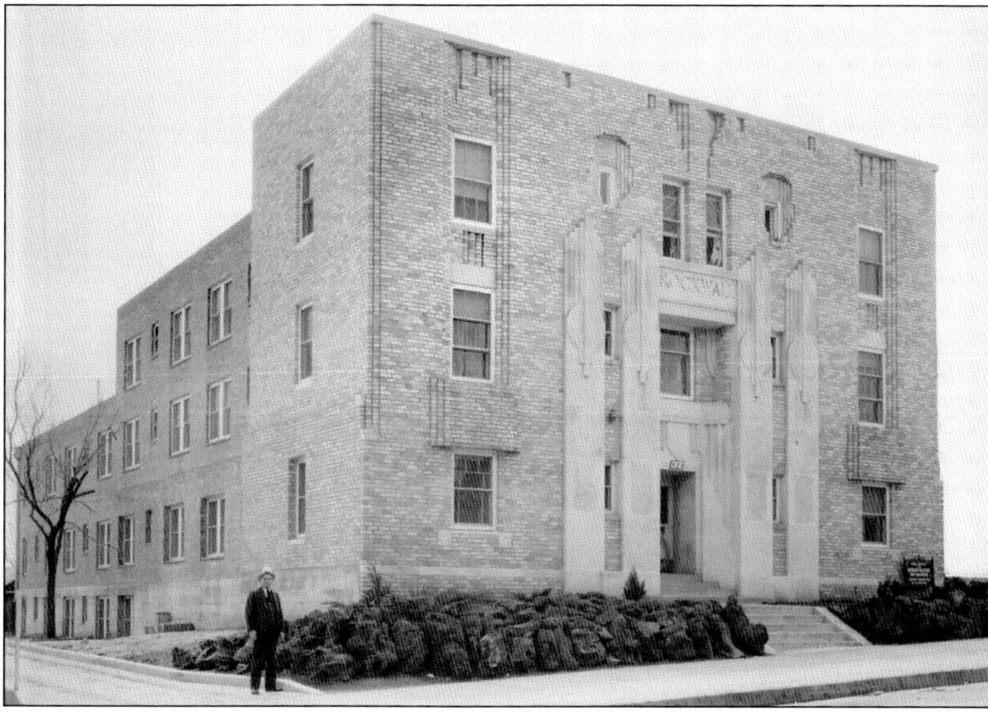

E.A. Hassman built the Rockwall Hotel at 424 Northwest Sixth Street in 1933. The name of the hotel may be derived from the unusual rock formations bordering its ornate Art Deco entrance. Some believe it may have something to do with Hassman's oil speculation in places like Rockwall, Texas that turned him from a telegraph operator to a rich oil tycoon. Hassman was an original '89er who arrived in Oklahoma with his Pforzheim, Germany family. Their homestead east of the city is now Hassman Park near Northeast Sixteenth Street and Interstate 35. Hassman's oil enterprises across Oklahoma, Texas, and Louisiana made him a successful oilman, who was responsible for the construction of several buildings in Oklahoma City. The Rockwall started as a hotel but has served as an apartment building for most of its life. Hassman passed away in 1954 at the age of 71. (Both, courtesy of the Oklahoma Historical Society.)

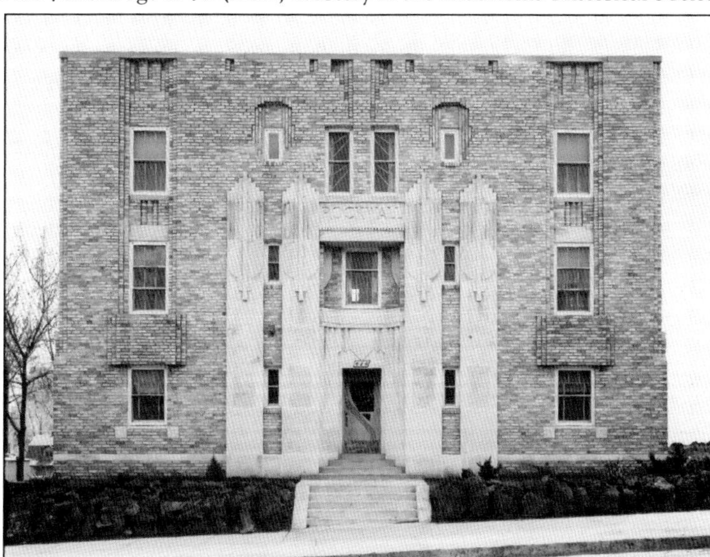

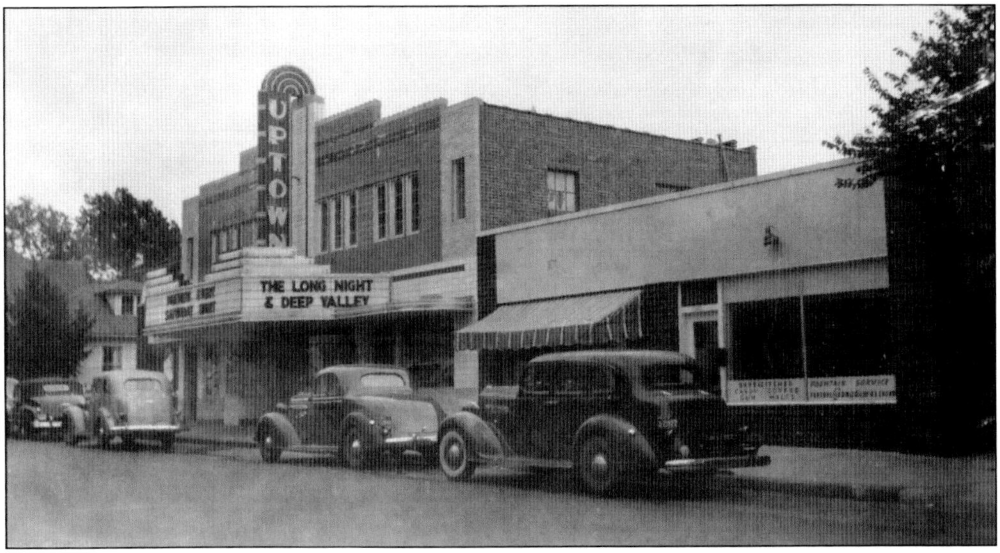

Designed by architect W.H. Schumacher and operated by the Ferris family chain, the Uptown Theater opened at 1212 North Hudson Avenue on February 6, 1941. The 700-seat theater operated until 1959, although it was partially converted into office space around 1955. It was later used as a medical laboratory. Above, the Uptown shows the 1947 films *Deep Valley* and *The Long Night*. Below, the Uptown is captured in a severe winter storm in January 1947 while showing *Angels with Dirty Faces* and *They Drive by Night*. In the background is a doctor's office, drugstore, three beauty shops, a candy store, the Uptown Grocery, and Ned's Grill. The Grill was a burger café until owner Ned Mutz closed it and opened Ned's Steakhouse near Classen High School in 1955. Many longtime city residents fondly remember Ned's for its pizza. (Both, courtesy of the Western History Collections, University of Oklahoma and the Oklahoma City Metropolitan Library System.)

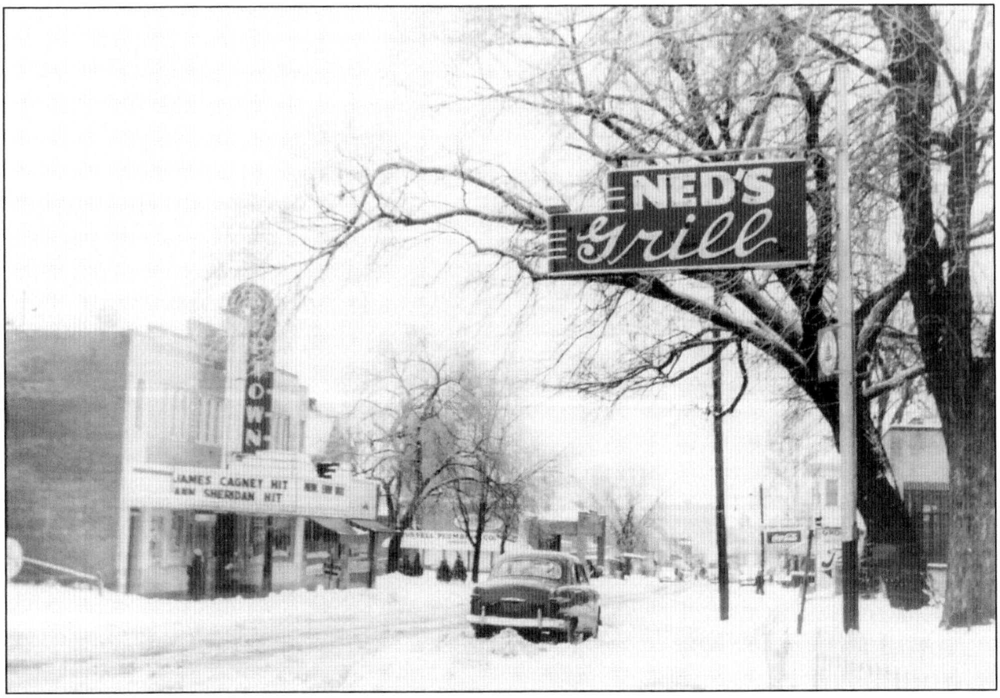

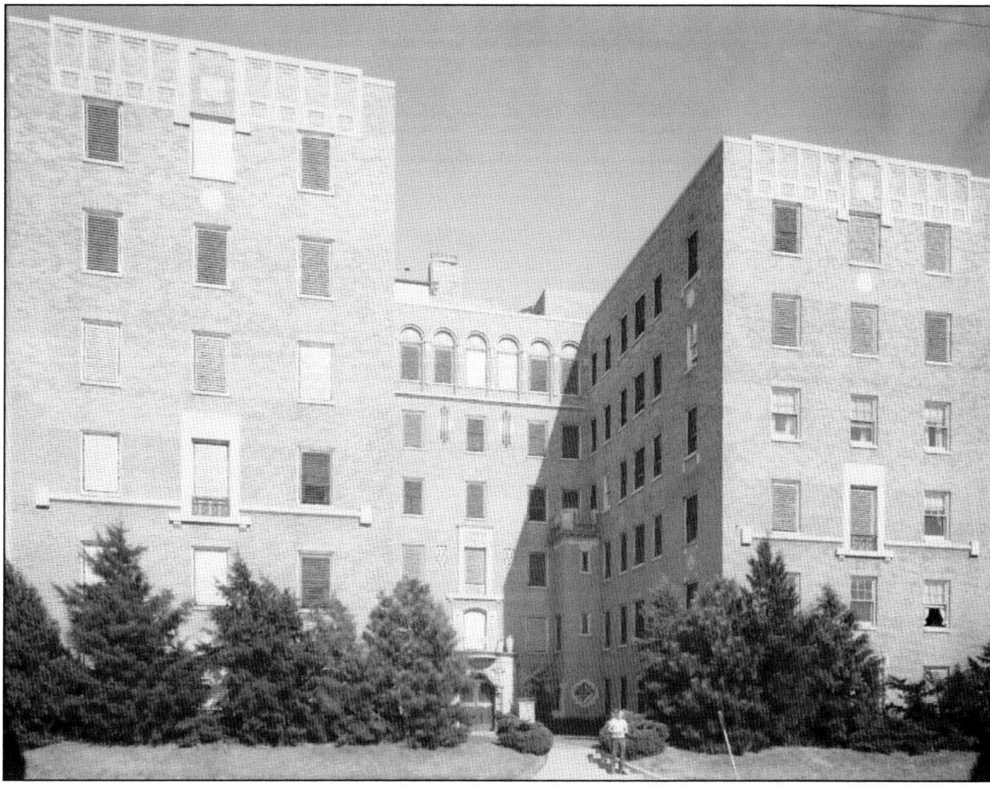

Named after physician Sir William Osler, one of four founders of the John Hopkins University Hospital and medical school, the Osler Medical building at 1200 North Walker Avenue opened in 1929. It was built in three phases eventually reaching seven stories in 1946—the first six being completed in 1929. Erected by the Physicians Holding Group, the Osler was the first suburban privately owned medical building in Oklahoma City. The Mission and Spanish Eclectic style designed by J.W. Hawk and J.O. Parr encompassed over 44,000 square feet of medical offices. Among them were physicians like Dr. Ray M. Balyeat, a pioneer in allergy and asthma medicine. Balyeat established the Oklahoma Allergy and Asthma Clinic, which is the oldest and most respected in the nation. Today, it is The Ambassador, a newly remodeled 54-room boutique hotel. (Both, courtesy of the Oklahoma Historical Society.)

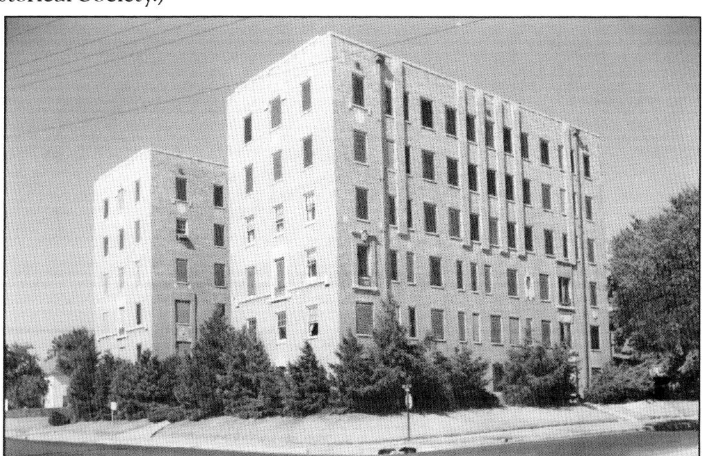

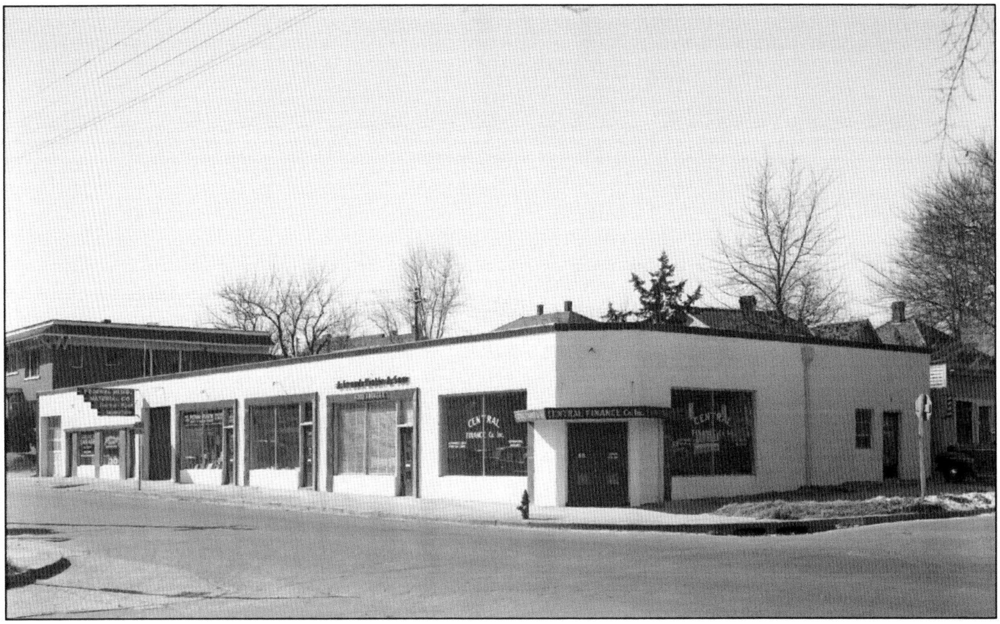

This c. 1947 photograph captures the Central Finance Company at 823 North Walker Avenue. The company was managed by James G. Ramsey, O.D. Thomas, and R.K. Sharp. Today, the property has changed very little and is occupied by McDaniel & Sons Rebuilt Generators and Motors Company. They continue to operate there 45 years after their startup in 1968. (Courtesy of the Oklahoma Historical Society.)

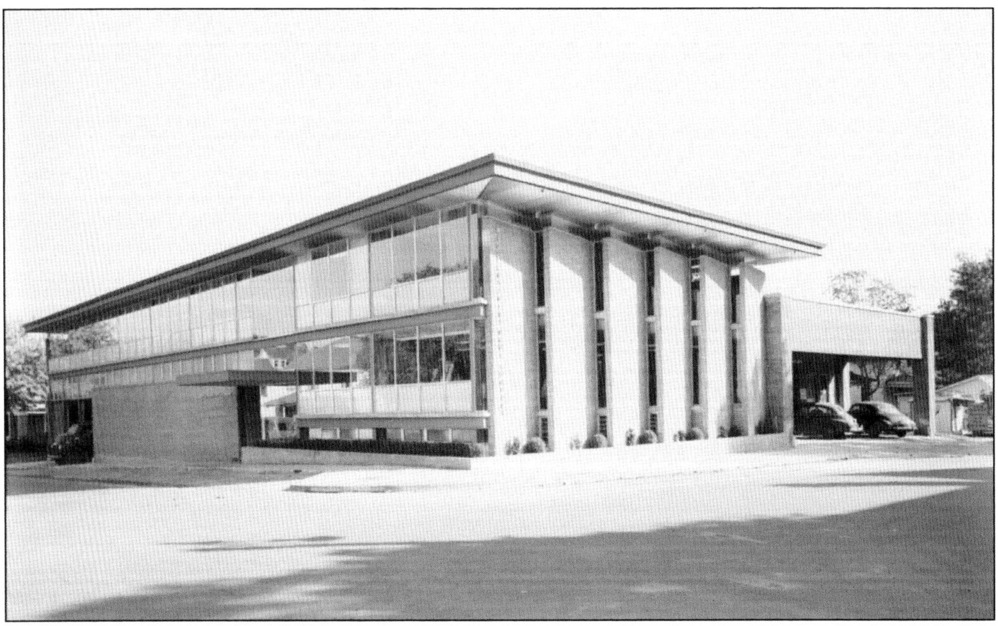

Owner Harvey P. Everest built the Mid-Continent News building in 1949 at 324 Northwest Eleventh Street. It was awarded an Outstanding Building Award from the American Institute of Architects in 1953. The agency was embroiled in a civil suit in the 1960s aimed at banning *Catcher in the Rye*, one of many books distributed by Mid-Continent News. Their offices were demolished in the 1990s. (Courtesy of the Oklahoma Historical Society.)

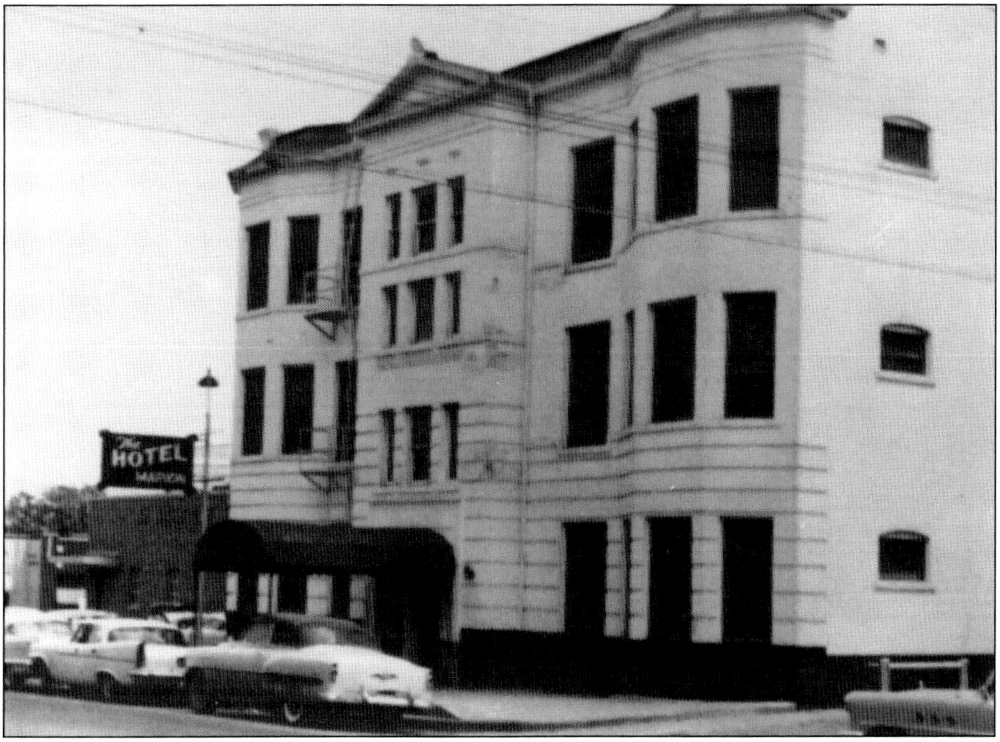

Popular Oklahoma City architect Edward Coady built the Marion Hotel for J.C. Hughes at 110 Northwest Tenth Street in October 1904. The pre-statehood neoclassical design features triangular pediments and a foyer of patterned floral mosaic tile work. A center courtyard is surrounded on all sides by its three-story edifice containing 40 rooms when it was first opened. (Both, courtesy of the Haney Estate.)

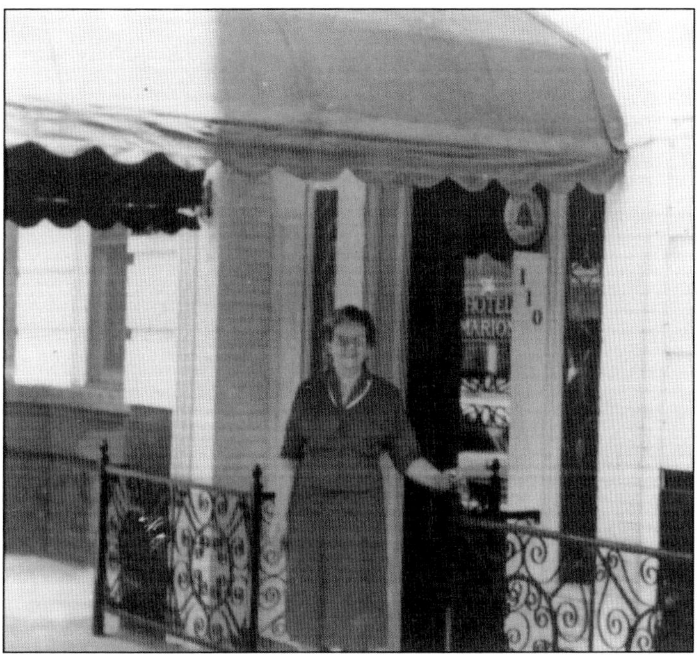

N.N. Gatlin leased the flats in 1909 and remodeled the building as a European Hotel "catering to the best and highest-class trade." The interior woodwork was painted a dark mahogany, the walls were papered, and ceiling decorations were a reflection of the tastes of Gatlin. The hotel was furnished throughout with Brussels- and Axminster-woven English carpets, and the rooms were trimmed differently in weathered oak, bird's-eye maple, and rich mahogany woods.

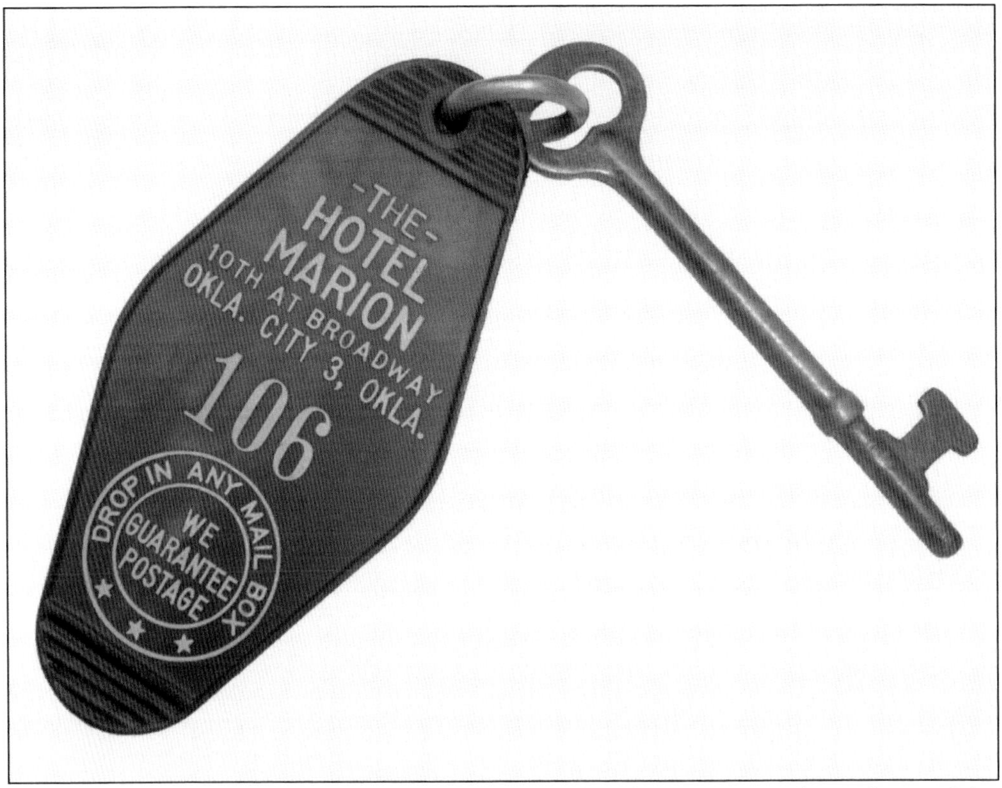

Bess Haney, as seen in the previous image, took over the hotel in 1946. According to her son John Haney, she was the warmest of people, which may have aided many soldiers being processed to serve in the Korean and Vietnam wars through an Army recruiting station across the street. An old soda machine dispensed cold drinks in the lobby. The hotel's slogan was "the nicest small hotel you'll find." The key pictured above belonged to Haney's room. (Courtesy of the author.)

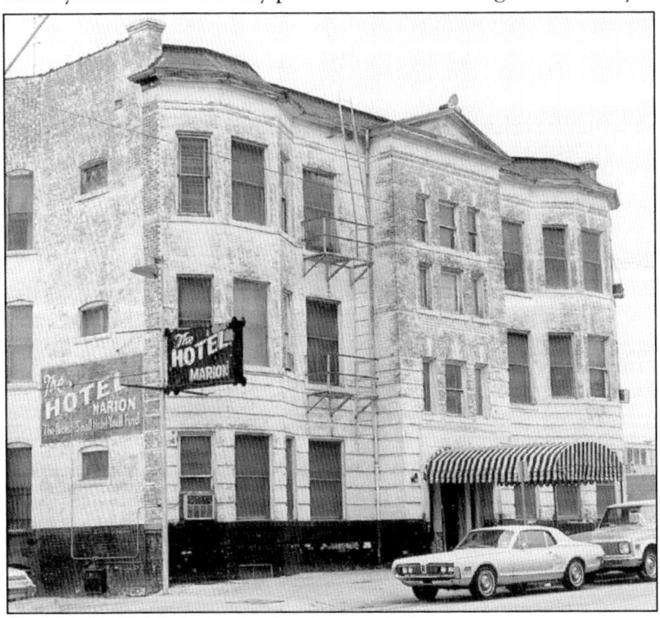

This c. 1979 image shows the Marion in a deteriorating state. Eventually, chain hotels drew guests away from places like the Marion, forcing Haney into retirement in the mid-1970s. The Marion remained vacant until Midtown Renaissance Developers acquired it. As of this writing, the Marion is about to undergo a complete restoration to be turned into high-end apartments, via a unique engineering effort by its owners. (Courtesy and Copyright 1979, OPUBCO Communications Group.)

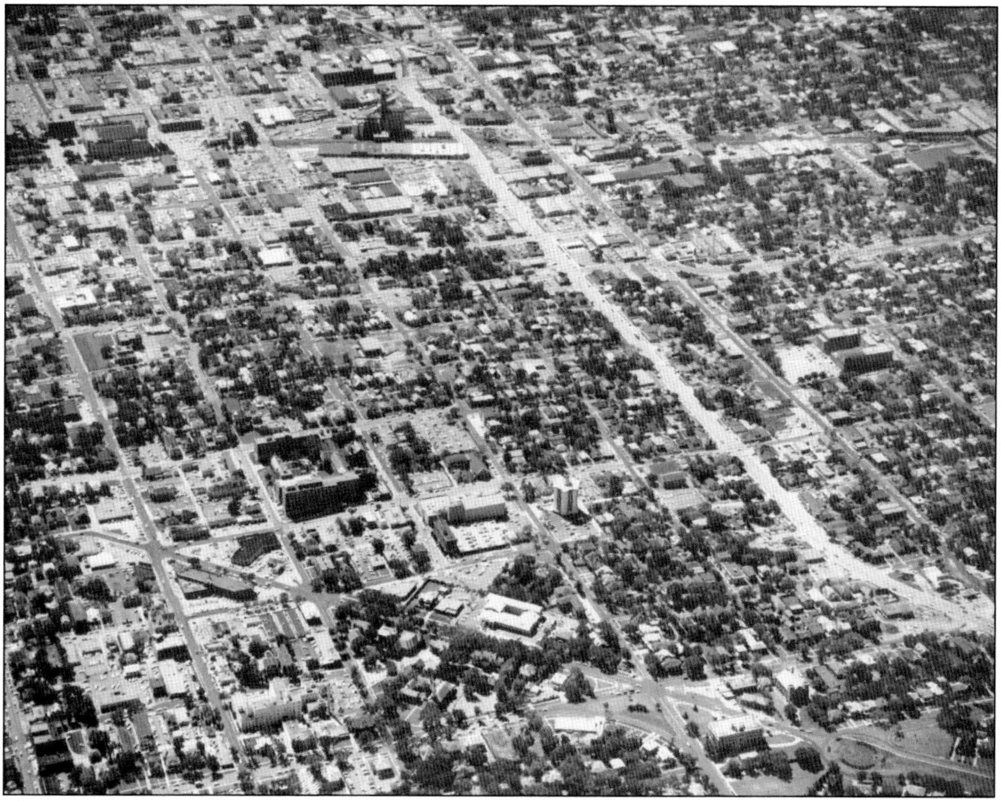

This aerial image looking south from St. Anthony Hospital, with Northwest Tenth Street in the foreground and the hospital along the left, captures a rare glimpse of the Cottage District, also known as SoSA. The district is composed of homes southwest of the hospital complex. Today, it consists of a unique collection of Modern-style residential architecture and restored territorial Victorian homes. (Courtesy of the Oklahoma Historical Society.)

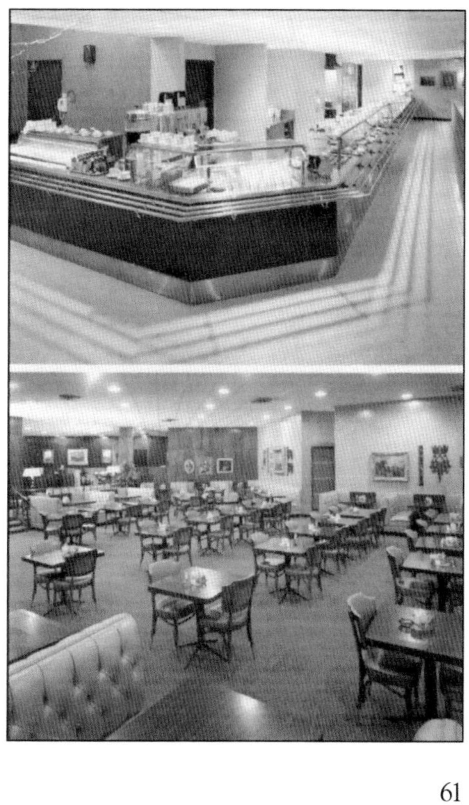

In 1948, John Schroer Sr. opened Boulevard Cafeteria near the Northwest Tenth Street rotary, currently home to the EMSA Ambulance administrative offices. At the time, Oklahoma City boasted 23 cafeterias, including the Queen Ann, also owned by Schroer. The cafeteria moved to 525 Northwest Eleventh Street in the 1970s. Very few images exist of Boulevard, and the postcard above shows the cafeteria after it opened. (Courtesy of the Oklahoma Historical Society.)

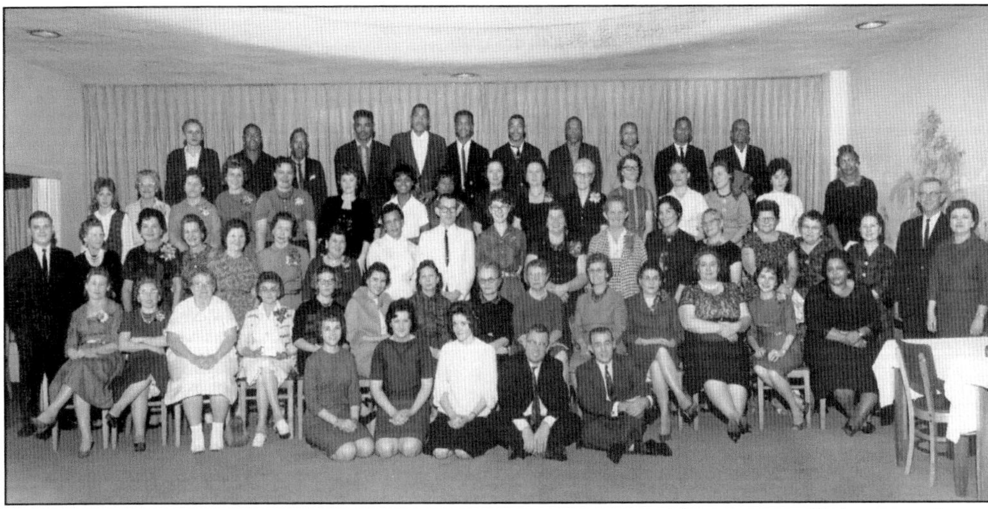

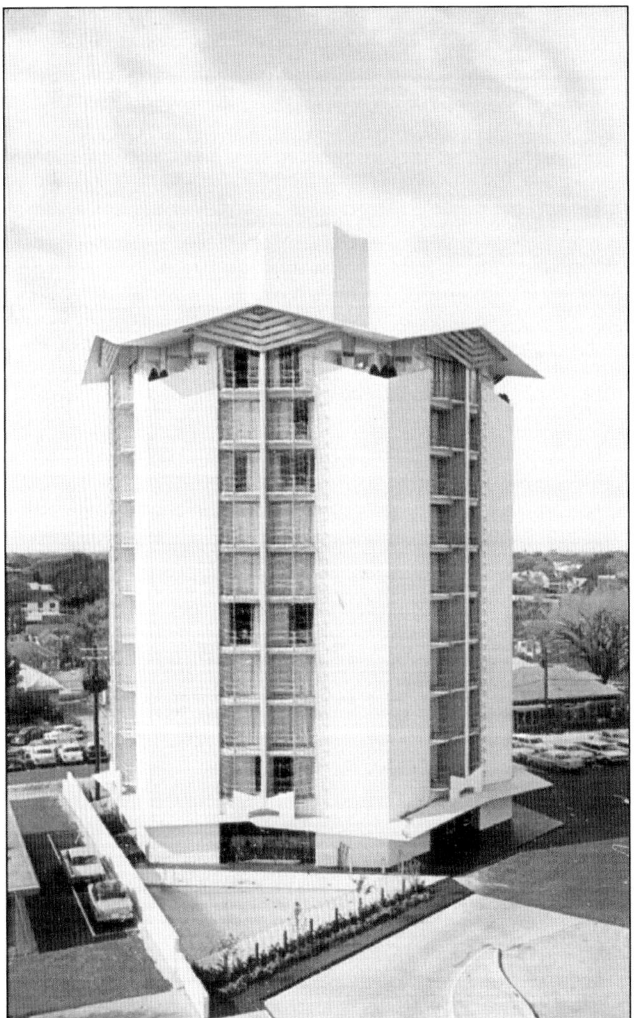

Above is a staff photograph from Christmas 1962. On the third row, far left, is John Schroer Jr., and John Schroer is on the far right, second row. Today, the cafeteria is managed by John Junior's sons Harrison and Stewart Schroer and still maintains the original family recipes dating back to the 1940s. (Courtesy of the Boulevard Cafeteria.)

Built by Bailey, Bozalis, Dickinson & Roloff, the Plaza Tower Hotel at 1117 North Shartel Avenue was a 10-story tower with 80 rooms, event space, dining, shops, and a unique triangular outdoor swimming pool with underground cabanas, as seen in the image above. Unfortunately, operations ceased after only a few years. The building housed nurses attending the St. Anthony School of Nursing from 1966 to 1967. (Courtesy of the Oklahoma Historical Society.)

Also known as the Hexagon Building, Plaza Tower, as described by the *Oklahoman* on March 8, 1959, was "designed using a diamond module to produce a hexagonal floor plan" with eight rooms on each floor in a modernistic structure. This image from a rare brochure lists the many amenities available, including an in-house doctor and laundry service. An unsuccessful plan to convert the space into an elderly retirement center fell through in 1986. Within a few years, the hotel was demolished. A new apartment complex has recently been proposed for the now vacant lot. (Courtesy of Okie Mod Squad at OKCMod.com.)

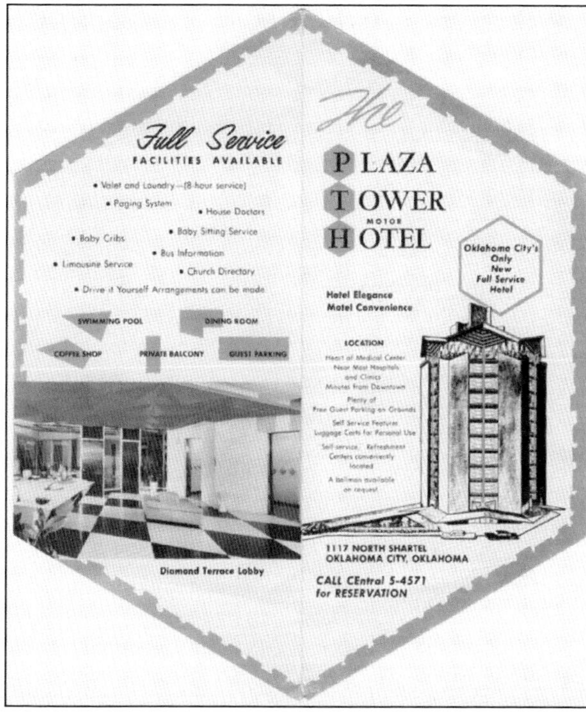

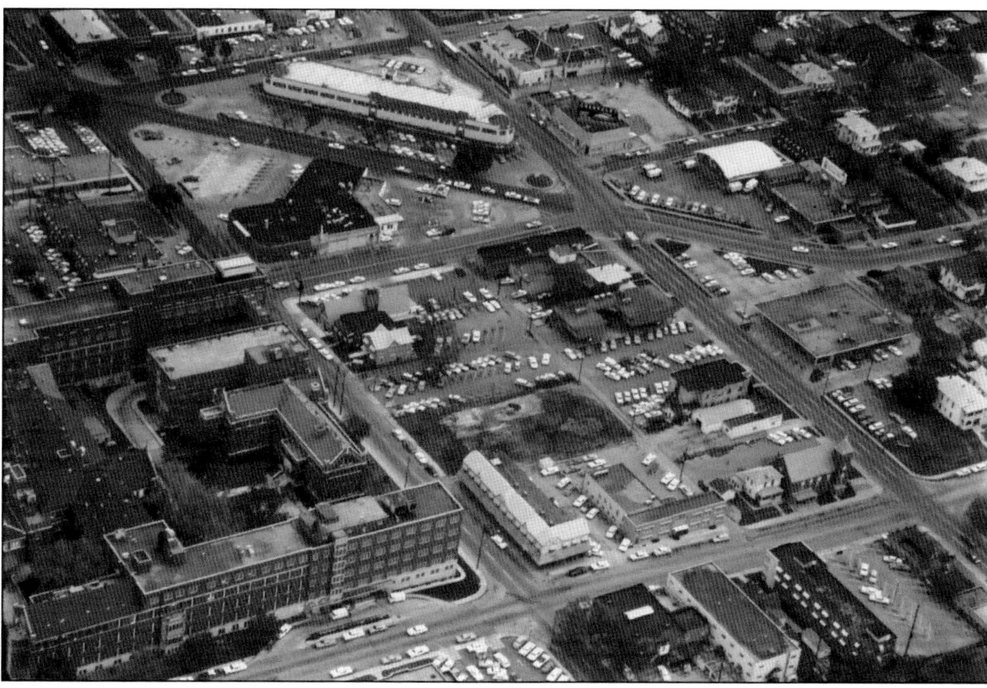

This aerial photograph captures west Midtown during the 1970s when Plaza Court was covered in siding. The St. Anthony complex sits in the lower left. Walker Avenue runs from bottom to top along the far right. This decade introduced much blight to the area. This continued until the mid-1990s, when bold private investors began to restore and renovate the properties still remaining. (Courtesy of the Oklahoma Historical Society.)

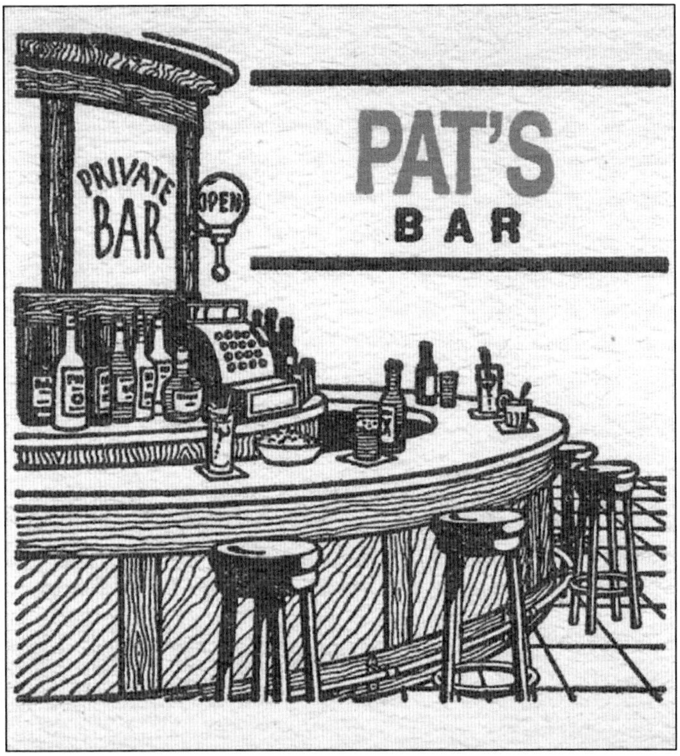

Pat's 10th Street Lounge was located in the west wing of the Packard building and was named after owner Pat Hyde. Hyde leased the space around 1996, although it had operated as a cocktail lounge since about 1943. He eventually closed up shop in 2006 after the property was acquired by the Midtown Renaissance group. Howard has since restored and redeveloped the Packard building into a successful mixed-use property as of this writing. This paper coaster is a lost remnant of Pat's, which was frequented by those along the Northwest Tenth Street corridor. The c. 1997 image below shows the Packard building and Pat's Bar. (Both, courtesy of the author.)

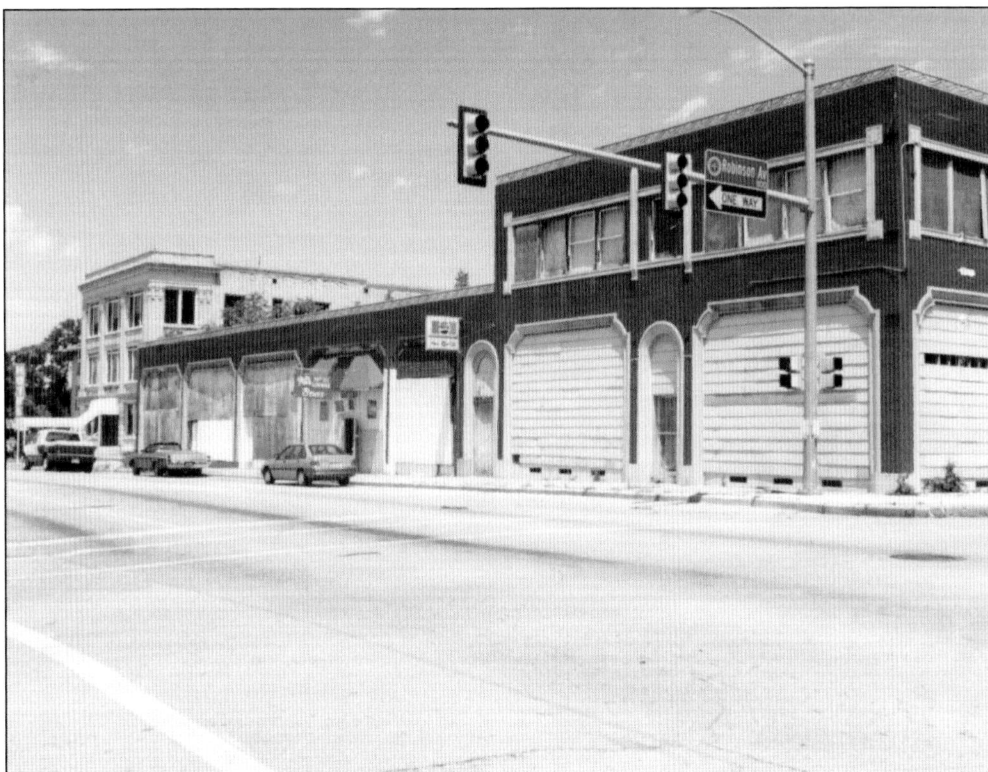

Three

Midtown Grace

Long before Oklahoma became a state, the territory was already hosting a score of people. Among them were Native American tribes, only five of which were local to the region, and numerous immigrant settlers from Mexico, Poland, Russia, and other European nations. With the exception of Native Americans who were forcibly relocated by the federal government, others began living in assigned lands to work in coal and metal mines operated by the railroads.

The work was dangerous. Numerous mining accidents occurred, prompting the area's rare Catholic-founded schools to close so that medical aid and support could be rendered. Over time, this effort resulted in the support and construction of other Catholic schools and hospitals. The first among them was St. Anthony Hospital in Oklahoma City, which opened as early as 1898. This work was taken on by three particular orders, who eventually settled their motherhouses in Oklahoma City's Midtown area.

The first among them were the Sisters of Mercy, who first appeared in 1884 at the invitation of Father Isodore Robot, the first prefect apostolic of the Indian Territory. Their work began with schools and later involved medical care. This order would go on to establish many schools across Oklahoma, including Mount St. Mary's on the south side of Oklahoma City in 1903. The Sisters of Mercy were also responsible for creating Mercy Hospital, which originally stood at Northwest Thirteenth Street and Walker Avenue, and is now part of a Catholic health care system that includes 32 hospitals and 300 outpatient locations.

The Sisters of St. Francis came to Oklahoma City to raise funds for their order's hospital in St. Louis, Missouri, but the immediate need for medical care in the post-land-rush city was tantamount. With the assistance of the local community, the state's first hospital was established in a former cornfield in 1898 and named St. Anthony. Today, the hospital has become part of a vast network of care facilities across the state that includes 19 rural hospitals, now operated by the Franciscan Sisters of Mary. The work of these three orders would establish a medical and educational care system within Midtown's heart that looked over Oklahoma City's earliest citizens, allowing them to survive many harsh moments including epidemic outbreaks, the Ku Klux Klan, and two world wars. Today, the effort of these sisters and the citizens they cared for is evident in the great city now surrounding them.

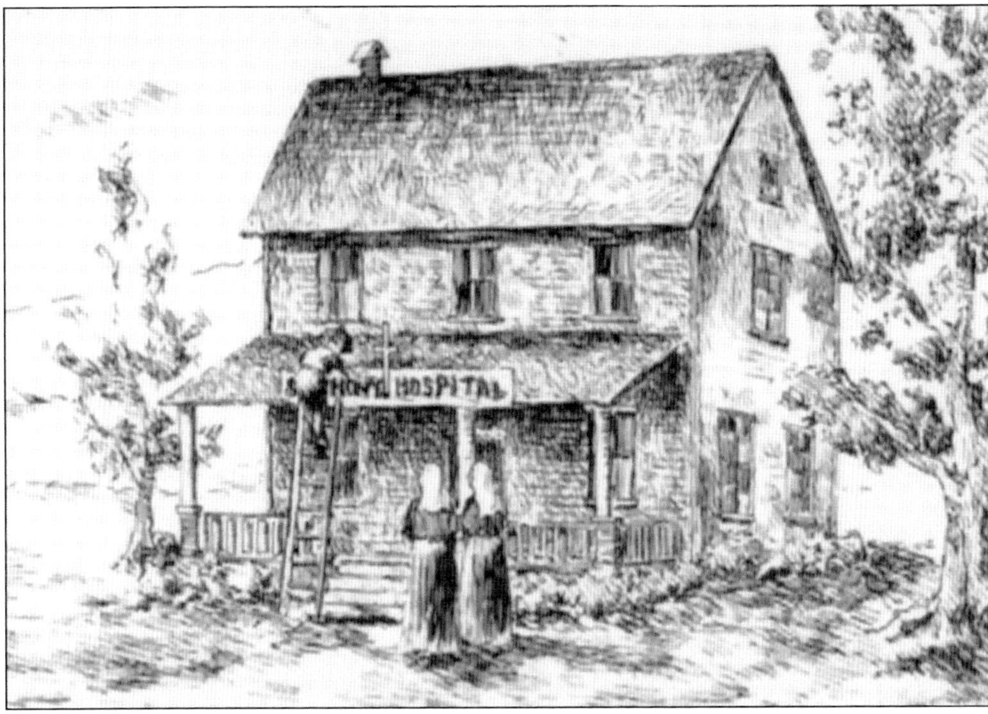

Two sisters of St. Francis of St. Louis, Missouri came to Oklahoma in 1889, seeking funds for their hospital in Merryville, Missouri. They asked permission from Father Lanslots of St. Joseph's to solicit funds, and he granted permission under the stipulation that funds raised would go toward establishing a hospital in Oklahoma City. This drawing depicts the early hospital. (Courtesy of St. Anthony and the Franciscan Sisters of Mary.)

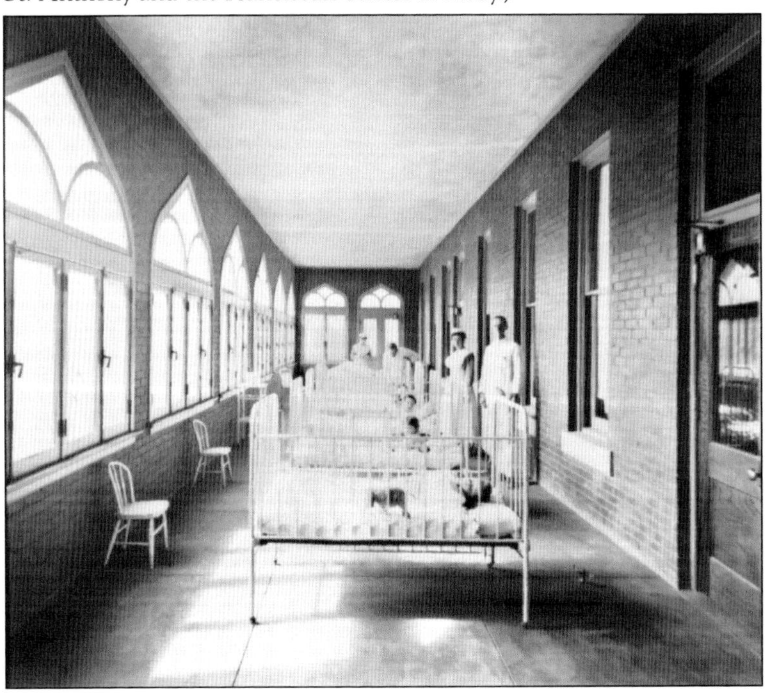

The 12-bed St. Anthony Hospital opened August 1, 1898, with a staff of six, including Dr. J.A. Ryan, a surgeon and unique rarity in frontier hospitals. The house was unsuited for patient care. It had a leaking roof, no gas or electricity, and was heated by coal stoves. This made it impossible to clean properly, forcing a shutdown for winter. (Courtesy of St. Anthony and the Franciscan Sisters of Mary.)

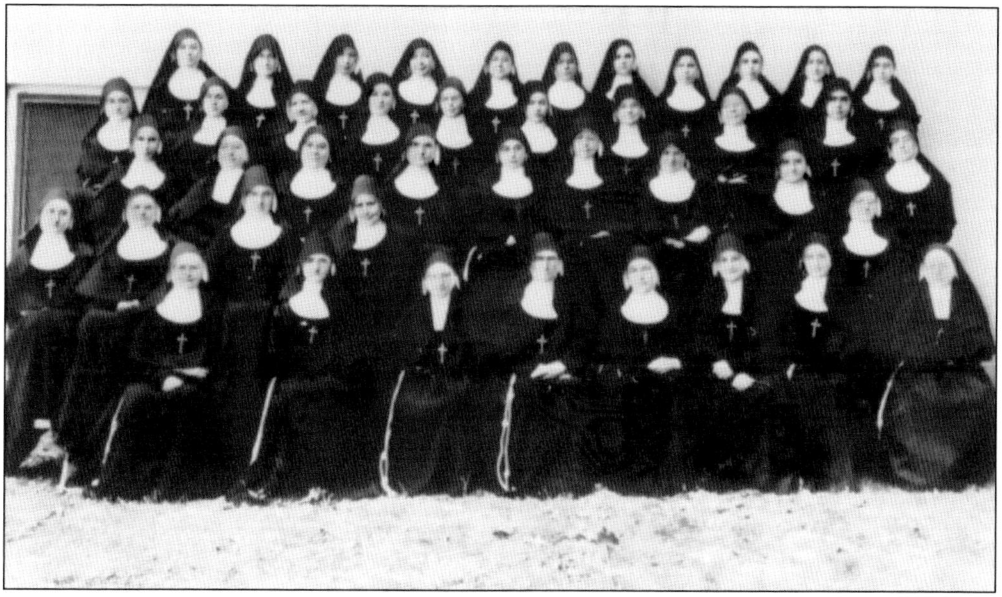

The sisters spent the winter seeking funds and preparing linens and dressings for the hospital. In 1899, a section of cornfield was acquired from homesteader Frank Gault through Thomas O'Keefe near Northwest Ninth Street and Lee Avenue for $600, thereby completing the contract for a new building. The cost for the new hospital was $11,200, which included land and all building materials but excluded plumbing, heating, and lighting. The new hospital, a two-story, 25-bed facility that featured a barn, barnyard, and vegetable garden, was dedicated on November 23, 1899. Patients and neighbors supplied livestock, seeds, and seedlings. (Both, courtesy of St. Anthony and the Franciscan Sisters of Mary.)

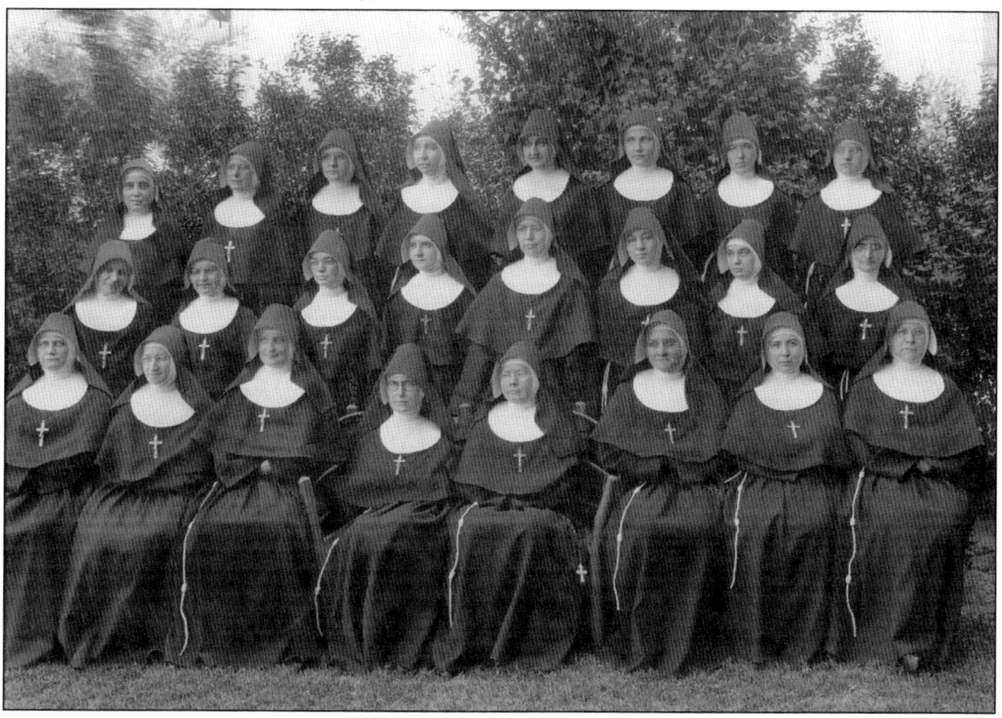

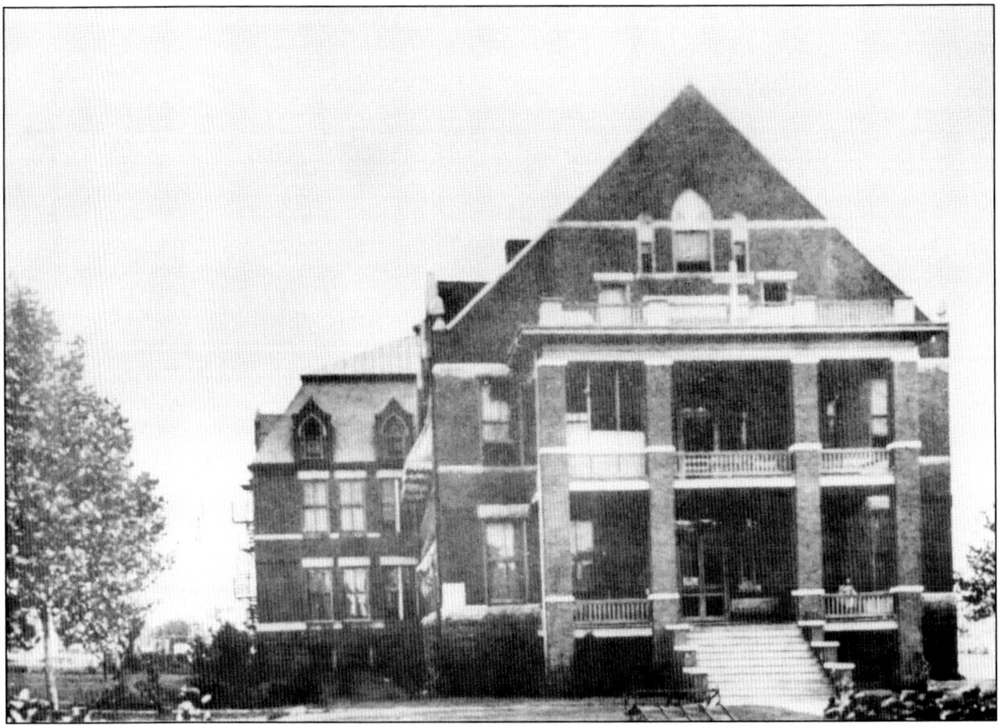

Despite it being a new building, problems persisted because the hospital lacked its own water and sewage system, used kerosene lamps for lighting, and needed coal for heating. A cesspool served as the sanitation system and was backed up after just six months. All water was hauled with the aid of a draft horse and a cart four blocks away. A windmill powered a pump when water was discovered below the property in 1904, but it was still hand-carried to the hospital. The hospital expanded in 1906, and the first x-ray machine was installed along with a steam laundry press the following year. During the winter of 1907, an epidemic of smallpox and scarlet fever swept over Oklahoma City. St. Anthony's barn was converted to accept and care for those patients. These images capture the hospital around 1906–1912. (Both, courtesy of St. Anthony and the Franciscan Sisters of Mary.)

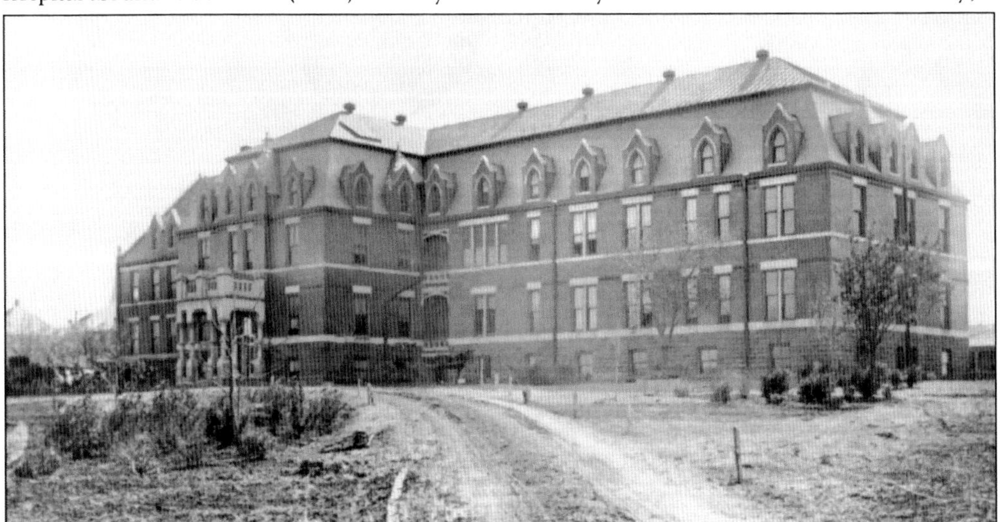

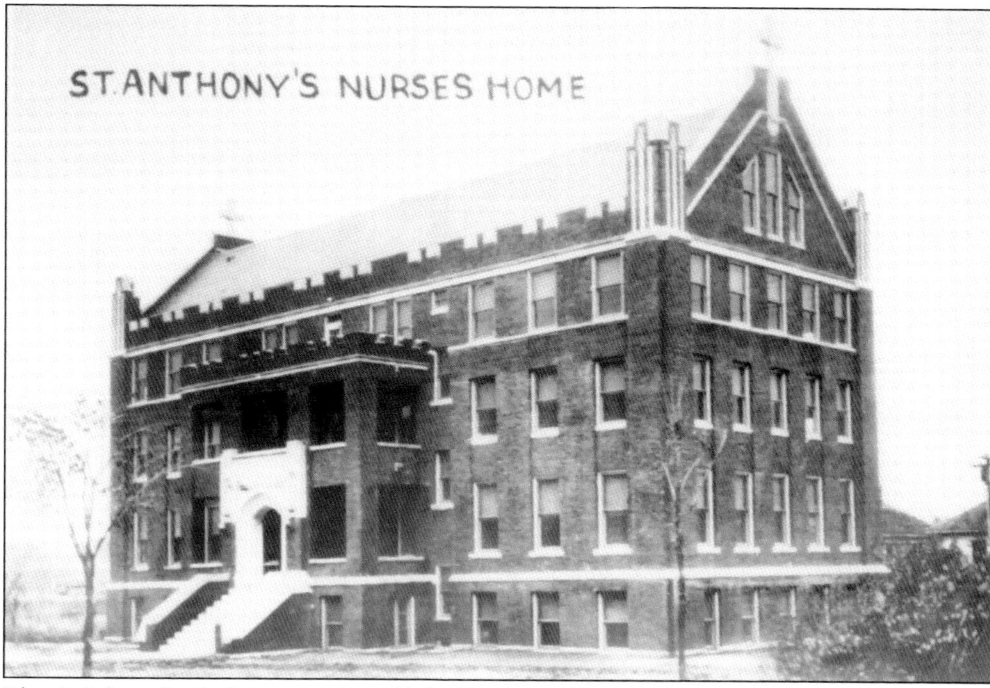

The city's first school of nursing was established by St. Anthony and opened in 1908. Nursing students lived in the hospital until a new facility was built for them in 1922. The hospital expanded once again in 1916, adding a new wing and bringing the bed capacity to 150. The expansion included the addition of a new surgery room, a clinical laboratory that offered facilities for bacteriology and pathology studies, a medical library, and classrooms. The new wing included eight private patient rooms and two separate pediatric wards for both males and females with private baths and sun porches. Sister Beatrice Merrigan became one of the country's first registered x-ray technicians in 1921 as she led the new radiology department. Above is an early image of the nursing home, near the current hospital's location. Pictured below is a small group of nursing graduates. (Both, courtesy of St. Anthony and the Franciscan Sisters of Mary.)

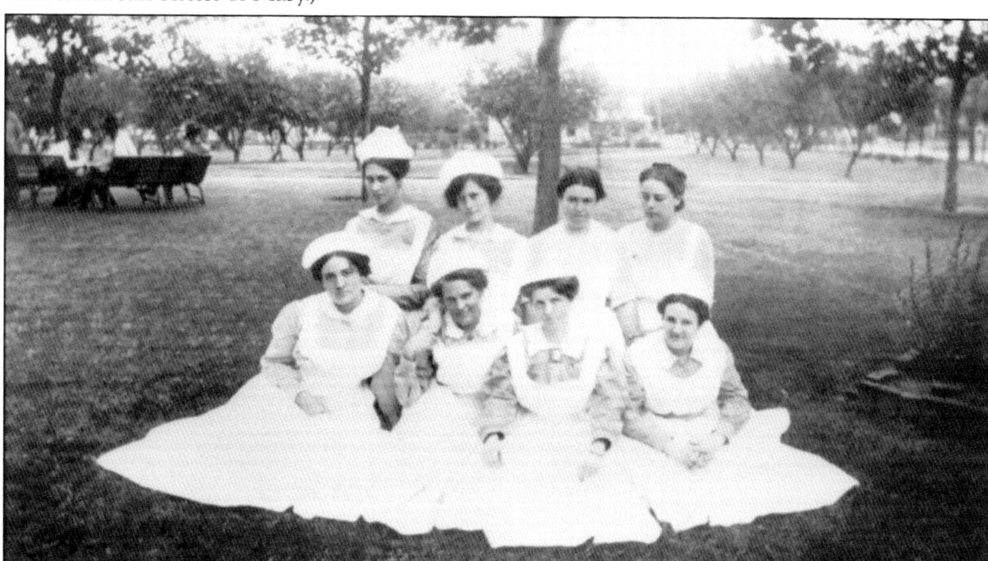

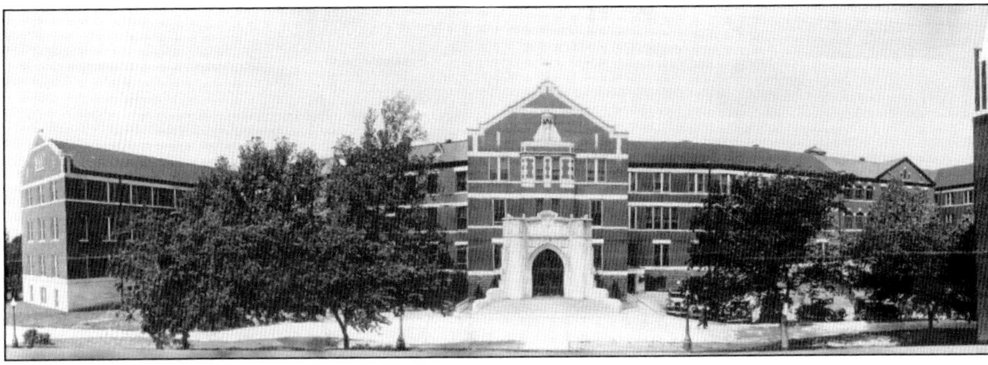

During the Great Depression (1930–1934), St. Anthony served over two million meals to over 6,000 poverty-stricken Oklahomans who lived in "Hoovervilles" along the banks of the North Canadian River (now the Oklahoma River). It was the sisters' motto to "turn no one away." The facility helped thousands of patients throughout these years, noting in their log "ODL," or Our Dear Lords, who were indigent or unable to pay for their services. Despite the Depression and growing debt, St. Anthony Hospital continued to develop its services and facilities. During World War II, doctors and nurses were called to the front lines while the sisters, along with the remaining staff, maintained the facility. The above image is the hospital in 1932, and below is one of the laboratories. (Both, courtesy of St. Anthony and the Franciscan Sisters of Mary.)

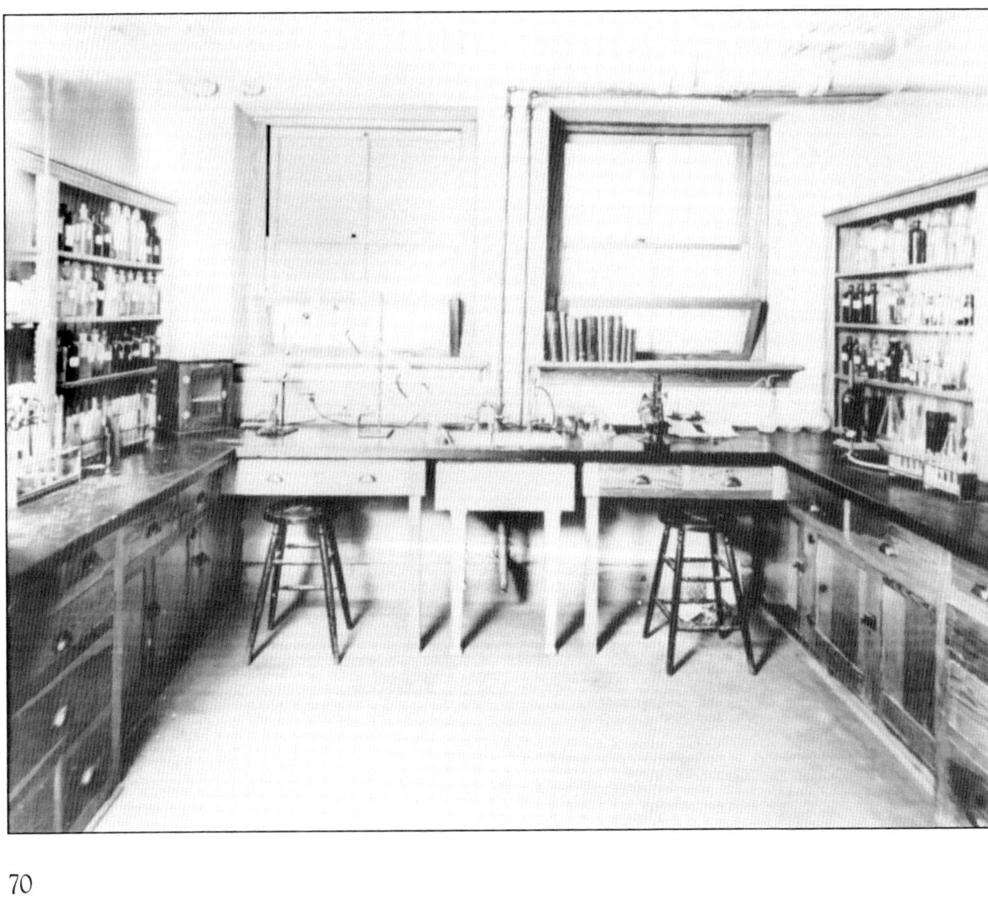

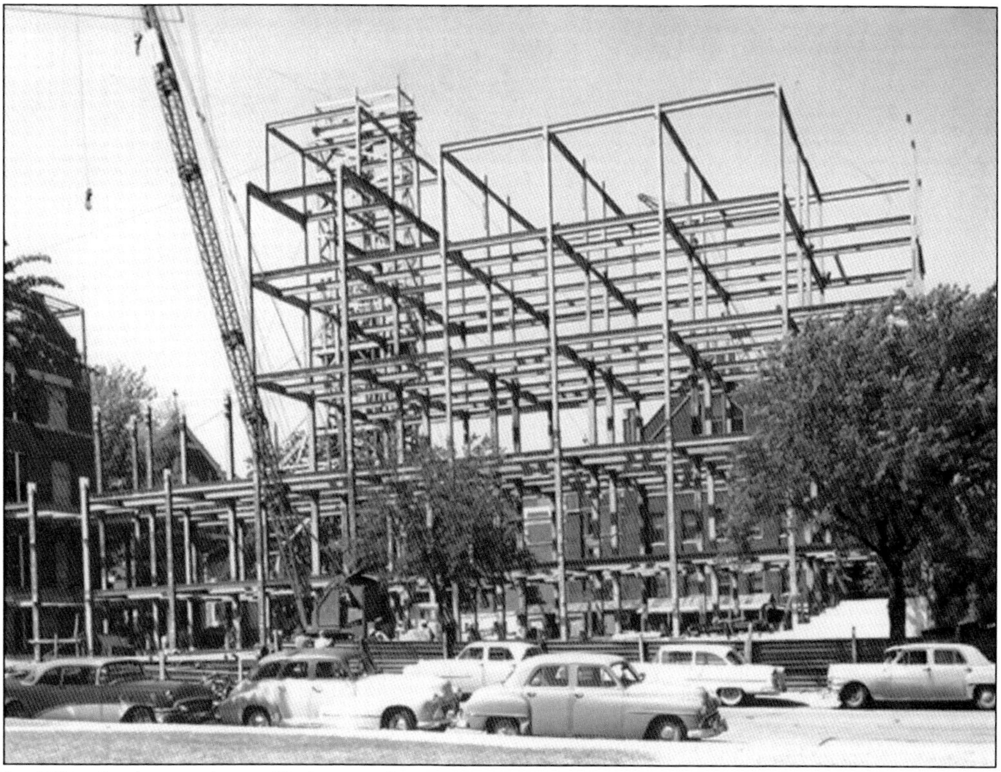

In 1954, the hospital installed central air-conditioning and began a three-phase building program. The new construction (pictured above) added 100 additional beds, a psychiatric unit, the first hospital-based occupational therapy unit in the state, an eye surgery unit, and a testing lab for cardiovascular irregularities such as heart murmurs. An expansion of the nursing residents, medical library, chemistry laboratory, dental unit, and new chapel were part of the final phase—called Marian Hall—as seen on the right. (Both, courtesy of St. Anthony and the Franciscan Sisters of Mary.)

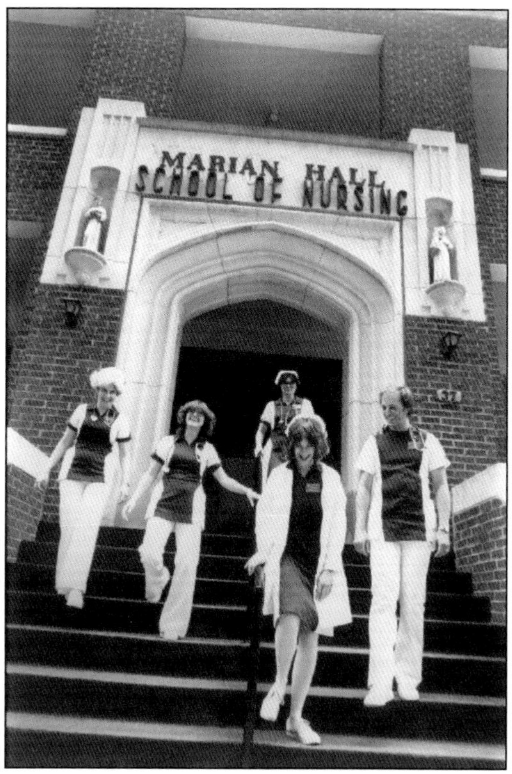

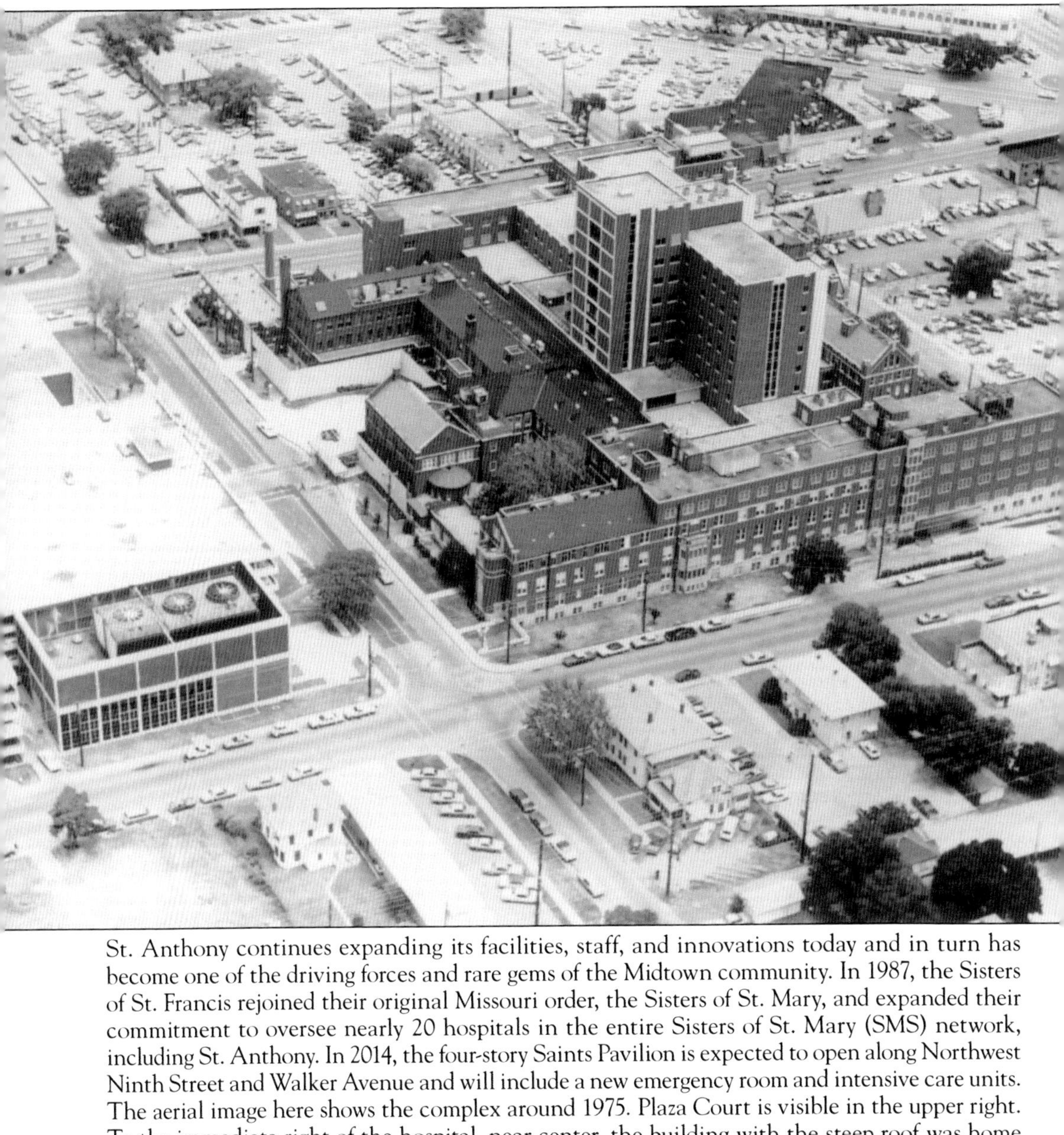

St. Anthony continues expanding its facilities, staff, and innovations today and in turn has become one of the driving forces and rare gems of the Midtown community. In 1987, the Sisters of St. Francis rejoined their original Missouri order, the Sisters of St. Mary, and expanded their commitment to oversee nearly 20 hospitals in the entire Sisters of St. Mary (SMS) network, including St. Anthony. In 2014, the four-story Saints Pavilion is expected to open along Northwest Ninth Street and Walker Avenue and will include a new emergency room and intensive care units. The aerial image here shows the complex around 1975. Plaza Court is visible in the upper right. To the immediate right of the hospital, near center, the building with the steep roof was home to Big Ed's Burgers. (Courtesy of St. Anthony and the Franciscan Sisters of Mary.)

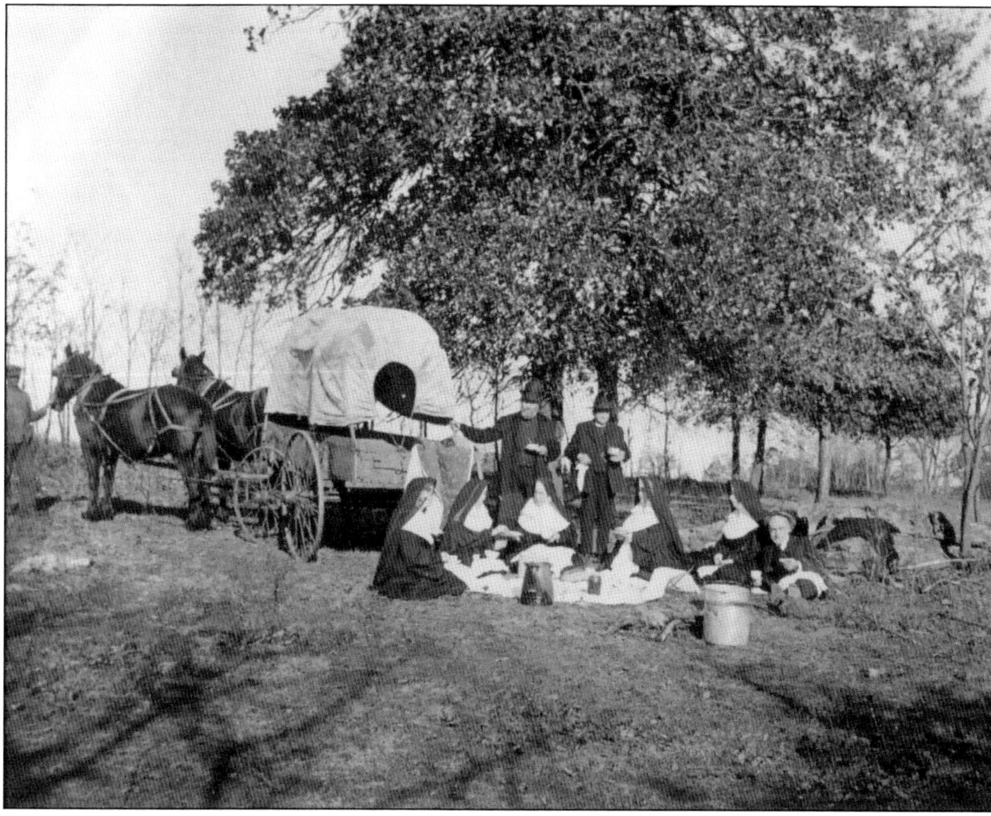

At the invitation of Rev. Isidore Robot, part of the Order of St. Benedict and the first prefect apostolic of the Indian Territory, five Sisters of Mercy traveled to Oklahoma from Lacon, Illinois, in 1884. The invitation asked the sisters to make the Sacred Heart Mission their new convent and help minister to and educate local Native Americans. Arriving "by the light of lanterns" in Atoka, Oklahoma, at 10:00 p.m. on the night of July 9, 1884, they were met by Father Robot and brother Dominic Lambert, accompanied by local Native Americans to see them safely through to Sacred Heart. After a morning mass the following day, they began their trek. Tragedy nearly struck when a horse was gripped in quicksand as the band tried crossing the Canadian River, but quick thinking prevented it. Within a year, they were joined by three additional sisters and established the St. Mary's Academy boarding school. (Both, courtesy of the Sisters of Mercy.)

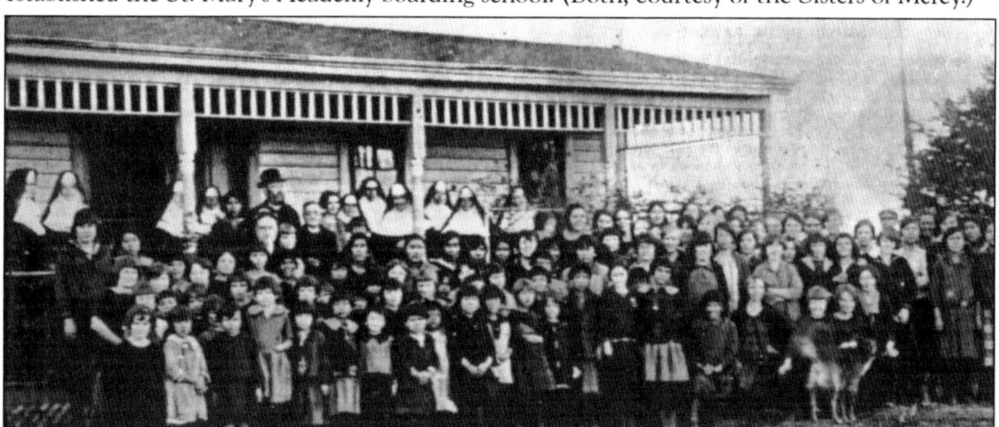

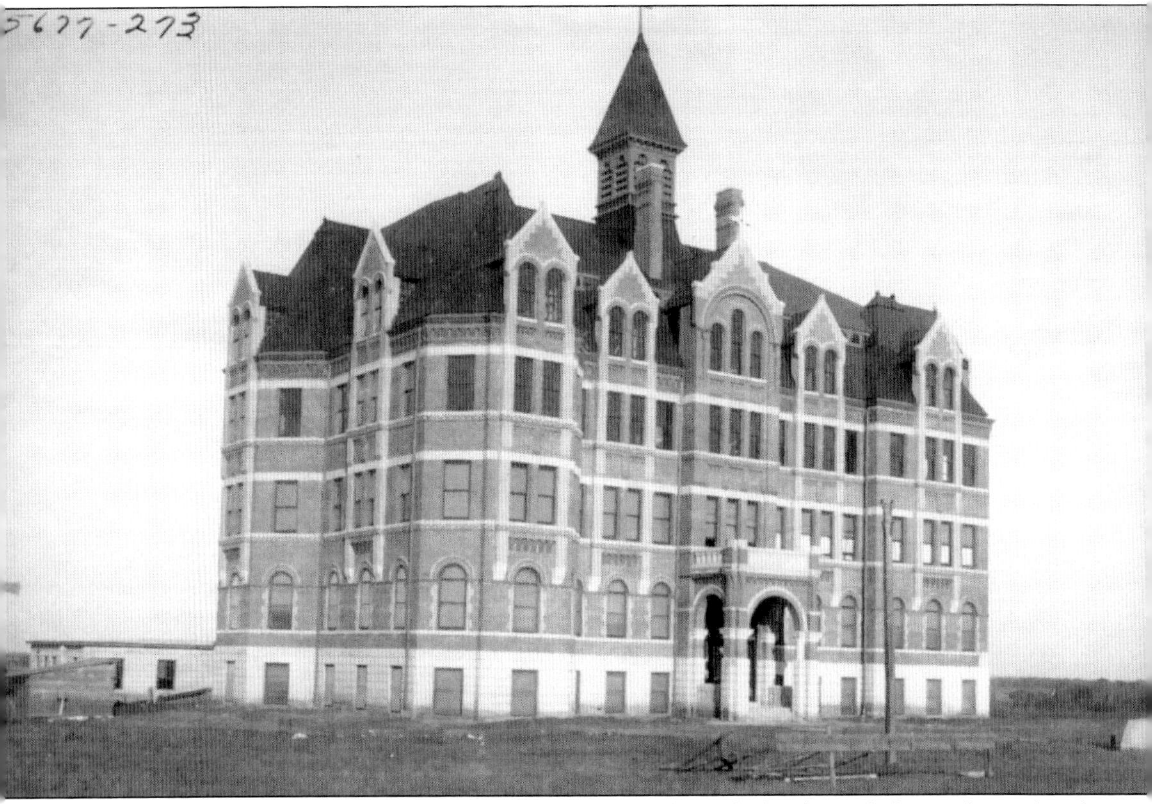

The Sisters of Mercy would go on to establish a long line of schools, including a day and night school in Krebbs, Oklahoma, in 1886. Schools in Ardmore, El Reno, Hartshorne, McAlester, Wilburton, and LaHigh, Oklahoma, followed in later years. In 1903, the order moved from Sacred Heart to Oklahoma City when property was donated for a new academy. In December 1903, the cornerstone was laid for what became Mount St. Mary's, which enrolled its first students in 1905, when this photograph was taken. It was was an all-girls school until 1950 when it became coeducational. The Mount became the first school in the nation to be cosponsored by an archdiocese and religious order. The school continues to operate at full capacity and with continual growth to this day. (Courtesy of the Sisters of Mercy.)

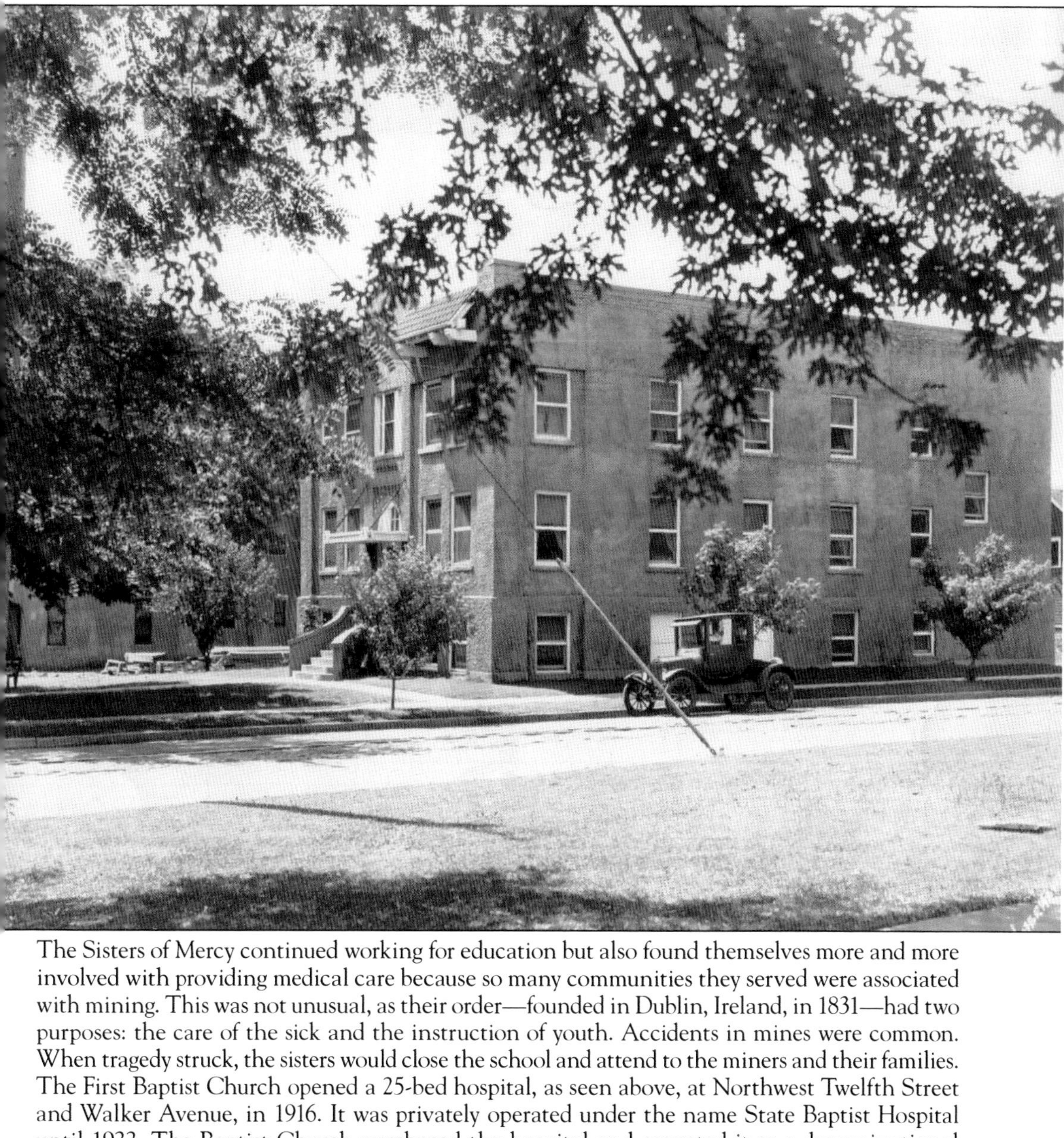

The Sisters of Mercy continued working for education but also found themselves more and more involved with providing medical care because so many communities they served were associated with mining. This was not unusual, as their order—founded in Dublin, Ireland, in 1831—had two purposes: the care of the sick and the instruction of youth. Accidents in mines were common. When tragedy struck, the sisters would close the school and attend to the miners and their families. The First Baptist Church opened a 25-bed hospital, as seen above, at Northwest Twelfth Street and Walker Avenue, in 1916. It was privately operated under the name State Baptist Hospital until 1922. The Baptist Church purchased the hospital and operated it as a denominational facility for two years, renaming it Baptist Hospital. Several doctors purchased the hospital and renamed it Oklahoma City General on December 8, 1923. It was expanded to accommodate 85 beds and 20 bassinets. The Sisters of Mercy acquired the hospital in 1947. (Courtesy of the Sisters of Mercy.)

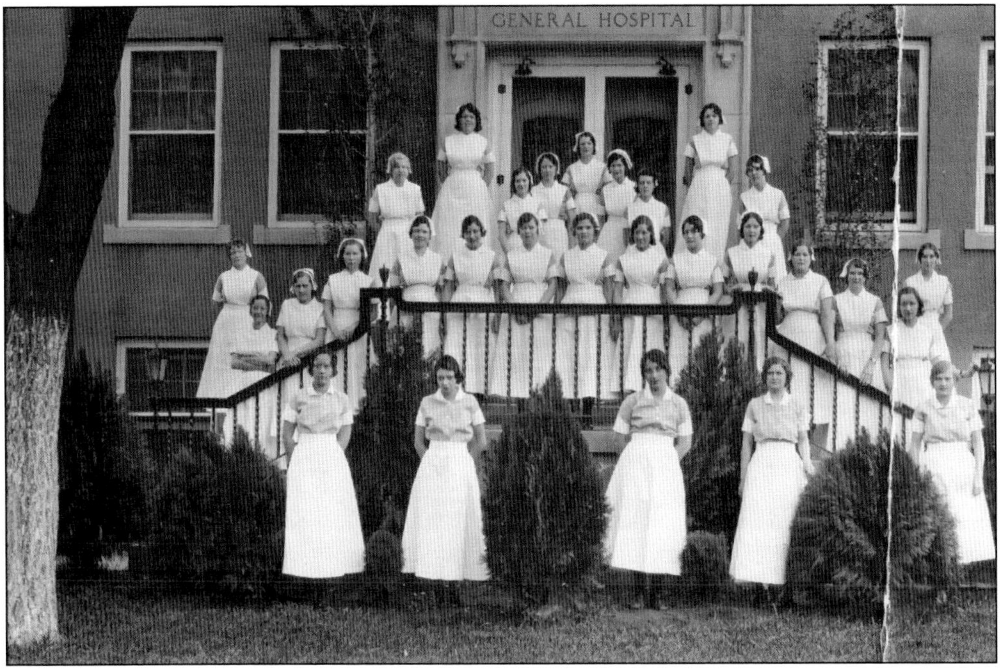

In the image above, student nurses are posing for a photograph along the west porch of the hospital. The image below shows a facility rate card from 1930 in its original frame. These would have been hung in each of the patient rooms. This card states that the rates were $3.50 per day. The rates increased gradually and in 1935 were $4.50 and in 1940, $6.50. The rates soared to $10 per day in 1945. (Both, courtesy of the Sisters of Mercy.)

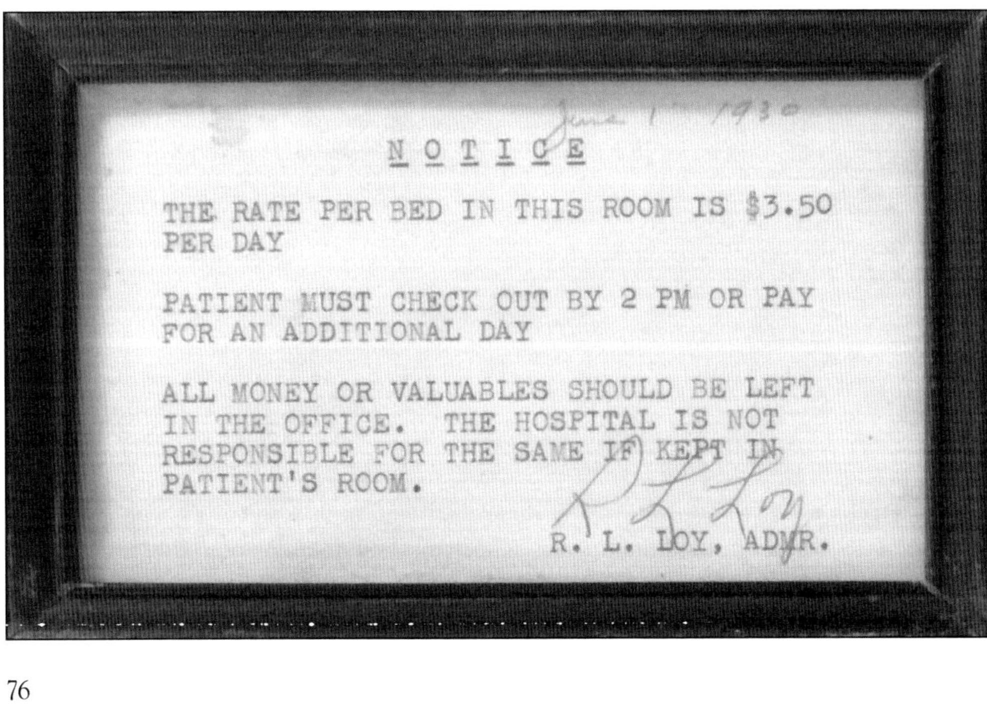

June 1 1930

N O T I C E

THE RATE PER BED IN THIS ROOM IS $3.50 PER DAY

PATIENT MUST CHECK OUT BY 2 PM OR PAY FOR AN ADDITIONAL DAY

ALL MONEY OR VALUABLES SHOULD BE LEFT IN THE OFFICE. THE HOSPITAL IS NOT RESPONSIBLE FOR THE SAME IF KEPT IN PATIENT'S ROOM.

R. L. LOY, ADMR.

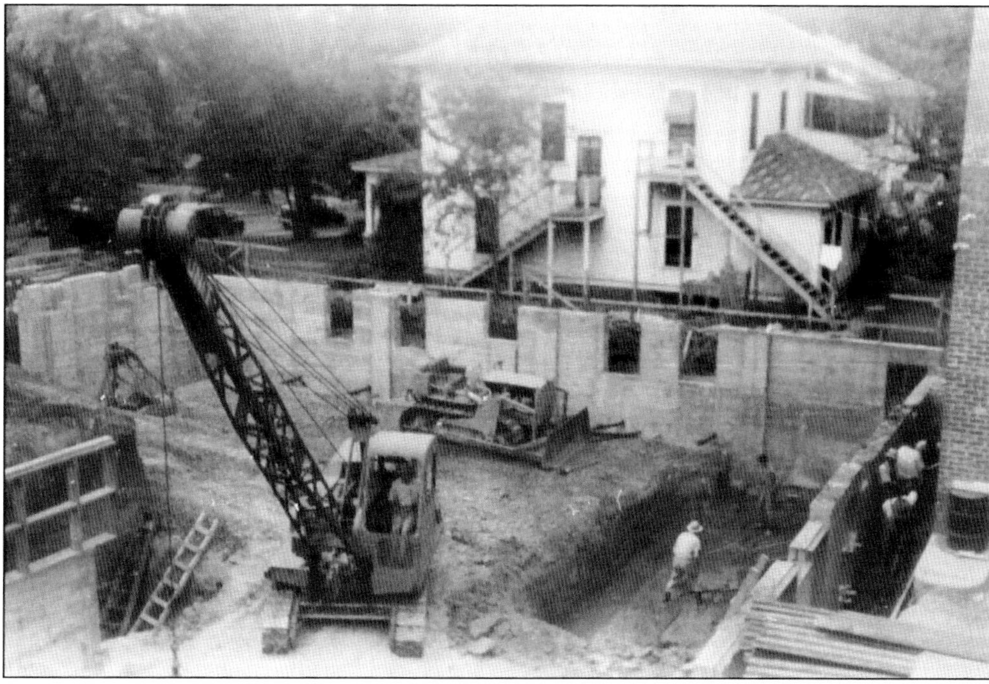

These two images show the construction of a new five-story wing added to Oklahoma City General before the Mercy sisters took over the facility on July 1, 1947. In the image above, workers build out the foundation and basement to the facility, while the image below depicts the steel skeleton of the new wing under construction in 1946. (Both, courtesy of the Sisters of Mercy.)

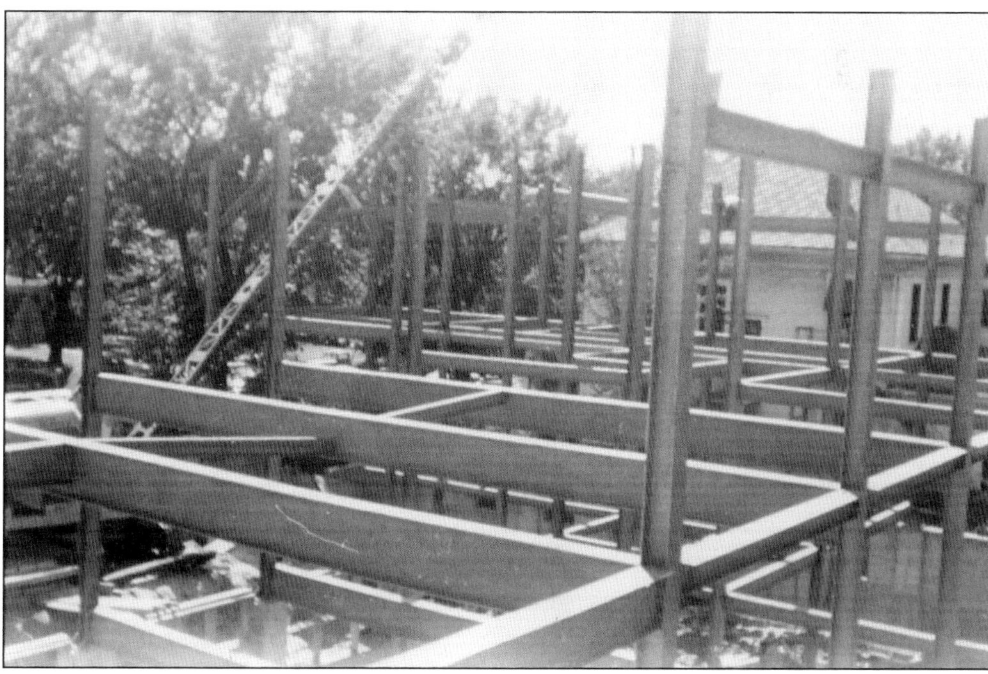

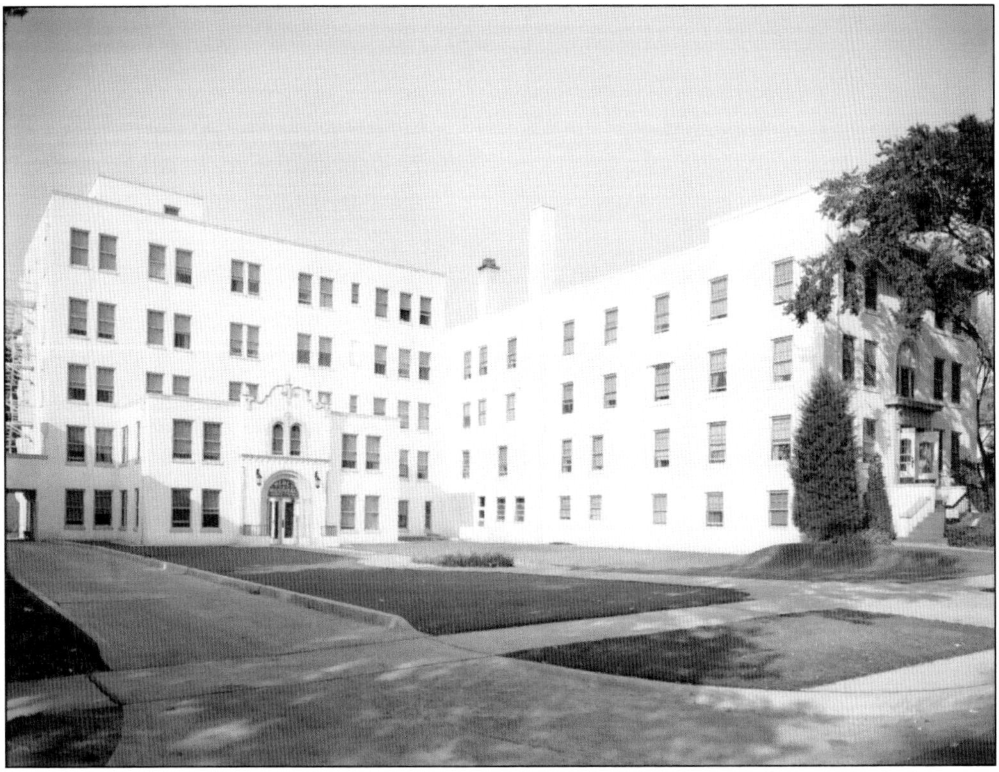

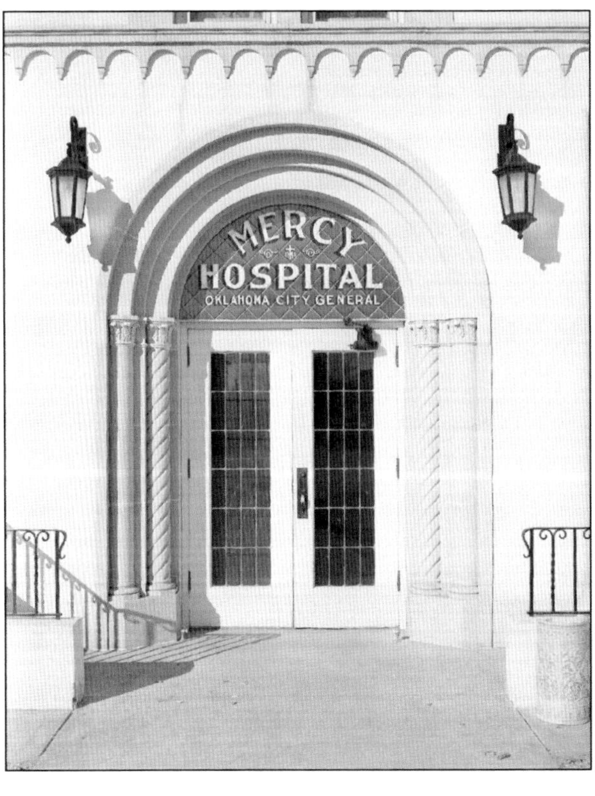

The Sisters of Mercy took charge of the hospital on July 1, 1947, after an additional five-story wing was added. They renamed the facility Mercy Hospital Oklahoma City General, although it became known as simply Mercy Hospital. The images above and below are of the hospital shortly after the new wing was added. The new name of the hospital can be seen in the image below. (Both, courtesy of the Sisters of Mercy.)

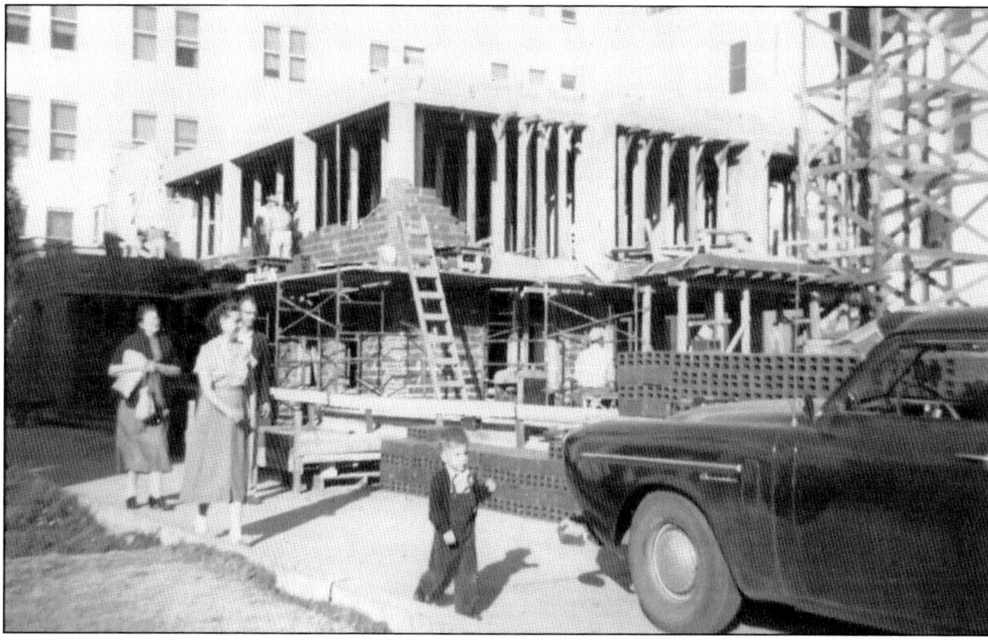

When the sisters took charge of the hospital, there were no spaces devoted to housing or classrooms for student nurses. A second story was added to a portion of the hospital to provide four classrooms. A four-story nurses' residence named McAuley Hall was added in 1950 and further featured classrooms, offices, a library, an assembly hall, and dormitories for 84 students. The hospital continued expansion through the years until 1966 when plans were presented to build a new facility north of the city along Meridian and Memorial Road. Here, the hospital is seen in various states of construction. (Both, courtesy of the Sisters of Mercy.)

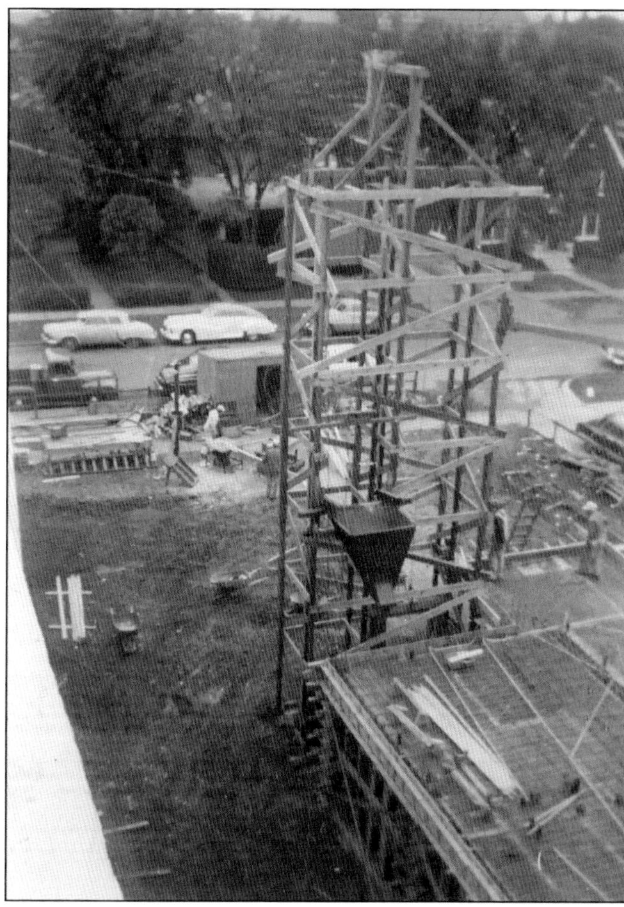

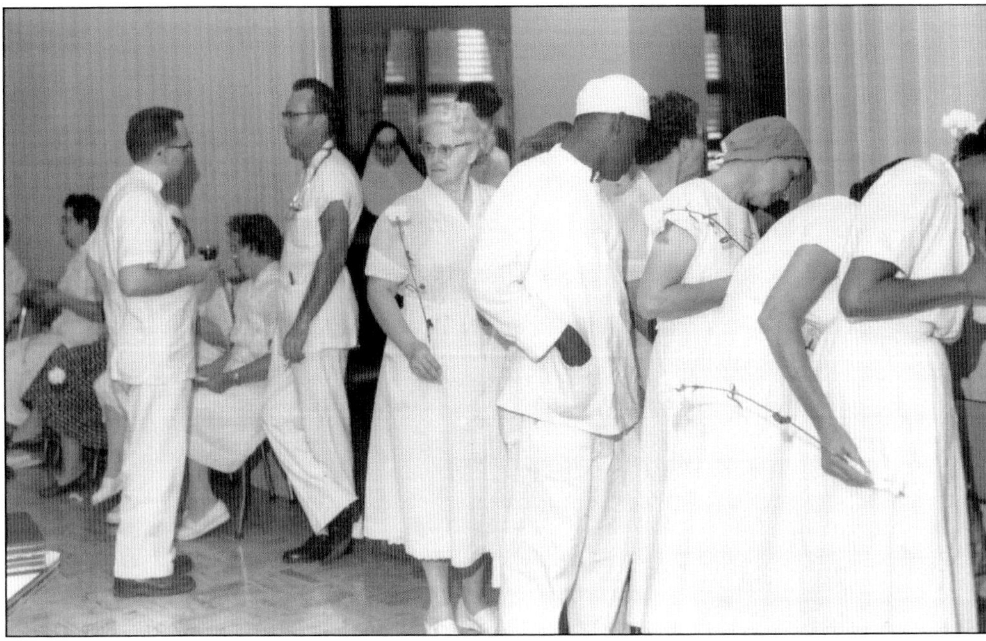

The Sisters of Mercy were the first employers in Oklahoma to integrate its staff after they took charge of the hospital in 1947. The staff consisted of 204 employees of both black and white personnel, yet African Americans only made up the maid and porter staff and were not allowed to work in other positions. The sisters immediately trained several black girls as nurse aides and assigned them to an African American section on the first floor of the hospital, whose staff mebers were reluctant to work with them. Patients thought highly of them. In 1955, the school of nursing enrolled its first black applicant. By 1961, out of 22 graduates 7 were black, with many staying to work at Mercy. Above, the integrated staff is shown at an employee event. Below, a nurse's aide is working in the newborn nursery in 1949. (Both, courtesy of the Sisters of Mercy.)

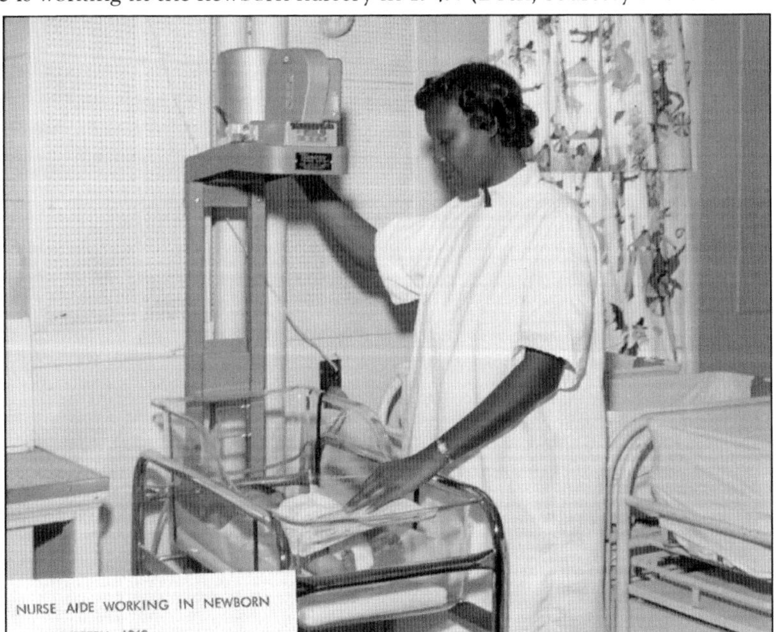

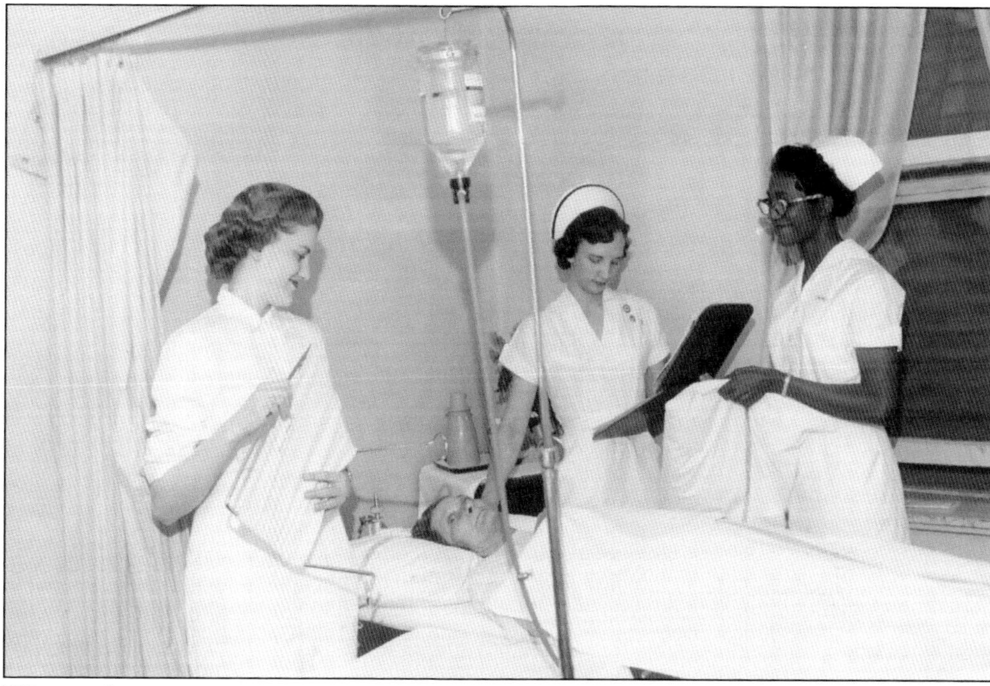

Efforts to eliminate discrimination persisted from 1946 until 1965. In 1949, a retired teacher was admitted with a heart attack. After he asked for a private room, the sister administrator assigned him to one on the second floor. The head nurse confronted the sister and stated that she could not care for a black patient and would resign if the issue were forced. The sister reassigned the patient to a first-floor, semiprivate room where better care would be given and then advised the nurse to look for another position. The Mercy philosophy was to allow no discrimination in the care of the sick because of their race, creed, or color. Above, from left to right, Lillie Emery, LPN; Carol Jean Johnson, RN; and Jacquita Mitchell, aide, have completed the care of Mrs. Bert Simpson in the Stryker Frame. Right, integrated staff eat in a break room. (Both, courtesy of the Sisters of Mercy.)

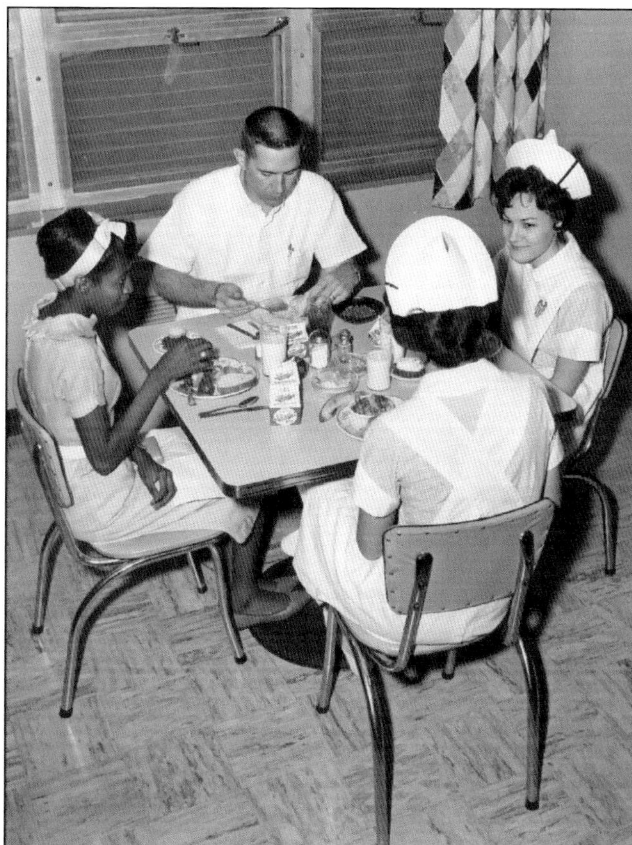

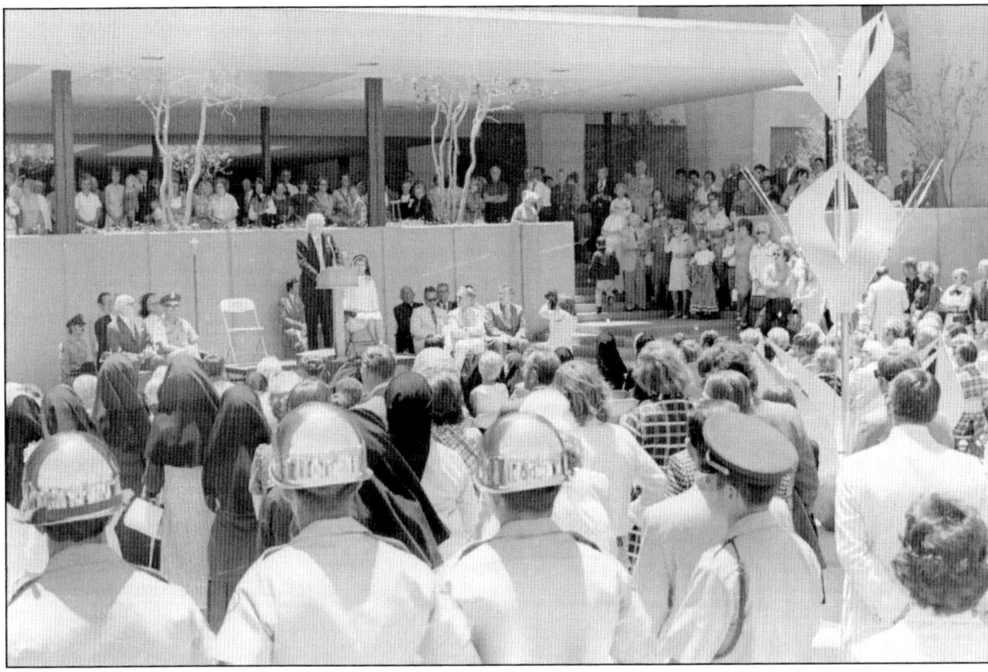

The old Mercy Hospital was finally closed in 1974 when construction of a new facility on Memorial Road was completed. The images above and below are of the dedication ceremony of the new Mercy Health Center on June 23, 1974, with Gordon A. Friesen at the podium. The old hospital on Northwest Twelfth Street was demolished in the 1990s, and as of this writing a new apartment complex named The Edge has begun construction. It will cater to increasing demands for residential and retail space within the Midtown area. (Both, courtesy of the Sisters of Mercy.)

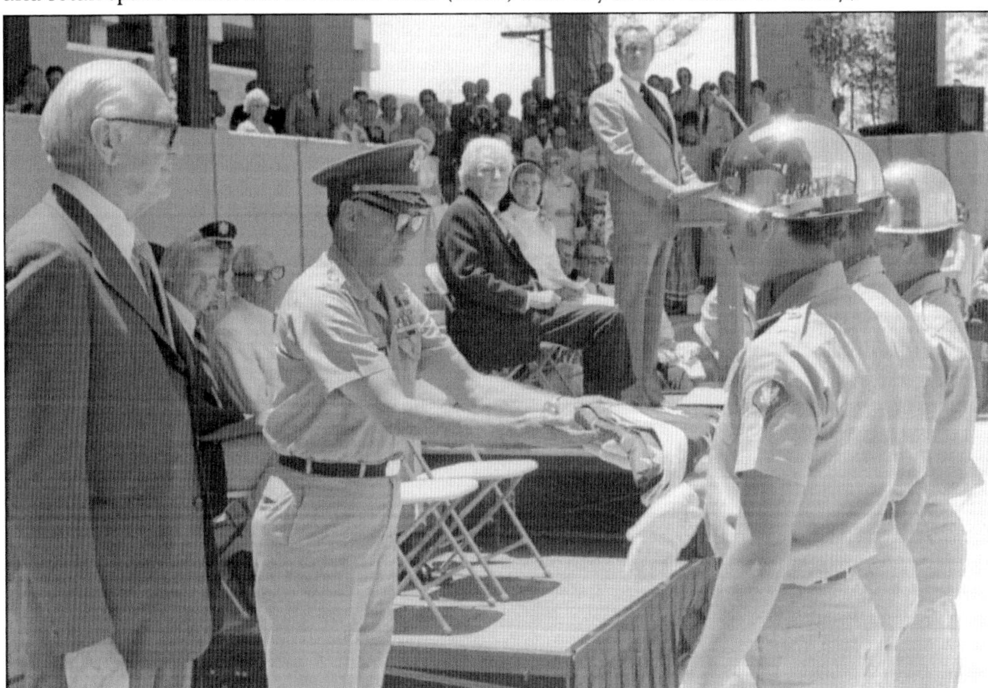

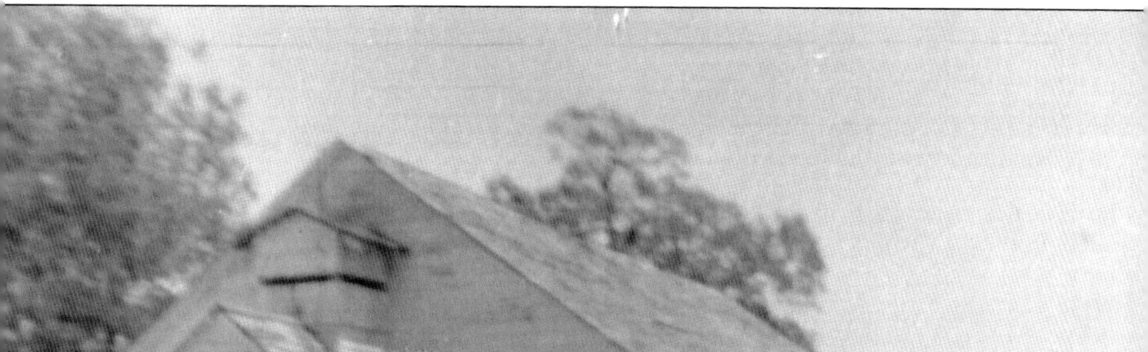

In 1916, Father Soler recruited three laywomen from Chicago while working with the Choctaw in Bentley, Oklahoma, and went on to found the convent of Carmelite Sisters of St. Therese of the Infant Jesus, which became the only Carmelite congregation organized in the United States sometime in 1917. The order focused on establishing a rudimentary education system in 1916, but their efforts were hampered as two of the three sisters returned to Chicago. Father Soler was able to recruit two more into the order from New England in April 1917. The coal-mining town of Bentley, with a population of only 100, was a hostile environment that consisted of a post office, general store, and a few log cabins. In addition to these hardships, bigotry and intolerance came from the locals who resented efforts to educate the Choctaw and European immigrants. The order instead gained strength from regional fears and managed to establish an early childhood education system. This image, although distorted, is the only image of the first Carmelite convent in Bentley, Oklahoma. (Courtesy of the Sisters of Villa Therese of the Infant Jesus.)

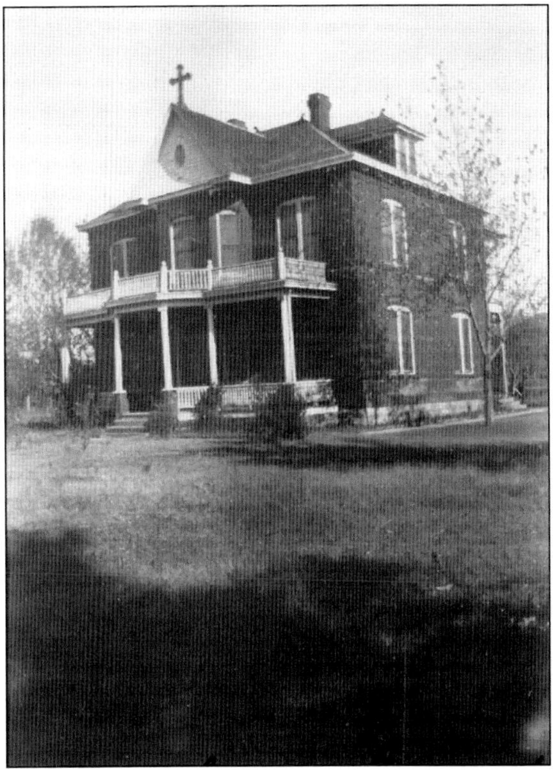

Eventually, the sisters were regarded as an organization of "teachers engaged in teaching." At the request of the state's Catholic Bishop Meerschaert, the order was relocated to Gowen, Oklahoma, and then to a school that was established by the Sisters of Mercy in Harsthorne, Oklahoma. The Mercy convent, turned Carmelite Motherhouse, is shown above. It was during this time that the sisters became the first Carmelites to specialize in early childhood education while teaching at the Jones Academy for Indian Boys. In 1927, the order relocated to Little Flower Church in Oklahoma City to continue their education and to combat the continued harassment from the Ku Klux Klan of all Catholic parishes, because the Klan despised the teachings to immigrants and nonwhite members of the community. The Little Flower convent is shown below. (Both, courtesy of the Sisters of Villa Therese of the Infant Jesus.)

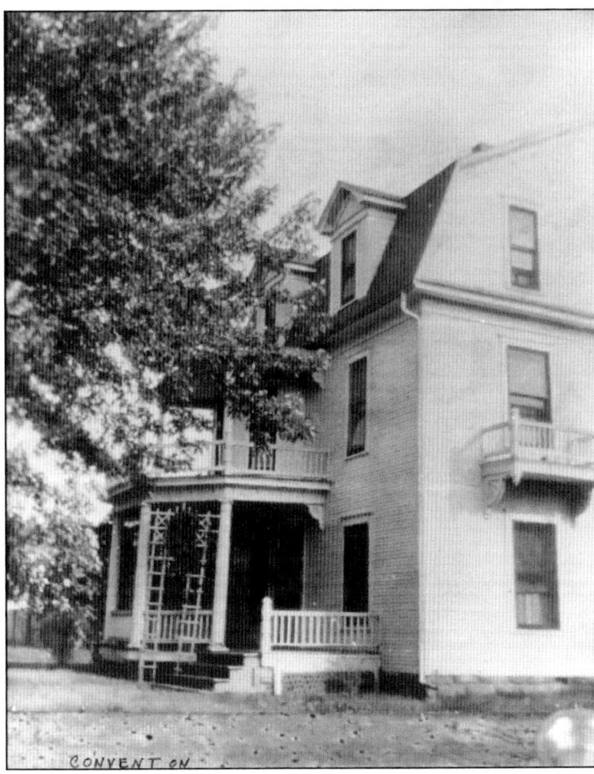

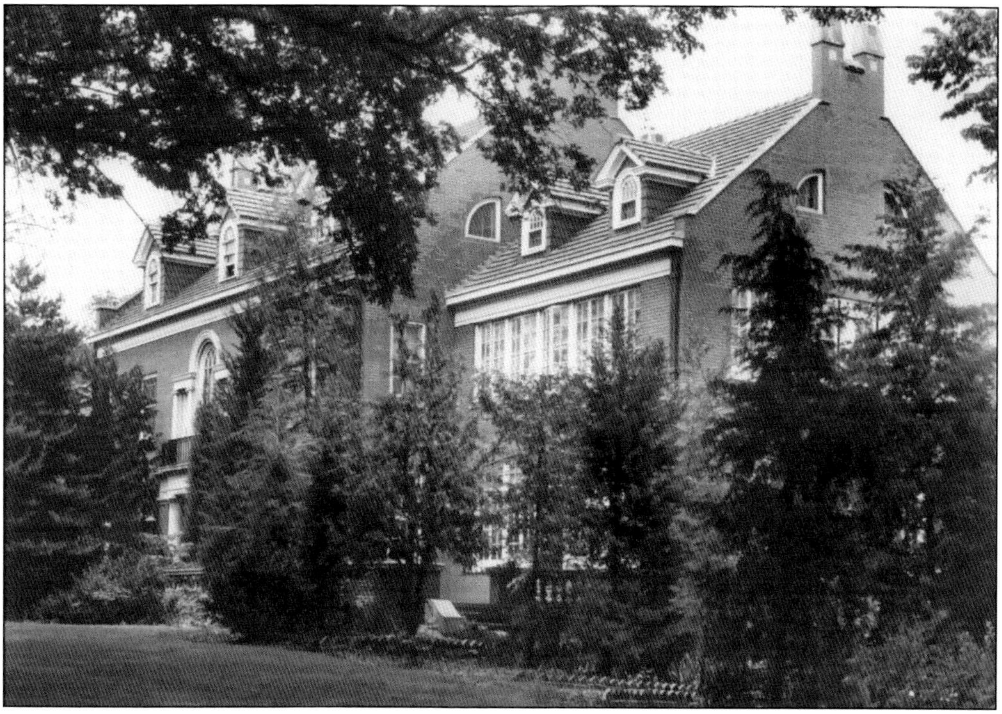

In 1930, the order was asked to take over the St. Joseph Orphanage, which they operated until 1933 when they purchased the Frank Anderson home at 1300 Classen Drive and moved their motherhouse from Little Flower to the new location. It was here that the sisters created a new school named Villa Teresa. The sisters began the first all-day kindergarten with before- and after-school care in Oklahoma City in 1933, during the Great Depression. This was a huge social development that enabled parents to keep working and provided steady meals for their children in a time of scarcity. (Both, courtesy of the Sisters of Villa Therese of the Infant Jesus.)

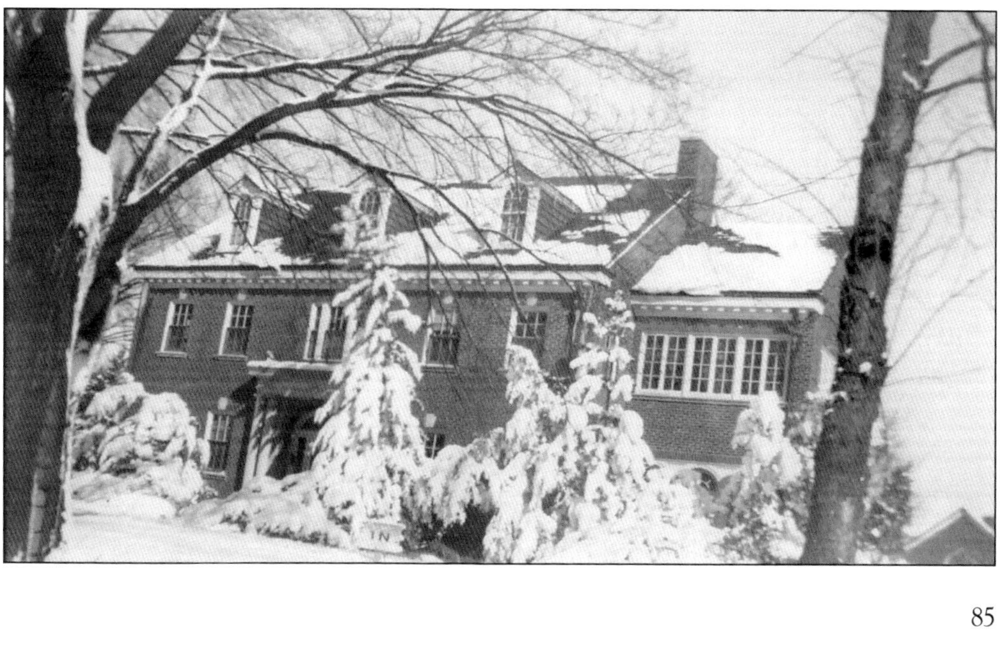

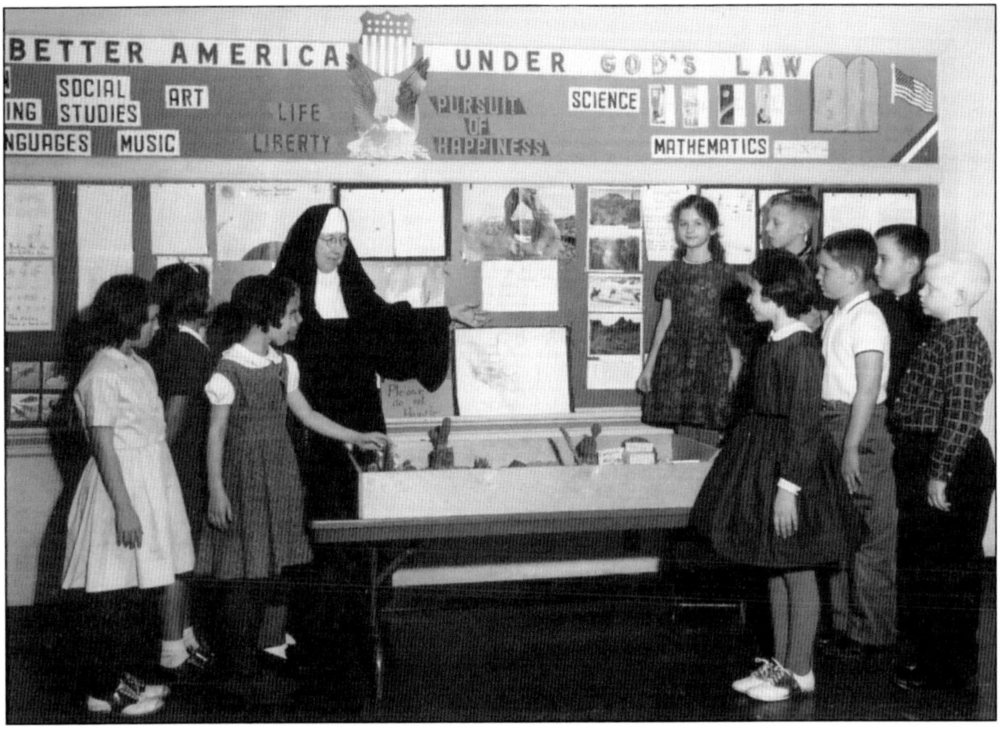

The order continued to provide the service throughout World War II to add the security of both education and safety as fathers served abroad and mothers worked in factories. The sisters created some controversy in 1958 when they integrated a young African American girl into their Villa Teresa School, resulting in a decreased enrollment of around 30 percent as parents took their children out of school, but most children returned soon after. The Carmelites further built and operated the first privately operated school established to educate the mentally handicapped. (Both, courtesy of the Sisters of Villa Therese of the Infant Jesus.)

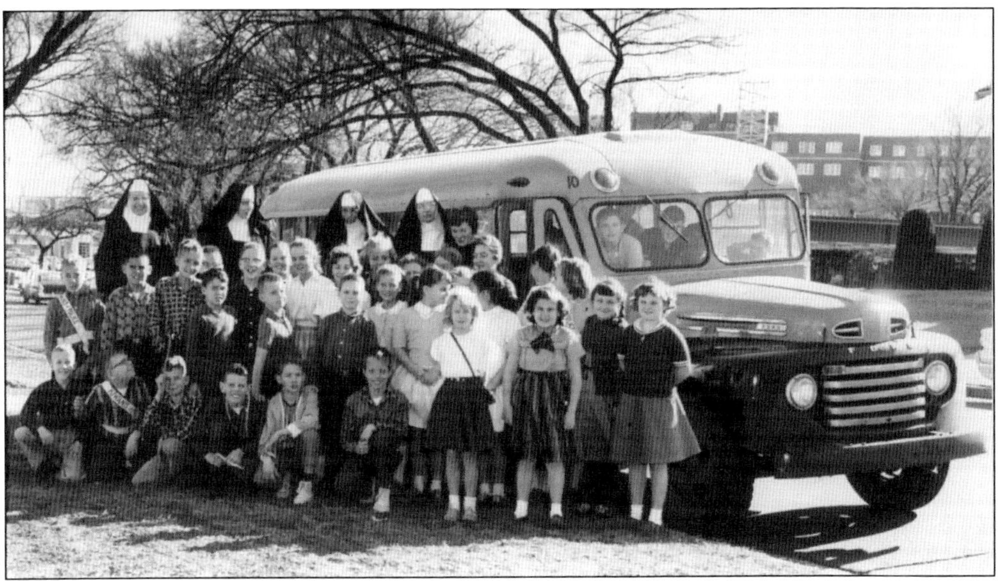

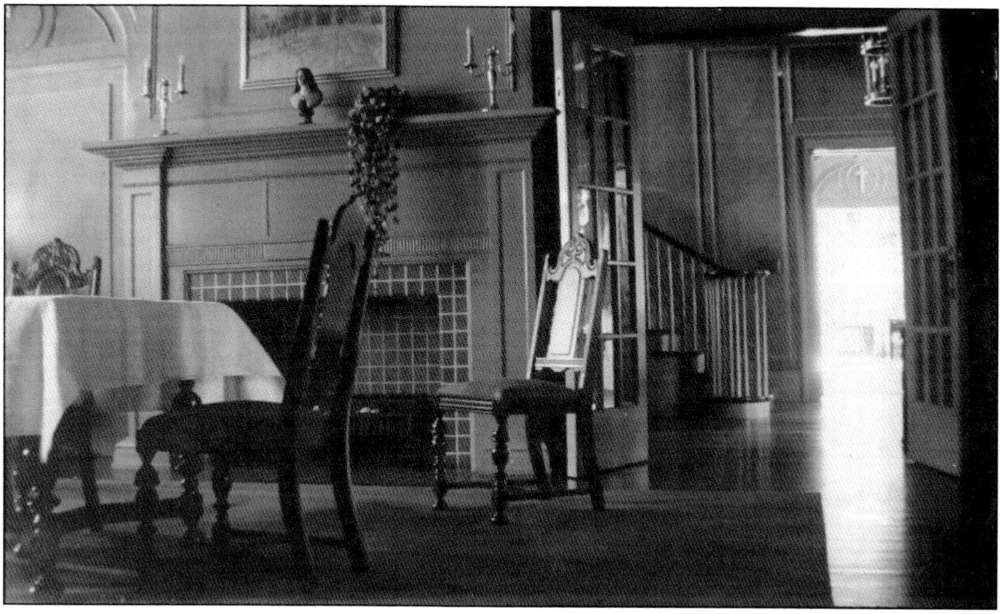

These c. 1938 images capture portions of the Villa Teresa motherhouse. Villa Teresa School operated for 79 years, 1933–2012, when finally the order's numbers were substantially reduced through time to only 13 sisters. The school could no longer provide the standard wage for teachers, could no longer operated with a majority staff from the order, and could not keep up with climbing maintenance costs. The motherhouse also became too difficult to maintain and to sustain the aging sisters, as it had never been designed for handicap access. Furthermore, the sisters of the order were finding themselves separated with some in nursing homes and unable to take care of each another. (Both, courtesy of the Sisters of Villa Therese of the Infant Jesus.)

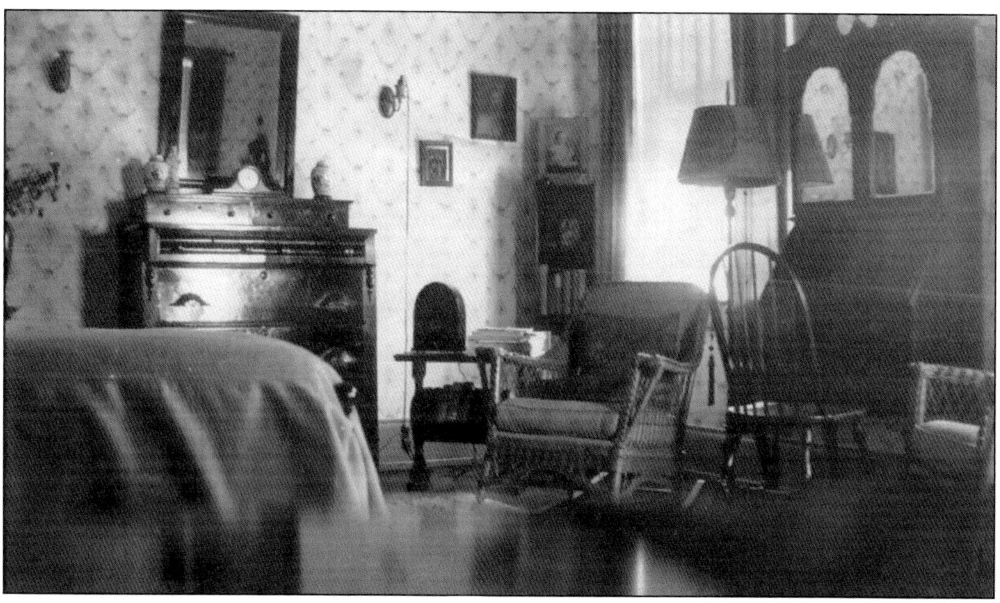

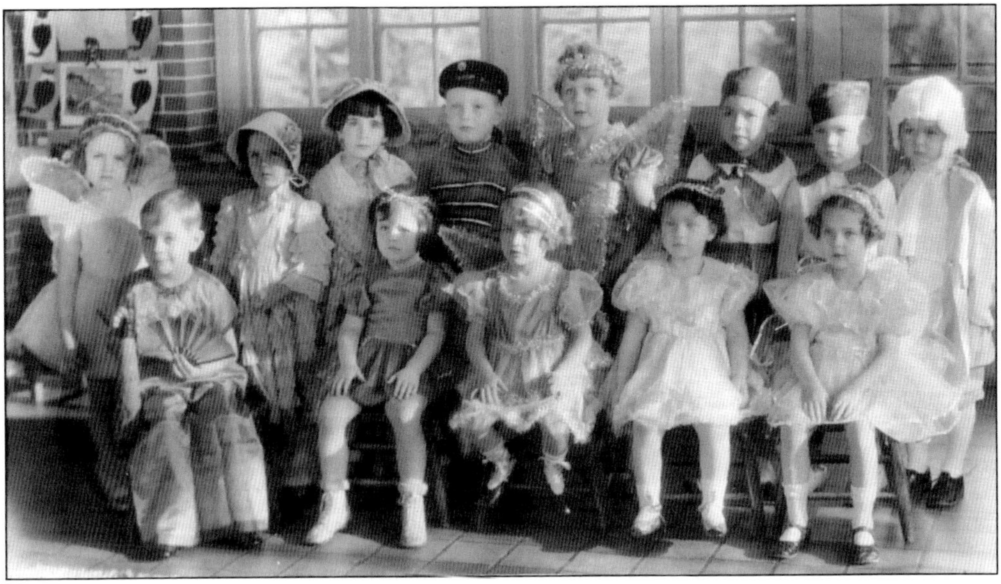

Villa Teresa was very active with programs, as seen in these images. Above, a class of young students participates in a play performance with elaborate costumes designed and hand sewn by the drama teacher in 1933. Below, upperclassmen perform square dancing routines around 1960 with one of the Villa Teresa sisters instructing. (Both, courtesy of the Sisters of Villa Therese of the Infant Jesus.)

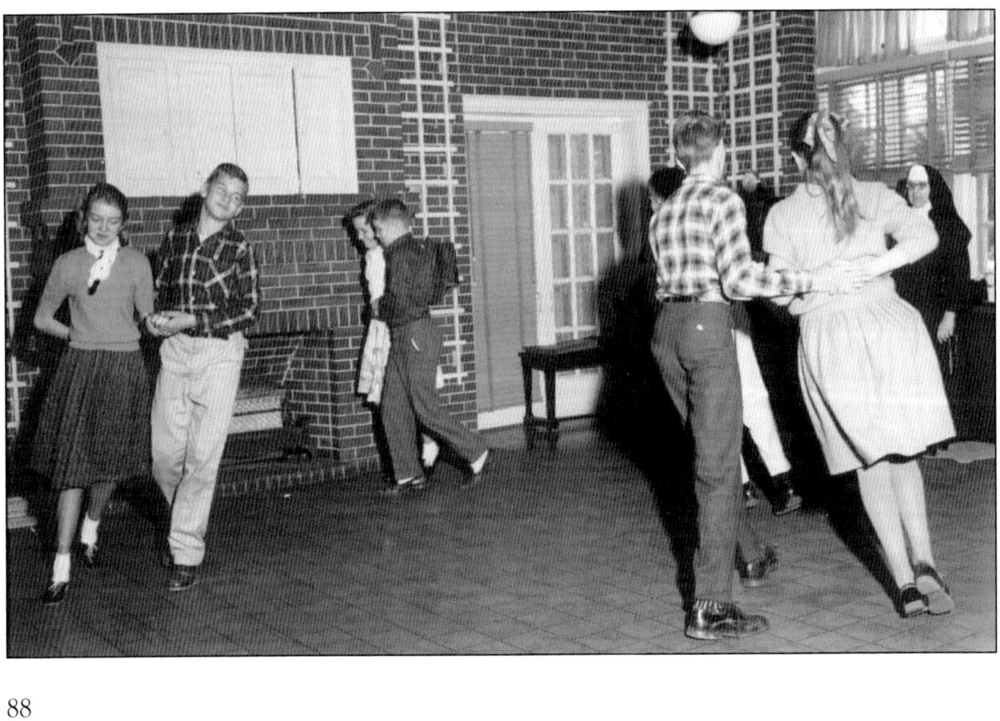

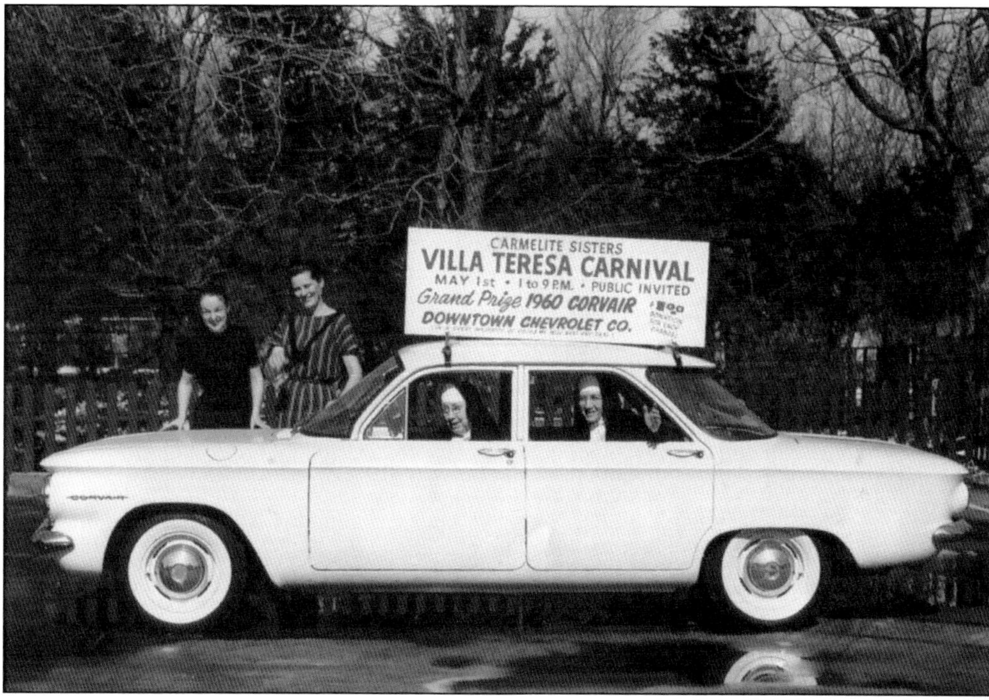

The images here show the sisters having a little fun promoting the school's raffle and its grand prizes from the 1959 and 1960 carnival events. In the 1960 Corvair above, are Sisters Hildegarde and Elizabeth. In the boat below from left to right are Sisters Patricia and Immaculata. Each sister came to be loved by the many children and supporters of Villa Teresa. (Both, courtesy of the Sisters of Villa Therese of the Infant Jesus.)

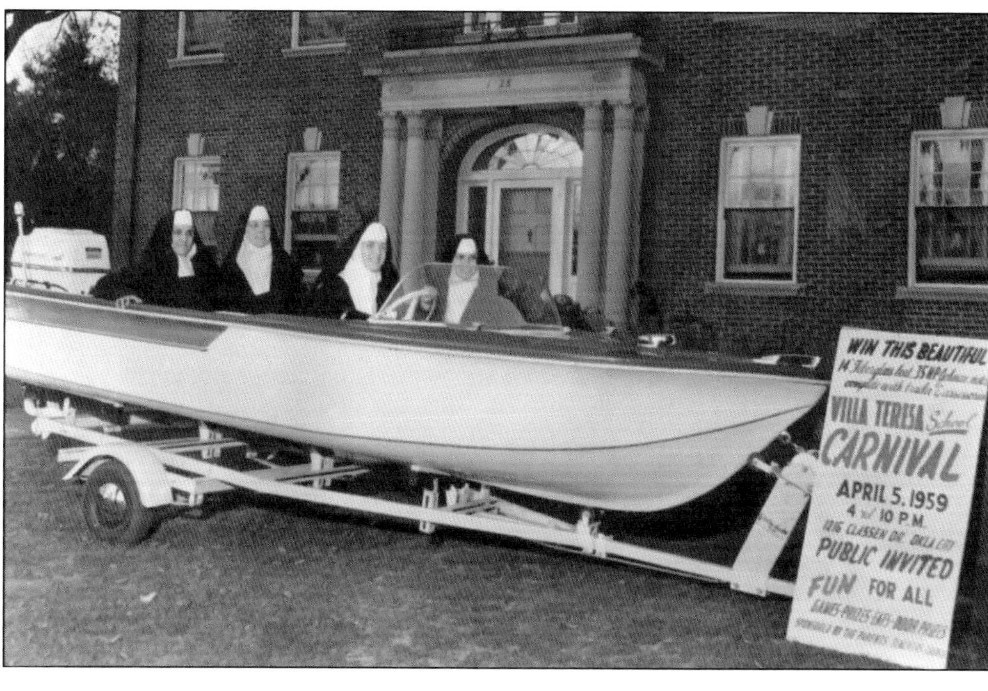

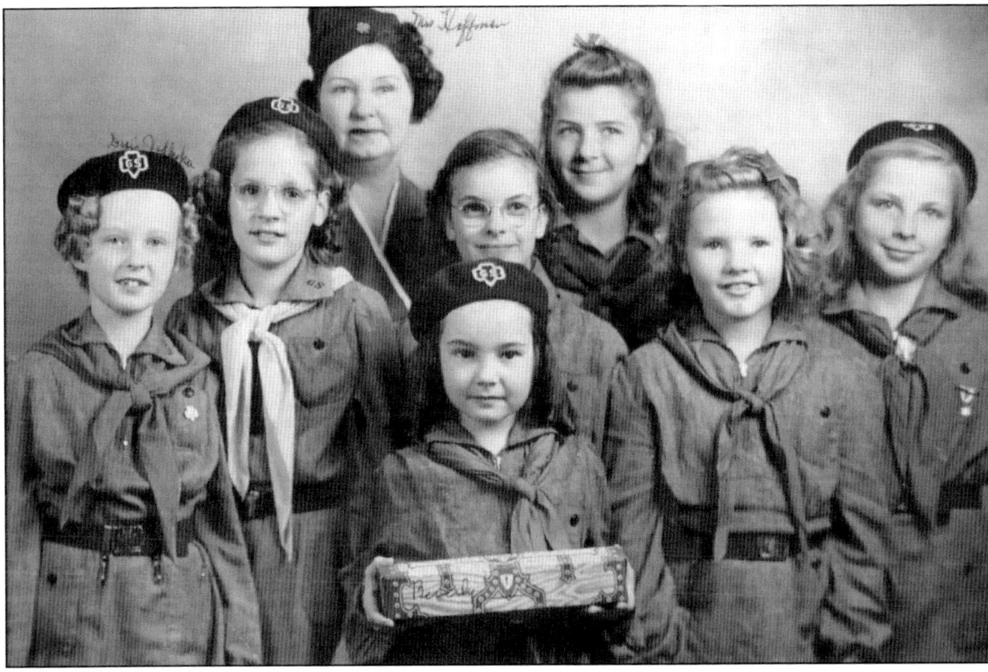

These images capture the Villa Teresa charted chapter of the Girls Scouts around the 1940s and Boy Scouts of America, Cub Scout pack in 1958. In 2012, the sisters announced the unexpected closing of Villa Teresa in a letter mailed to the entire student body, school alumni, and supporting members. Later, it was also announced that the sisters would be relocating to a new retirement facility that would be constructed alongside St. Anne's. The sisters went on retreat with one another for the first time in decades in 2013 and, at the time of this writing, have returned to their motherhouse until they make their final move sometime in 2014–2015. (Both, courtesy of the Sisters of Villa Therese of the Infant Jesus.)

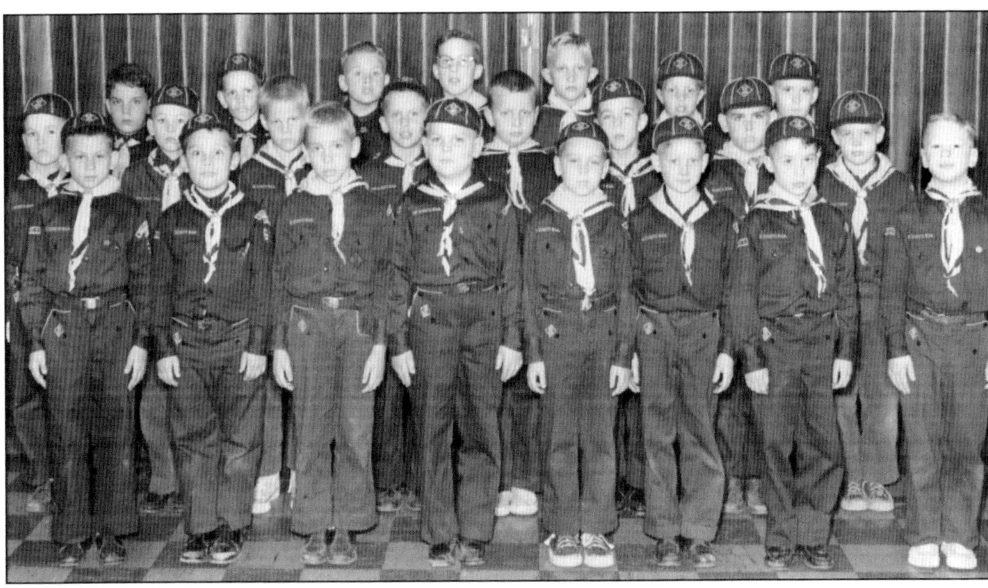

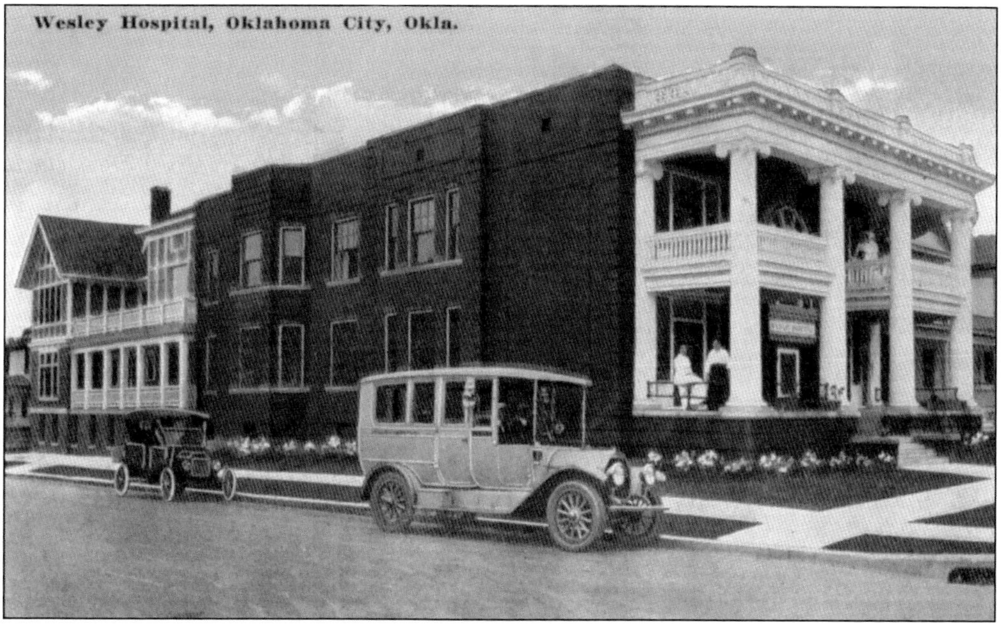

Wesley Hospital was founded by Dr. F.K. Camp on two floors of the Herskowitz Building at Broadway and Sheridan Avenue in 1910 until a permanent structure opened to patients on December 1, 1911, at Northwest Eighth–Ninth Streets and Harvey Avenue as seen above. The hospital boasted in newspaper ads that it had the latest emergency care equipment and that its ambulance service was available to pick up patients at the train station. The hospital was very successful and eventually partnered with the Washita Presbytery, who renamed it Presbyterian Hospital in 1964. Below, staff members are seen in front of Wesley Hospital in 1963. A new Presbyterian Hospital was built in 1973 at Northeast Thirteenth and Lincoln Avenue, now part of the Oklahoma University Medical Center. (Both, courtesy of the Oklahoma Historical Society.)

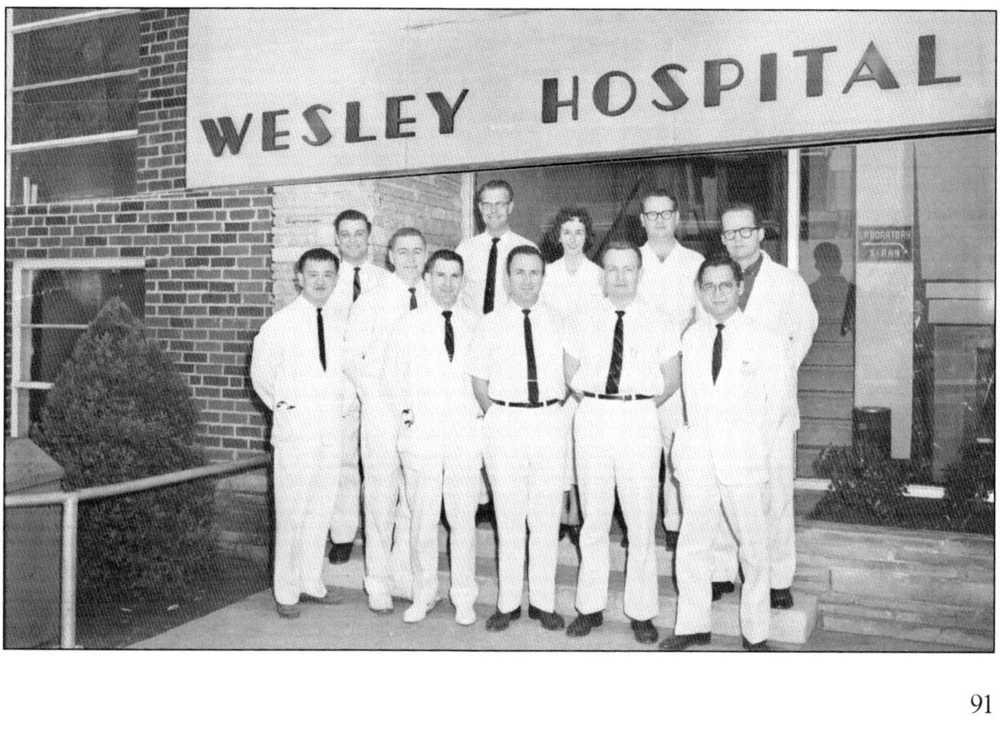

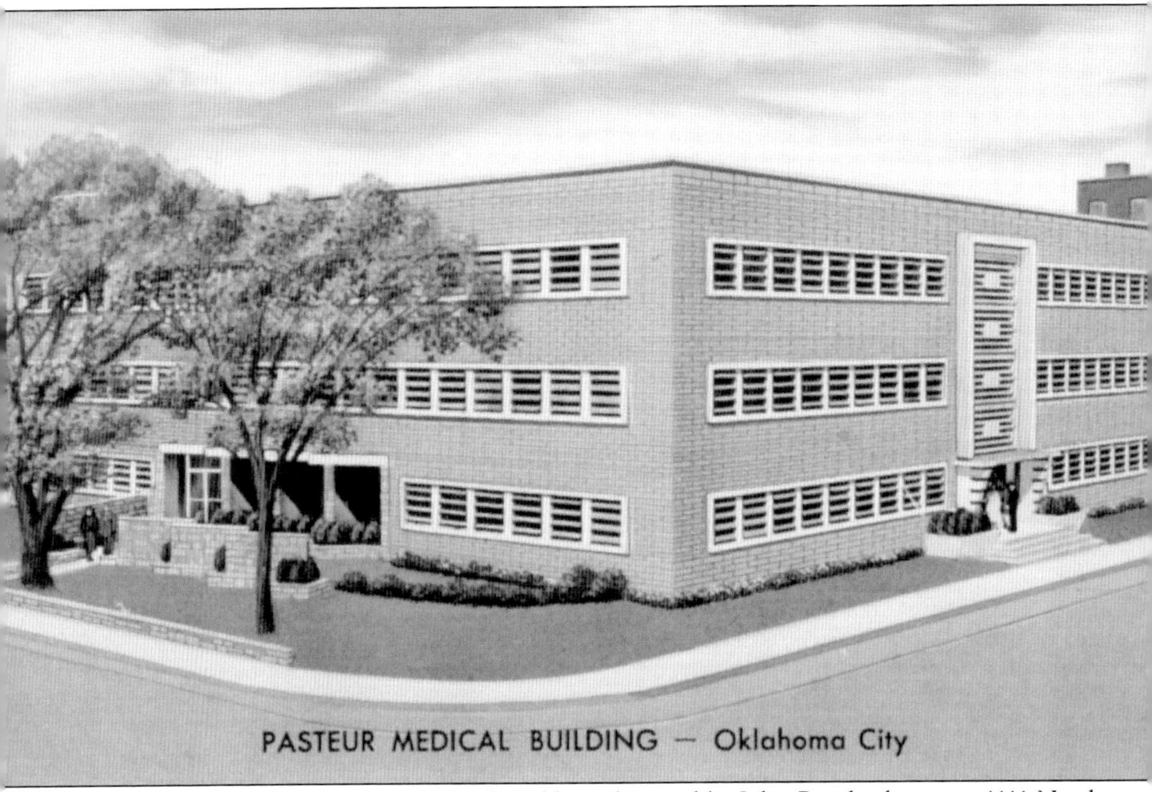

Construction of the Pasteur Medical Building, designed by John Bozalis, began at 1111 North Lee Avenue on March 26, 1950, after six frame houses were removed from the Classen Marquette Addition. Opening December 9, 1951, at a cost of $750,000, the building was hailed in the *Oklahoman* as the most modern medical facility created "in the interest of public health." One peculiar design feature was the Pasteur's louver-covered windows, which could supposedly be closed in the event of atomic fallout and protect the inhabitants. Among those who organized the Pasteur Medical Building Corporation was John W. Nichols. When the value of PMBC reached $3.3 million in the early 1960s, Nichols suggested using it as "equity money" to borrow against drilling programs. The result created Devon Energy in 1971, today among the most prominent oil and gas producers in the world. Its CEO is Larry Nichols, son of John Nichols. Devon's construction of a 925-foot-tall business tower in 2012 resulted in an entire overhaul of downtown Oklahoma City streets and infrastructure. (Courtesy of the Oklahoma Historical Society.)

Four

MIDTOWN FAITH

In no other place in the state—perhaps in no other city in the nation—is there a portion of town so saturated with the faithful than Church Row in Oklahoma City. For unknown reasons, nearly every Christian denomination has gathered their flocks inside stately edifices along north Robinson Avenue for over 100 years. Perhaps it is because of this faith base that Oklahoma City survived through the Dust Bowl, the Great Depression, urban renewal, the 1980s oil bust, and the tragic 1995 terrorist bombing of the Alfred P. Murrah Federal Building, which did a great deal of damage to the entire cityscape. Ironically, it was the latter event that strengthened and inspired this Midtown community to rebuild and restore these rare structures.

While assessing the numerous properties damaged or destroyed by the shockwave of that terrible 1995 tragedy, the city rediscovered the rich history left standing. Yet—long before the bombing—these magnificent churches, as well as many other buildings, were nearly destroyed by age and apathy. As their congregations picked up the broken pieces and swept up the shattered remains of their stained-glass windows, the churches reexamined their properties and the historical value each one offered the city.

The Robinson Avenue churches grew in spurts, and during those early days each congregation often met in public houses, courthouses, businesses, or temporary frame homes. Most of these were either razed to make room for larger edifices or in a couple of instances, destroyed by accident in a fire. In only a few years, larger and more permanent houses of worship were constructed, creating the row of impressive structures standing there today.

Each church struggled in some way to acquire the lots for their permanent houses of worship. In some cases, those lots were worth only between $100–$600 each. Today, the property and the churches on it are valued in the millions of dollars.

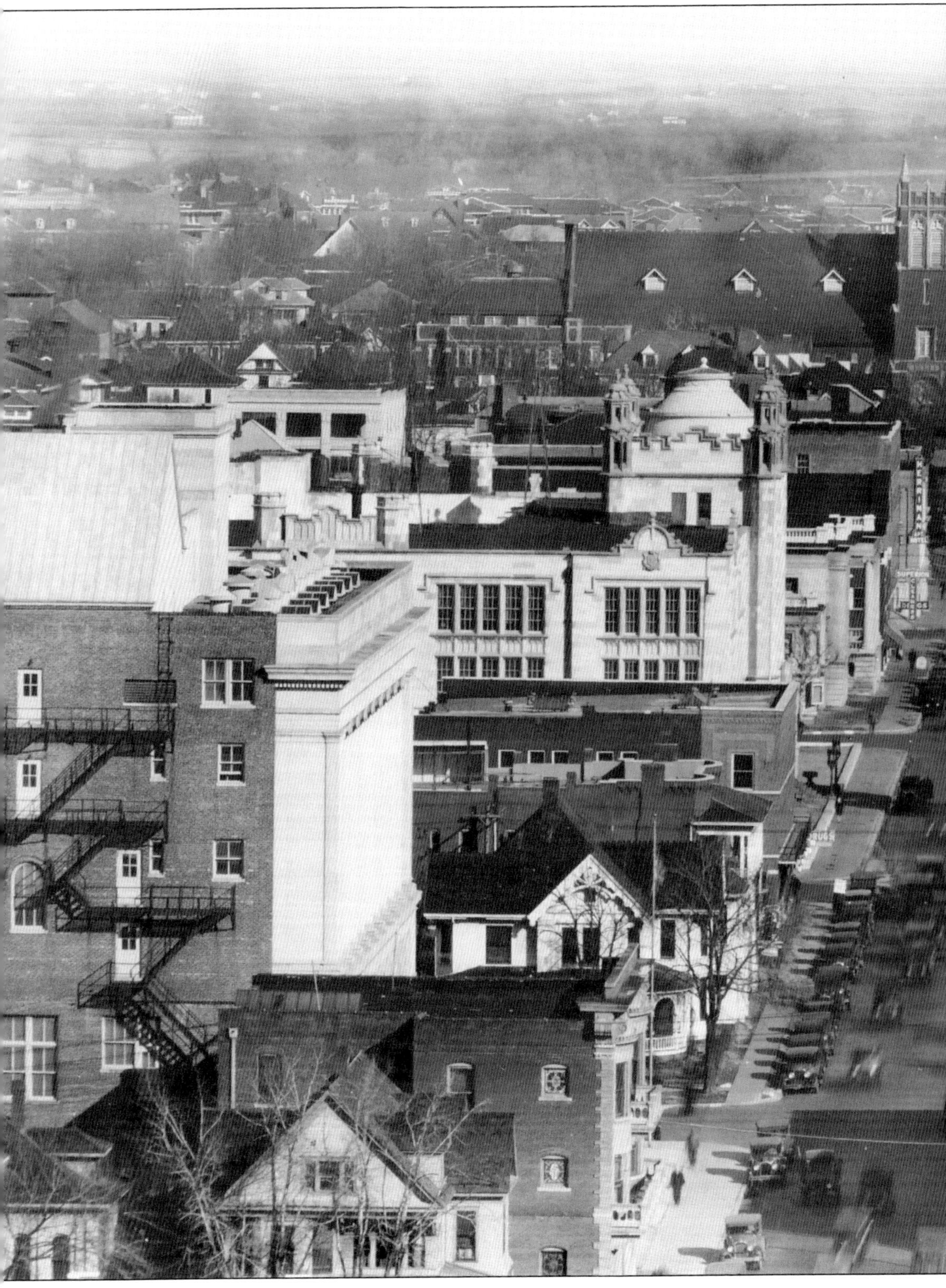
SUPERIOR
DRUGS

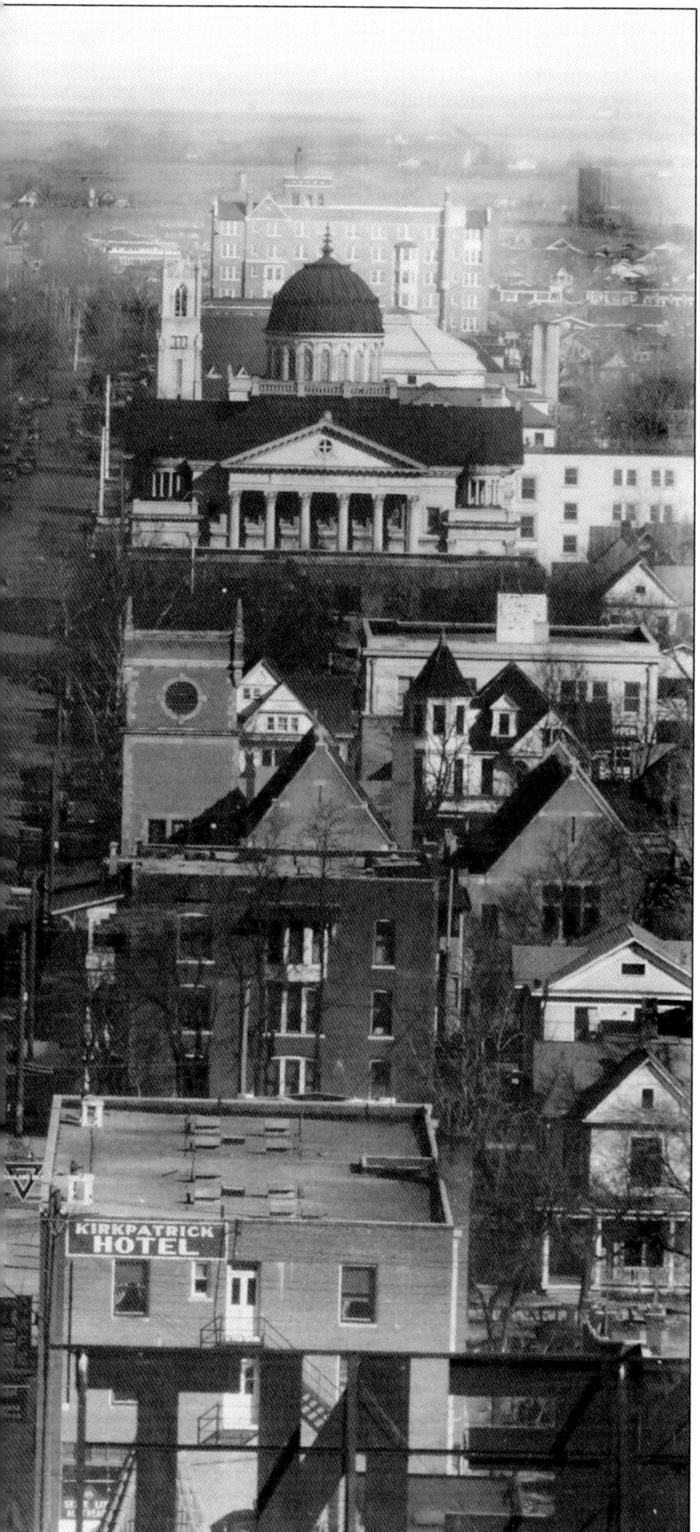

This amazing c. 1925 image captures the hustle and bustle of North Robinson Avenue, looking northbound from Northwest Fifth Street, along what was affectionately called Church Row. The name stems from the street being lined with churches starting from as early as 1901 and representing nearly every Christian denomination. In the lower right is the Kirkpatrick Hotel, and looking down Robinson numerous churches and the Central High School are clearly visible. Looking further in the distance, the stark contrast between the city and farms is distinct and offers a unique view into Oklahoma City's growth. Today, many of these structures are no longer standing or have been replaced with modern businesses. (Courtesy of the author.)

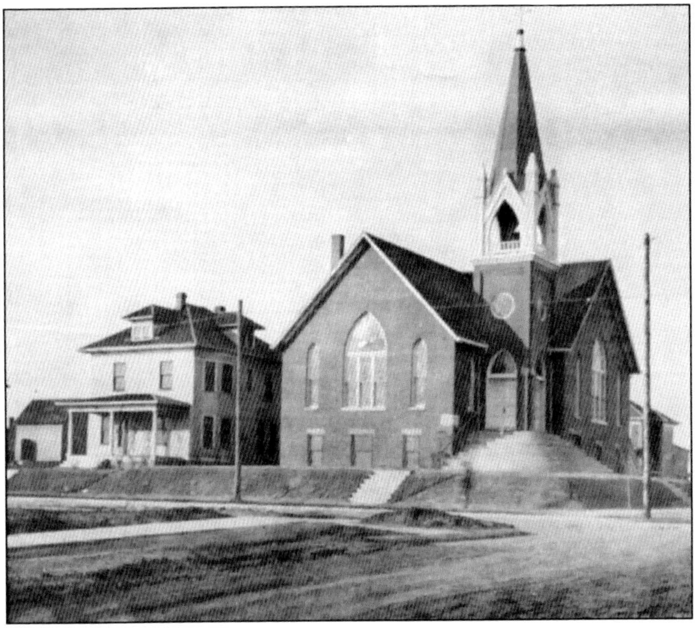

Skilled craftsmen among the First German Methodists, aided by elder Anton Classen, built their church at Northwest Eighth Street and Lee Avenue on August 18, 1907. Included were 19 handcrafted pews, a 29-pipe German Hinners organ, an oil painting depicting Jesus's "Walk to Emmaus," and 22 stunning Jacoby stained-glass windows with one panel inscribed in German: "donated by Anton Classen, in memory of his mother." (Courtesy of Skyline Urban Ministries.)

The First Church of Christ, Scientist, was established in Oklahoma City after 1889. Services were scattered along Main Street, the courthouse, Overholser Opera House, and along Robinson Avenue until 1906 when the wood framed church (pictured) was built at 1202 North Robinson Avenue. In the fall of 1919, construction started on 1200 North Robinson Avenue with the most expensive building project of the year. (Courtesy of the Oklahoma City Metropolitan Library System.)

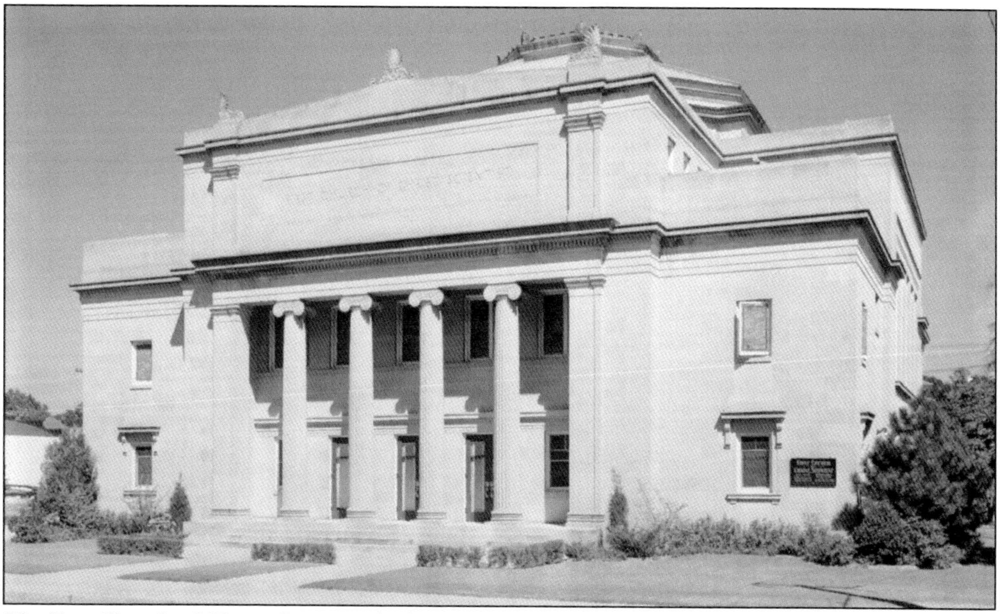

The First Church of Christ, Scientist, laid its cornerstone on July 17, 1920. Its west foyer was decorated with wood paneling, its ceramic tile floor was covered in a square pattern joined at the corners with intertwined swastikas, and a Kimball pipe organ was near the stage. A massive octagonal domed skylight fills the central portion of the roof, and its eight sections of glass depict a triangular floral pattern of white, gold, and blue. Limestone finials decorated the dome's cornice up until a shockwave from the Alfred P. Murrah Federal Building bombing on April 19, 1995, destroyed them and 13 of the building's stained-glass windows. The property was utilized by its congregation until 1988 when it was sold to a neighboring business. These images show the church's exterior on August 28, 1945, and its interior in July 1951. (Both, courtesy of the Oklahoma Historical Society.)

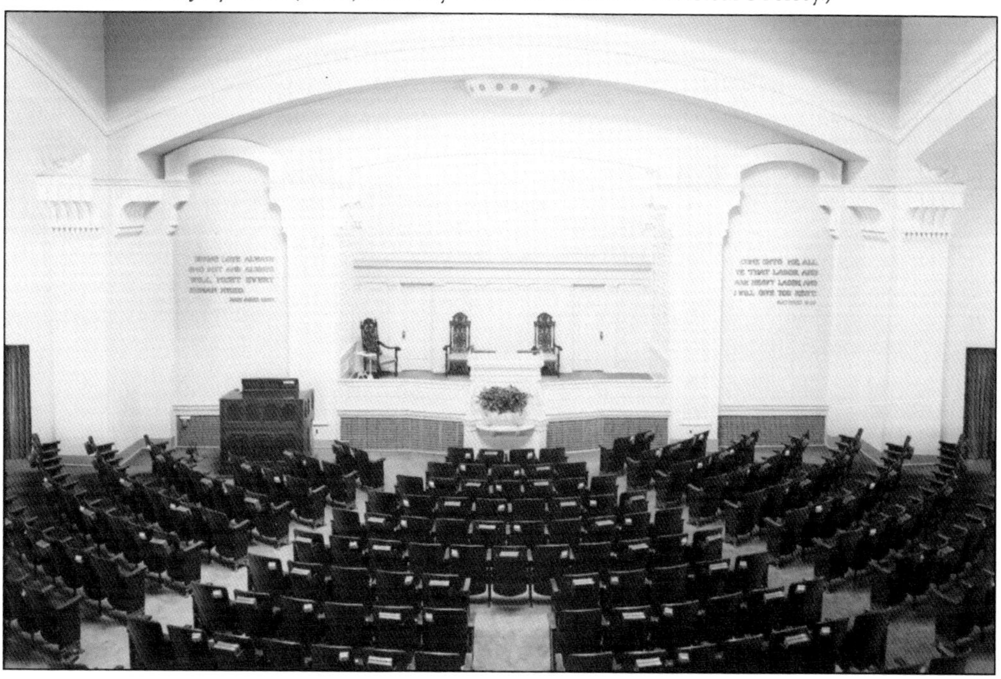

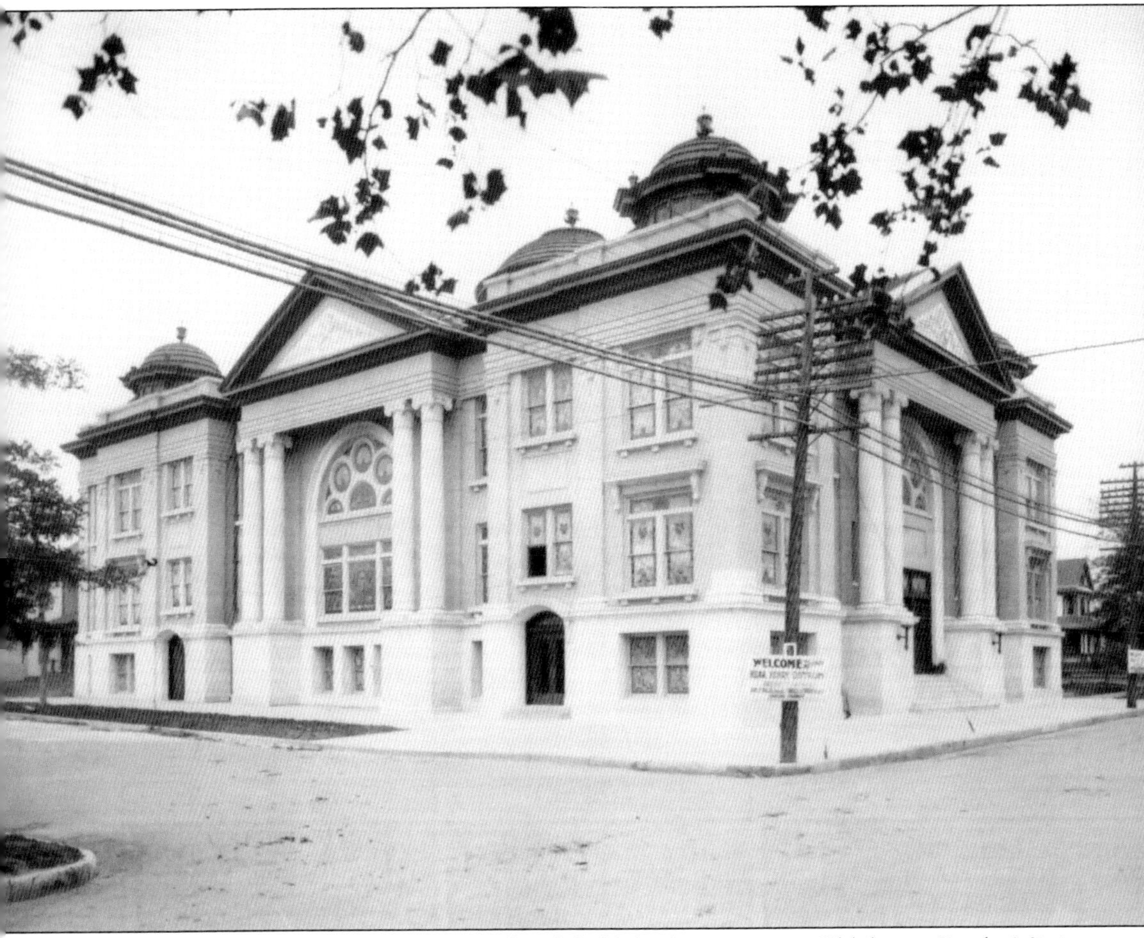

On April 28, 1889, First Presbyterian Church held the first service in Oklahoma City by Minister Charles C. Hembree around the only water well in town at Broadway and Main Street. After the sermon, the first mayor, Capt. William Lewis Couch, supposedly slapped Hembree on his back, stating, "Well, parson, you certainly have given our city a fine start!" J.C. Adams killed Couch in a duel involving a homestead claim dispute on April 21, 1890. The congregation became a chartered mission church on November 3, 1889. It was instrumental in establishing the first welfare agency in the city, the Provident Association. The c. 1911 image above is of their third home at Northwest Ninth Street and Robinson Avenue. Steady growth contributed to building First Presbyterian Church at 1001 Northwest Twenty-fifth Street in the mid-1950s. The building pictured here was demolished around the same time. First Presbyterian also became a landmark to find the large and stately Fairlawn Cemetery north of the church, featuring grave markers from as early as 1892 and many elaborate mausoleums. (Courtesy of the Oklahoma Historical Society.)

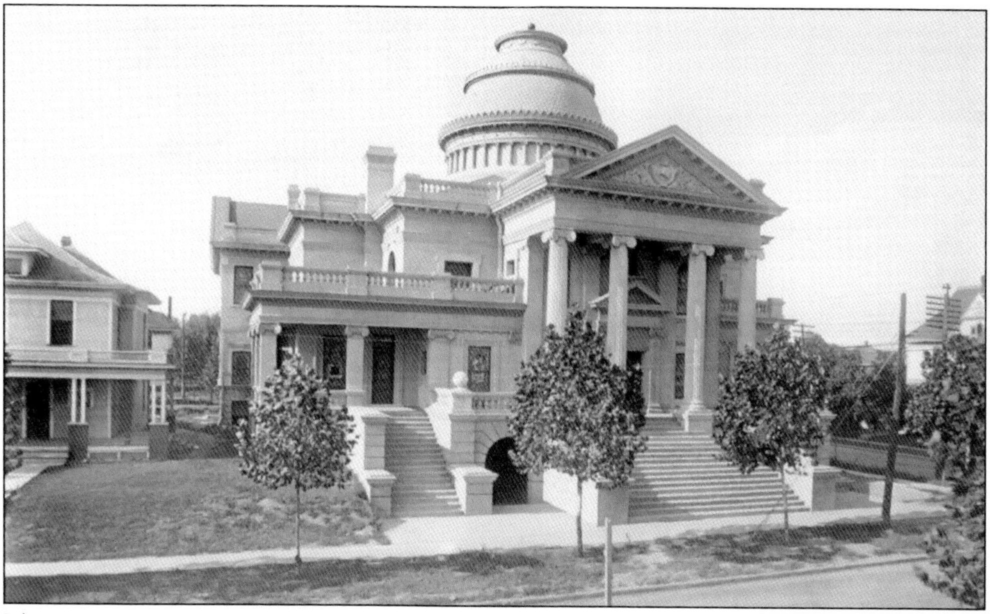

The First Methodist Episcopal Church, South formed on June 23, 1889, near Main Street and Broadway was a lean-to of lumber and canvas that was erected to serve the "Tabernacle Church's" first house of worship. In 1904, the name was changed and St. Luke's Church was built at Northwest Ninth Street and Robinson Avenue. A larger church was built in 1947 at Northwest Fifteenth Street and Robinson Avenue. (Courtesy of the Oklahoma City Metropolitan Library System.)

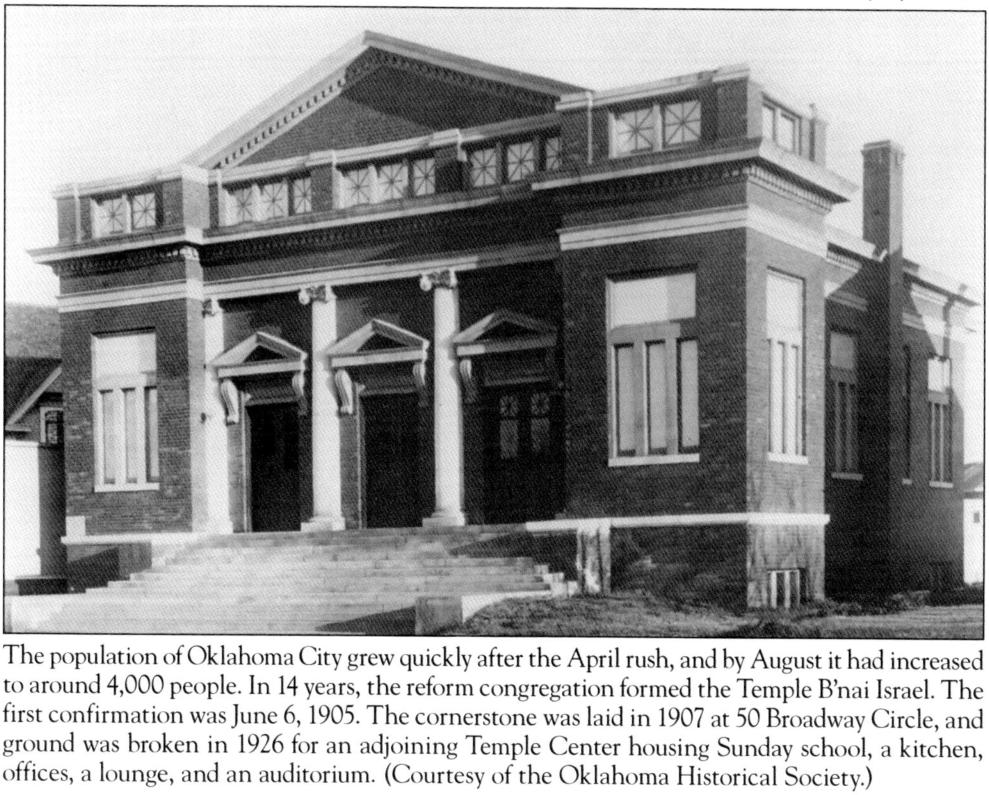

The population of Oklahoma City grew quickly after the April rush, and by August it had increased to around 4,000 people. In 14 years, the reform congregation formed the Temple B'nai Israel. The first confirmation was June 6, 1905. The cornerstone was laid in 1907 at 50 Broadway Circle, and ground was broken in 1926 for an adjoining Temple Center housing Sunday school, a kitchen, offices, a lounge, and an auditorium. (Courtesy of the Oklahoma Historical Society.)

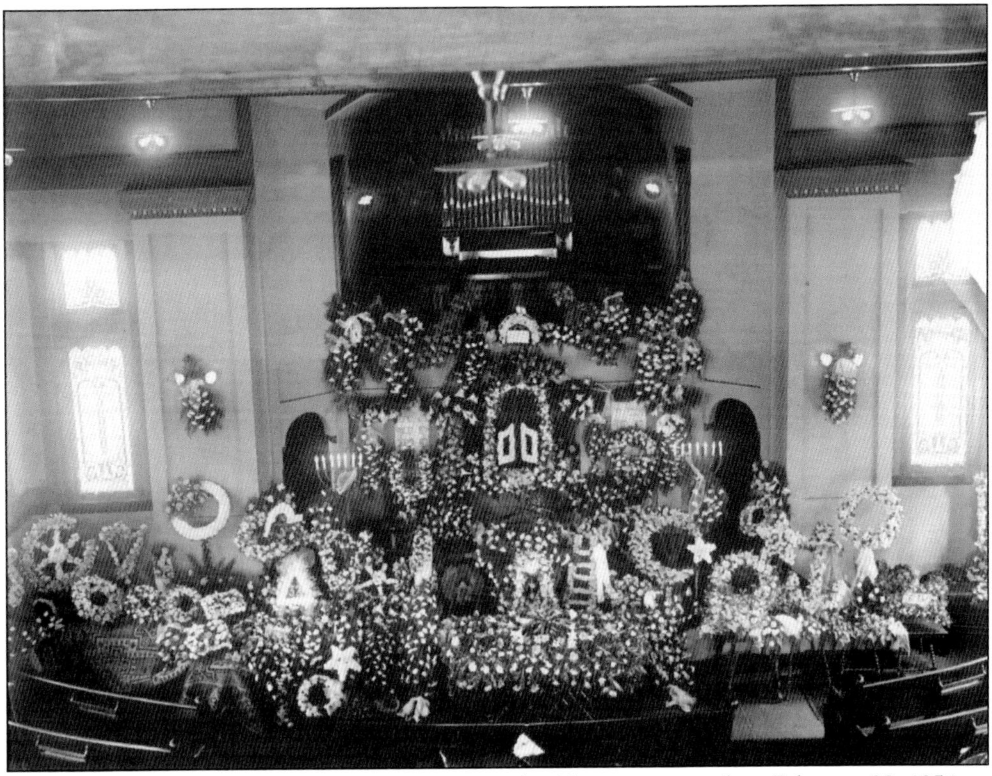

When the congregation outgrew its home, a new building was started on February 28, 1954, at 4901 North Pennsylvania Avenue. Above, a large funeral arrangement is inside the temple in 1912 for Seymour Caesar Heyman, who became a popular civic leader. Heyman served as director for the Commercial Club, which became the Oklahoma City Chamber of Commerce. Heyman was also one of three Oklahoma delegates that traveled to Washington, DC, seeking admission of the Oklahoma Territory as a new state, which occurred in 1907. The image below is of the temple on April 30, 1956, after it became a Masonic center. (Both, courtesy of the Oklahoma Historical Society and the Oklahoma City Metropolitan Library System.)

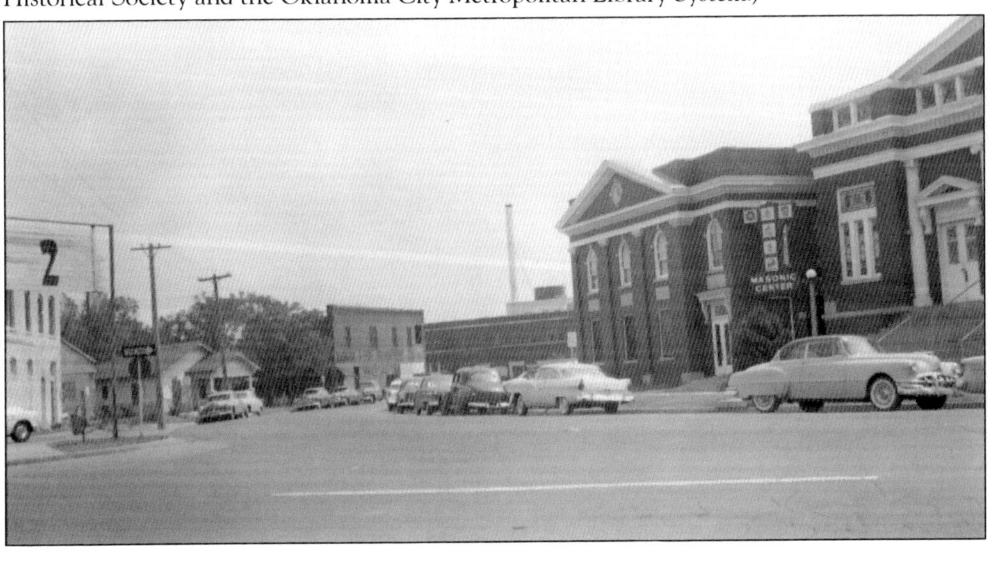

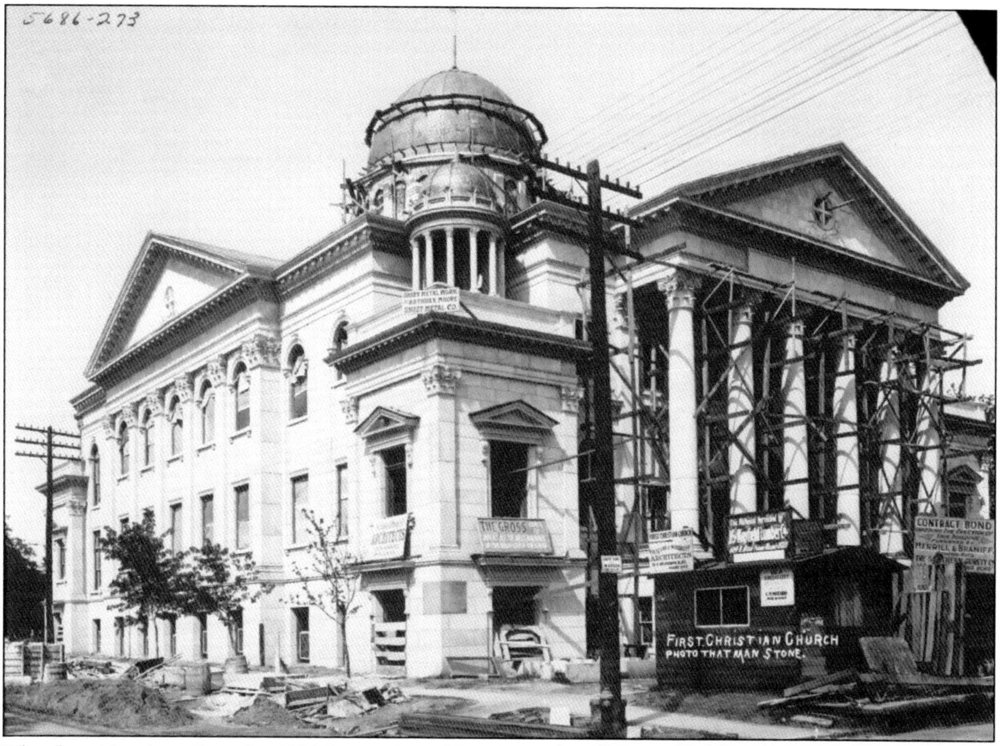

The first Sunday after the Oklahoma Land Rush on April 28, 1889, nondenominational church services were held for all who could be drawn by bugle around the only water well in the city at Broadway and Main Street. Nine of the congregation began discussing the formation of a new church afterwards, which became First Christian Church. Accompanied by 200 cavalrymen to watch over the proceedings, Rev. T.J. Head held a baptismal service along the North Canadian River on June 2, 1889. The congregation built a church at Northwest Third Street and Harvey Avenue by 1894 and moved to a new red-brick building at Northwest Third and Robinson Avenue in 1902. The denomination split into Church of Christ and Disciples of Christ in 1906, with the latter building a massive new church at 1104 North Robinson Avenue. It can be seen in the image above and as a completed structure in 1911 below. (Both, courtesy of the Oklahoma City Metropolitan Library System.)

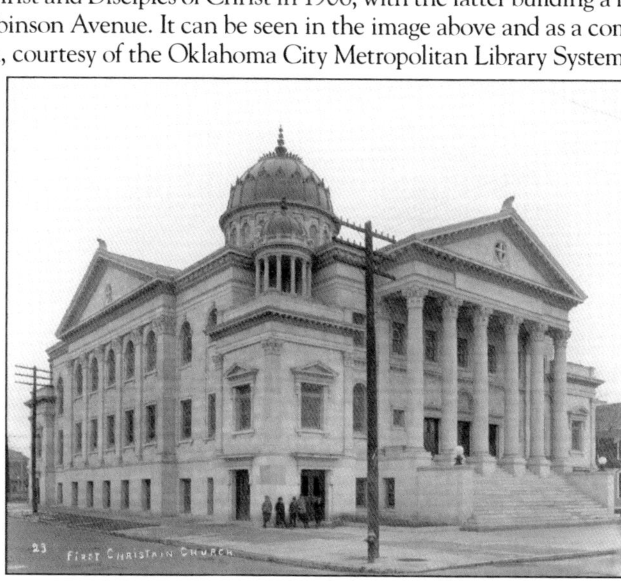

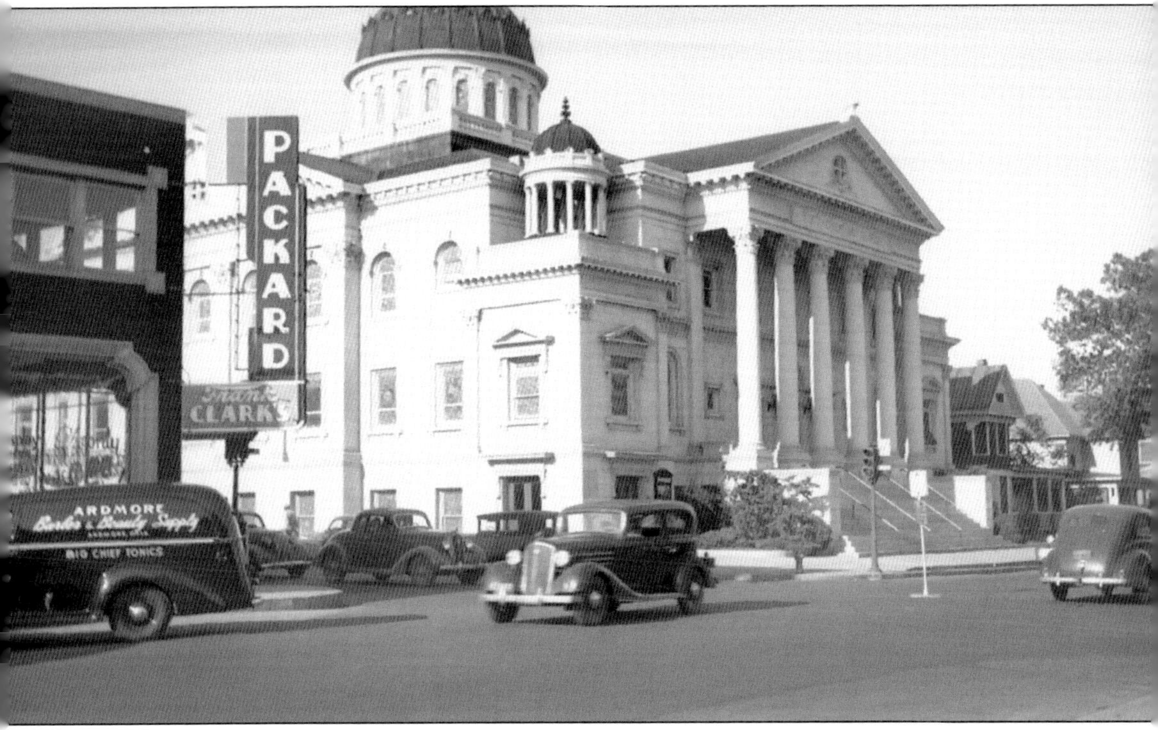

The congregation stayed in a temporary wooden structure at Northwest Eighth Street and Broadway until construction was completed. The congregation dedicated the neoclassical church on December 3, 1911. The building featured an ornate raised dome, three cupolas, and pilasters at the corners with Corinthian capitals. "First Christian Church / 1911 / Christ the light of the world" is inscribed over the three sets of its south facing doors. In 1946, Pastor Bill Alexander convinced the church board to purchase a former golf course near Northwest Thirty-sixth Street and North Walker Avenue for a new church and extensive grounds to serve its congregation and community. First Christian remained in the Robinson Avenue church until 1956. The images here are from May 31, 1940. Today, the former First Christian Church is occupied by Frontline Church, who completed extensive restoration to the building in 2011 after years of neglect and abandonment. (Courtesy of the Western History Collections, University of Oklahoma.)

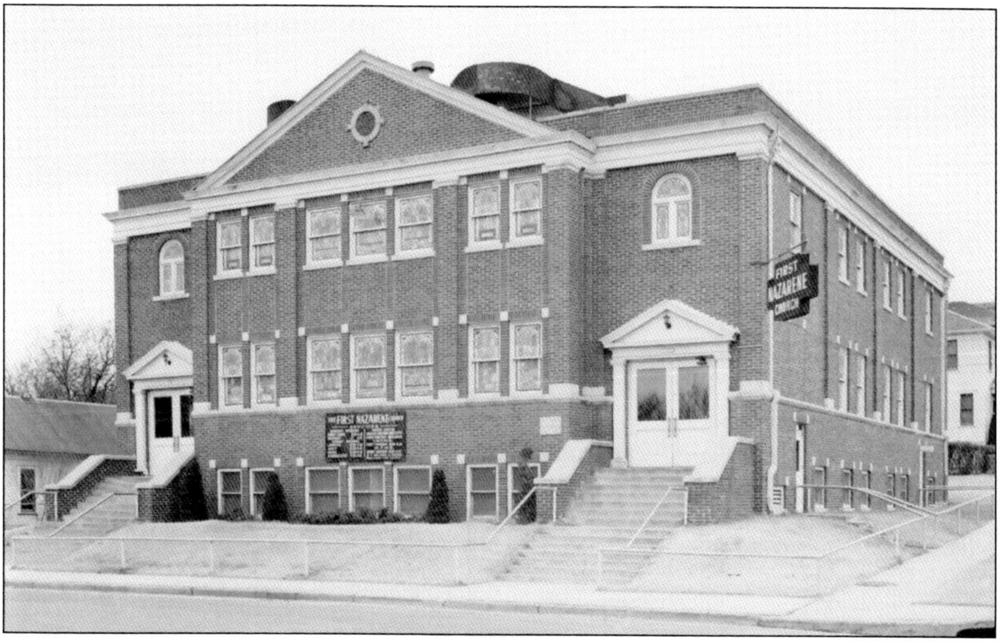

"Uncle" Bud Robinson, who suffered from a speech impediment, hosted a revival meeting in the Sunshine Mission at Reno and Shartel in May 1910 that led to the formation of the First Church of the Nazarene on March 29, 1912. The Nazarene congregation continued services on Shartel until the mid-1930s when they relocated to a new three-story brick building at 901 Northwest Sixth Street, a location that eventually earned the moniker "The Singing Church" from the 1940s–1950s. In the 1960s, city zoning changed the neighborhood surrounding the church to a commercial area, which drove church leaders to think about relocation. A new facility was constructed at 4400 Northwest Expressway and opened in 1970. The First Church of the Nazarene celebrated its 100-year jubilee in 2010. The image above shows First Nazarene as it looked around 1945. Below is the same building in October 1963. (Both, courtesy of the Oklahoma Historical Society.)

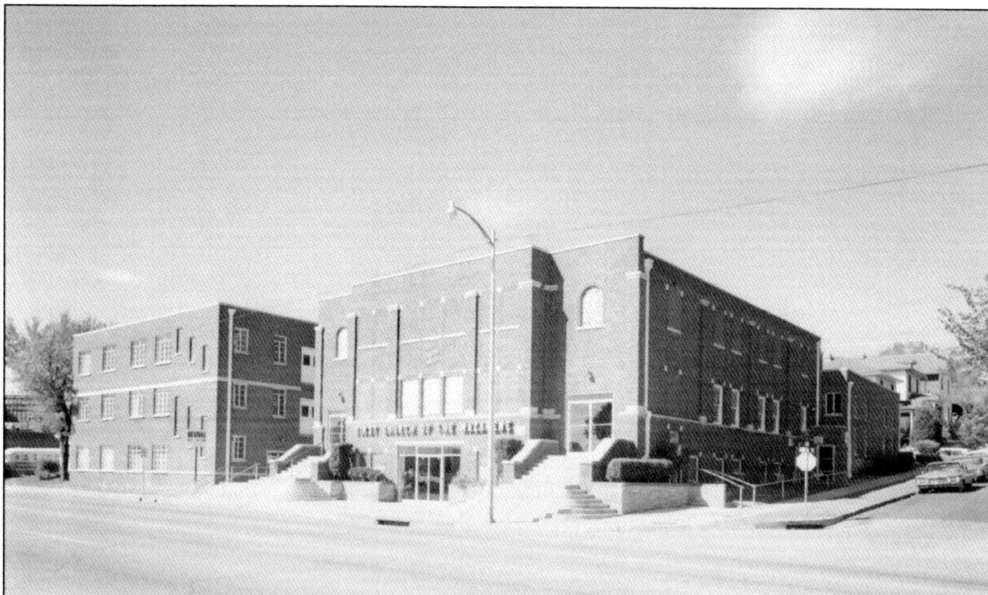

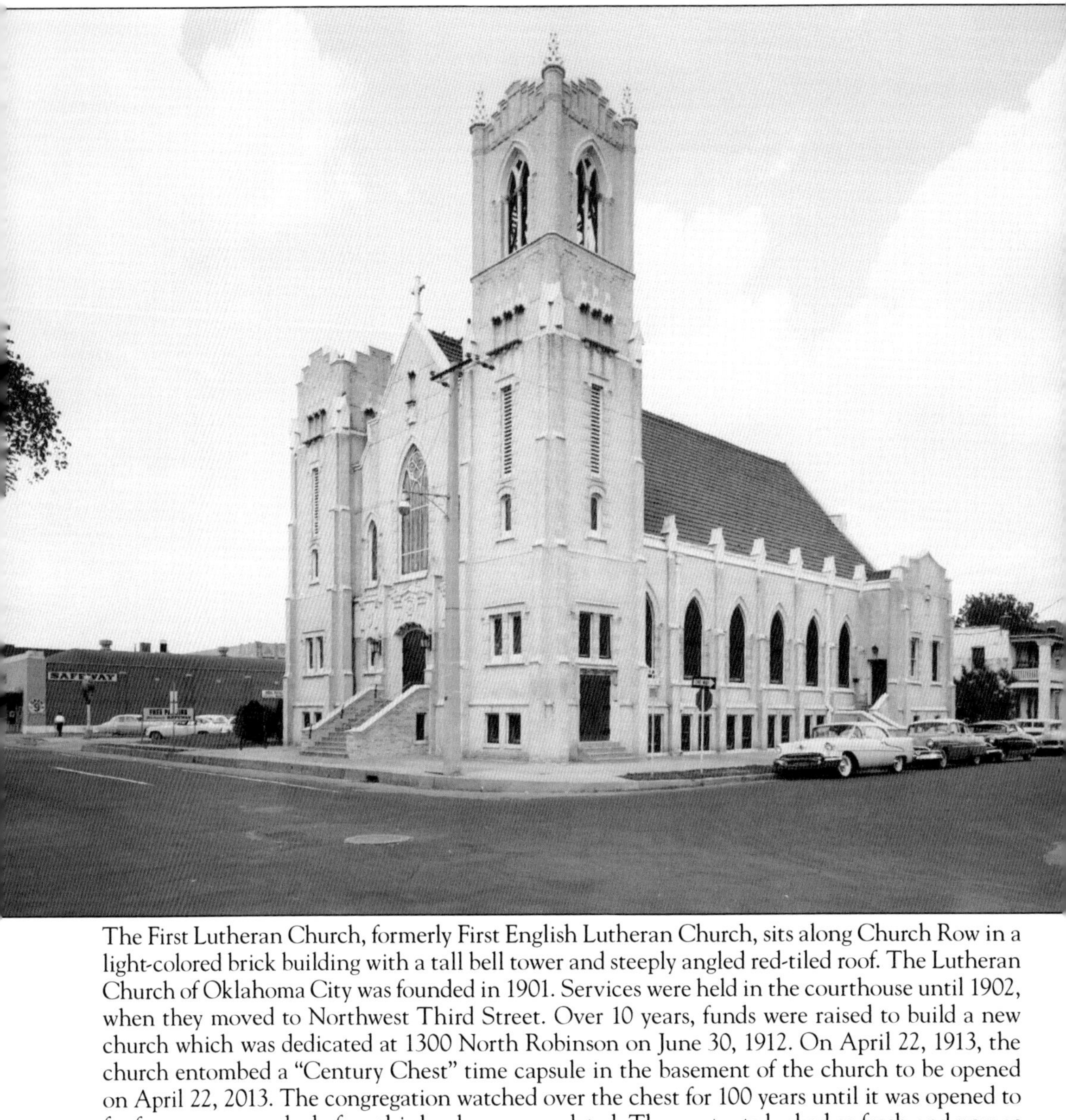

The First Lutheran Church, formerly First English Lutheran Church, sits along Church Row in a light-colored brick building with a tall bell tower and steeply angled red-tiled roof. The Lutheran Church of Oklahoma City was founded in 1901. Services were held in the courthouse until 1902, when they moved to Northwest Third Street. Over 10 years, funds were raised to build a new church which was dedicated at 1300 North Robinson on June 30, 1912. On April 22, 1913, the church entombed a "Century Chest" time capsule in the basement of the church to be opened on April 22, 2013. The congregation watched over the chest for 100 years until it was opened to fanfare, mere months before this book was completed. The contents looked as fresh and new as the day they were interred and revealed many surprises and numerous messages from important citizens about the city's past. The artifacts, as of this writing, are still being catalogued by the Oklahoma Historical Society. (Courtesy of the Oklahoma Historical Society.)

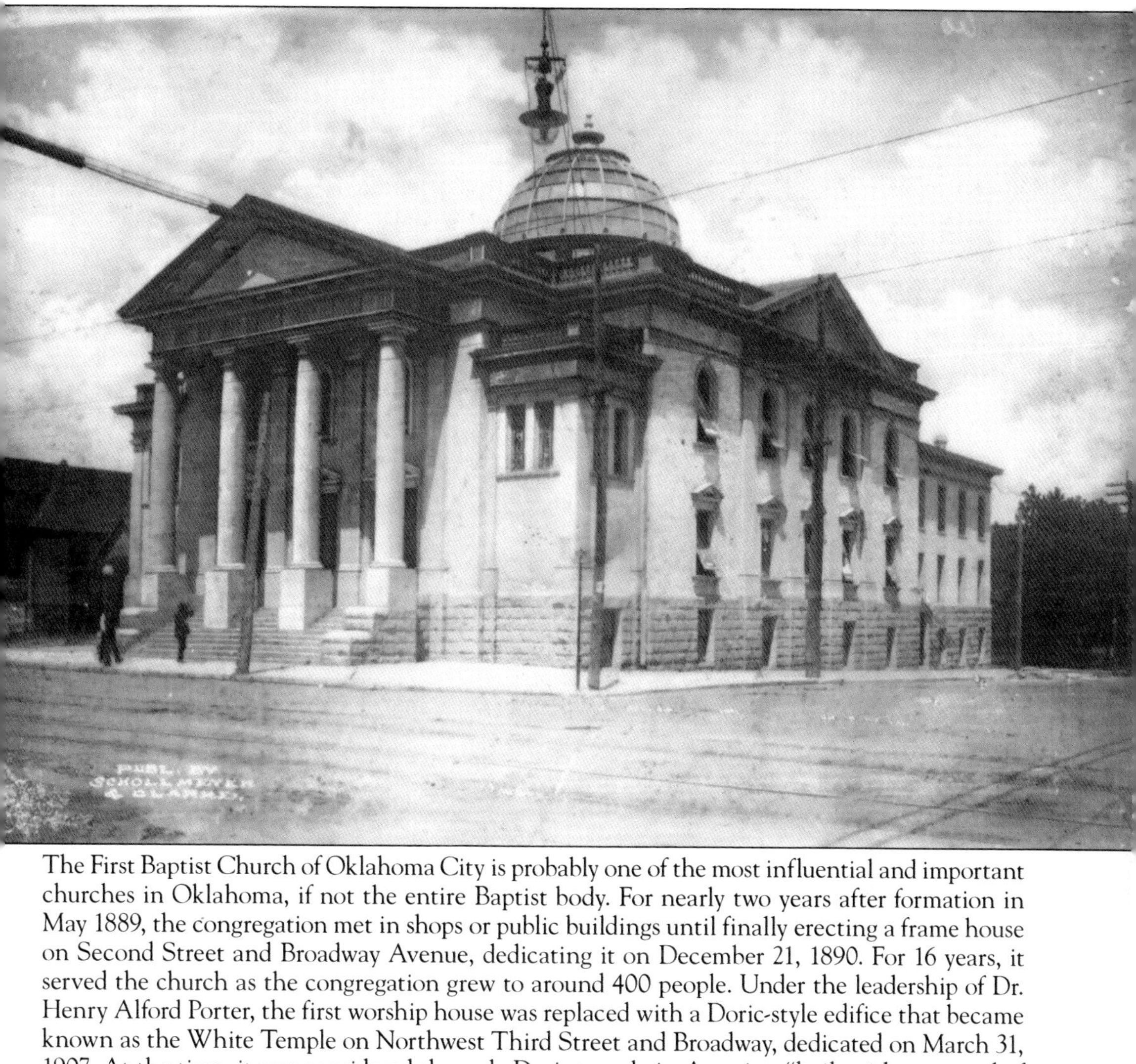

The First Baptist Church of Oklahoma City is probably one of the most influential and important churches in Oklahoma, if not the entire Baptist body. For nearly two years after formation in May 1889, the congregation met in shops or public buildings until finally erecting a frame house on Second Street and Broadway Avenue, dedicating it on December 21, 1890. For 16 years, it served the church as the congregation grew to around 400 people. Under the leadership of Dr. Henry Alford Porter, the first worship house was replaced with a Doric-style edifice that became known as the White Temple on Northwest Third Street and Broadway, dedicated on March 31, 1907. At the time, it was considered the only Doric temple in America, "built without sound of hammer or buzz of saw." (Courtesy of the Oklahoma Historical Society.)

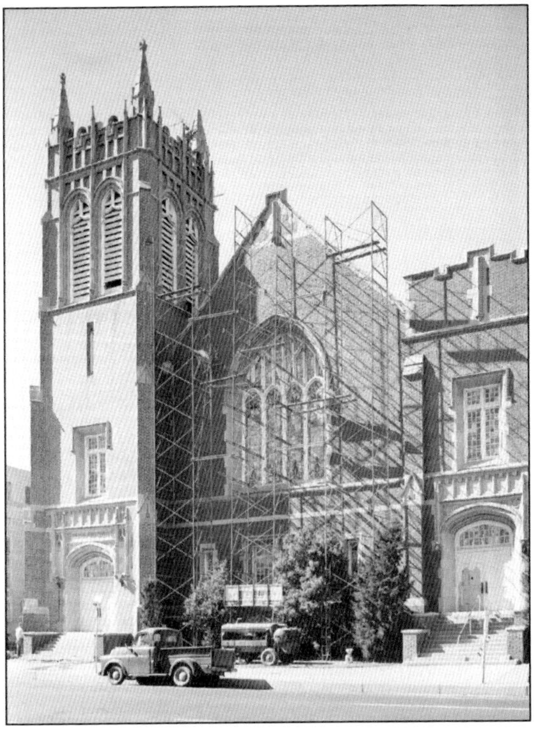

The first meeting of Baptists took place above Winningham Brothers Hardware Store at 123 West Grand Boulevard, May 18, 1889. Alice E. Mitchell, L.J. Perring, and Mrs. Hull were tasked to find other families toward efforts to establish Oklahoma City's first Baptist church. The first Sunday school started on July 28, 1889. Elected officers organized the church on November 16, and Reverend W.H. Nichols took the pastorate on February 5, 1890, preaching his first sermon April 6, 1890. In three years, membership outgrew the temple. Under then-pastor Dr. Carter Helm Jones, a new home was completed and dedicated in 1912 at Northwest Eleventh Street and Robinson Avenue. The church operated from the First Presbyterian Church building at Northwest Sixth Street and Broadway Avenue from June 1911 because the White Temple was sold to the Masonic Fraternity of Oklahoma, Lodge No. 36. (Both, courtesy of the Oklahoma Historical Society.)

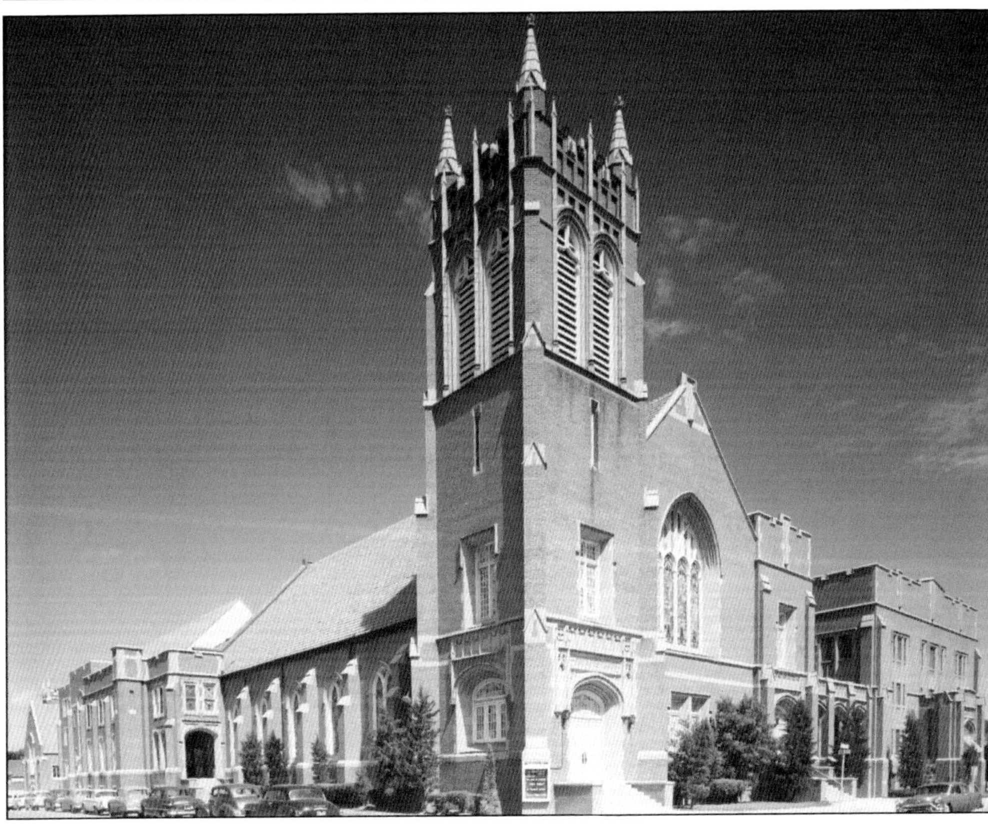

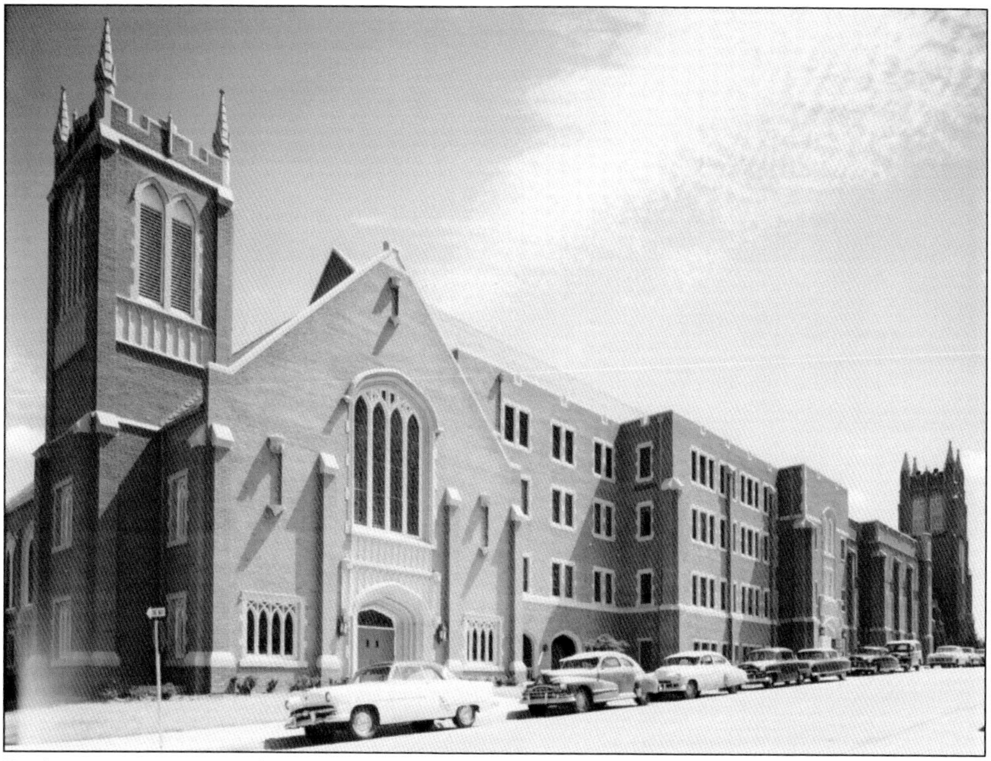

Further expansion was needed by the late 1920s. Over the course of two years, plans and recommendations were made for a new educational building, which was built on four adjacent lots west of the church. The new building was constructed for around $100,000 and dedicated on April 12, 1931. The church tower on Robinson Avenue became known as the "Lighthouse on the Corner" because of a light that had burned for decades prior to the bombing of the Alfred P. Murrah Federal Building on April 19, 1995. The bombing's shockwave caused extensive damages, which included the collapse of a chandelier on top of the sanctuary piano. It still bears the scars of the damage sustained. First Baptist Church has served as a beacon of hope in Oklahoma with its mission work and heavy community involvement for over 100 years. (Both, courtesy of the Oklahoma Historical Society.)

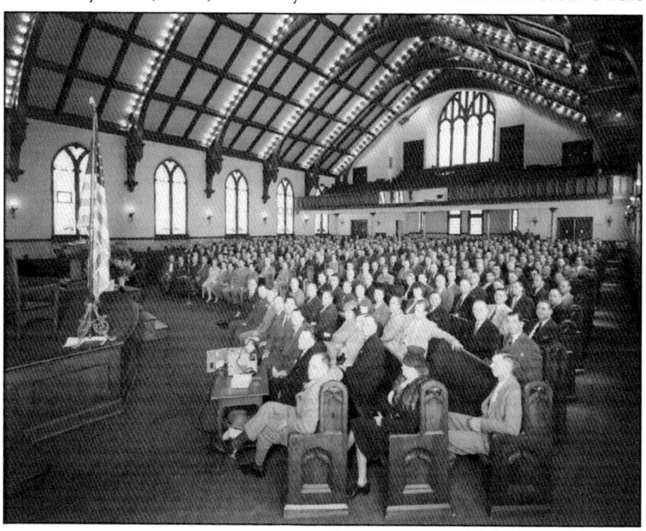

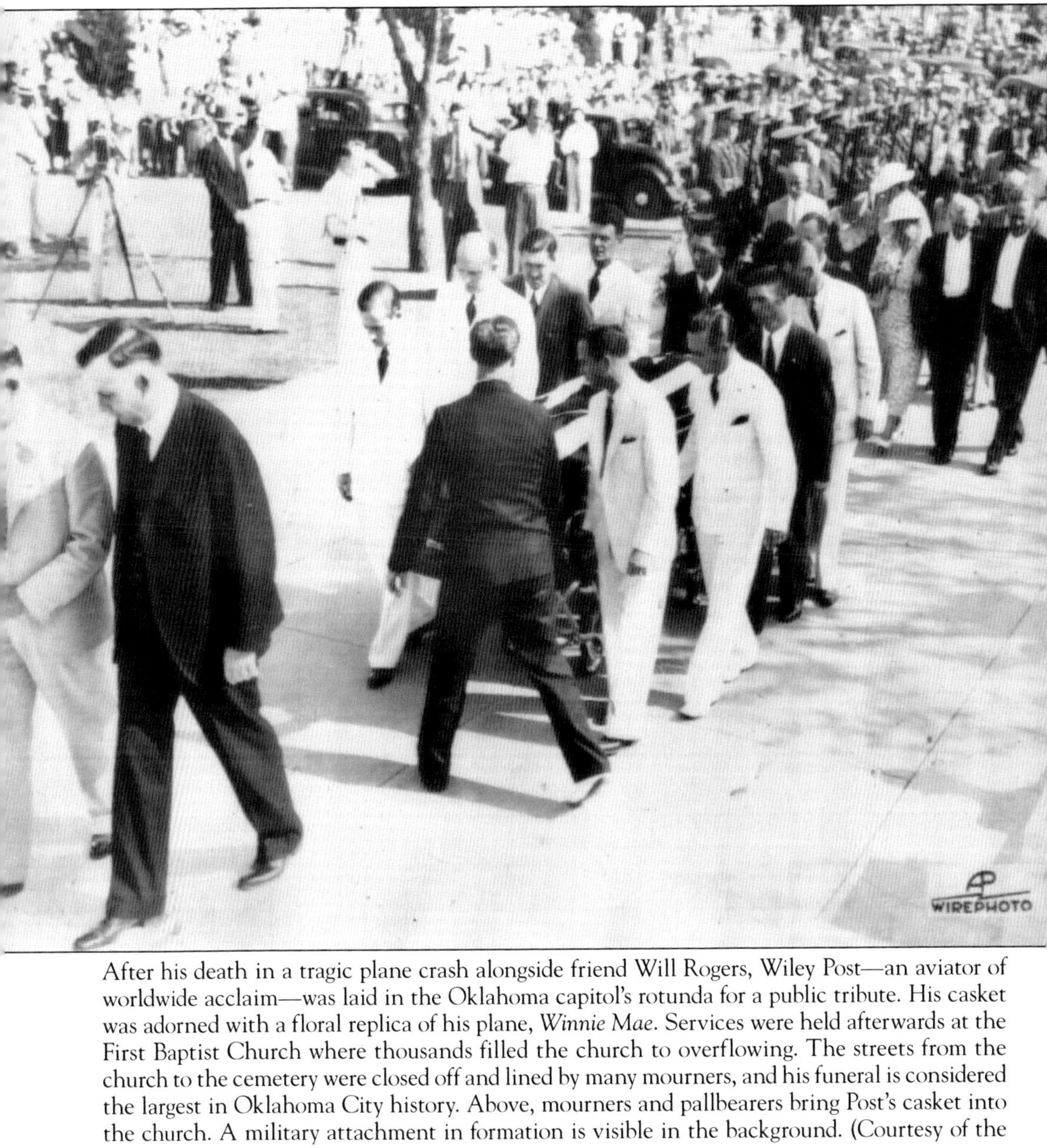

After his death in a tragic plane crash alongside friend Will Rogers, Wiley Post—an aviator of worldwide acclaim—was laid in the Oklahoma capitol's rotunda for a public tribute. His casket was adorned with a floral replica of his plane, *Winnie Mae*. Services were held afterwards at the First Baptist Church where thousands filled the church to overflowing. The streets from the church to the cemetery were closed off and lined by many mourners, and his funeral is considered the largest in Oklahoma City history. Above, mourners and pallbearers bring Post's casket into the church. A military attachment in formation is visible in the background. (Courtesy of the Oklahoma Historical Society.)

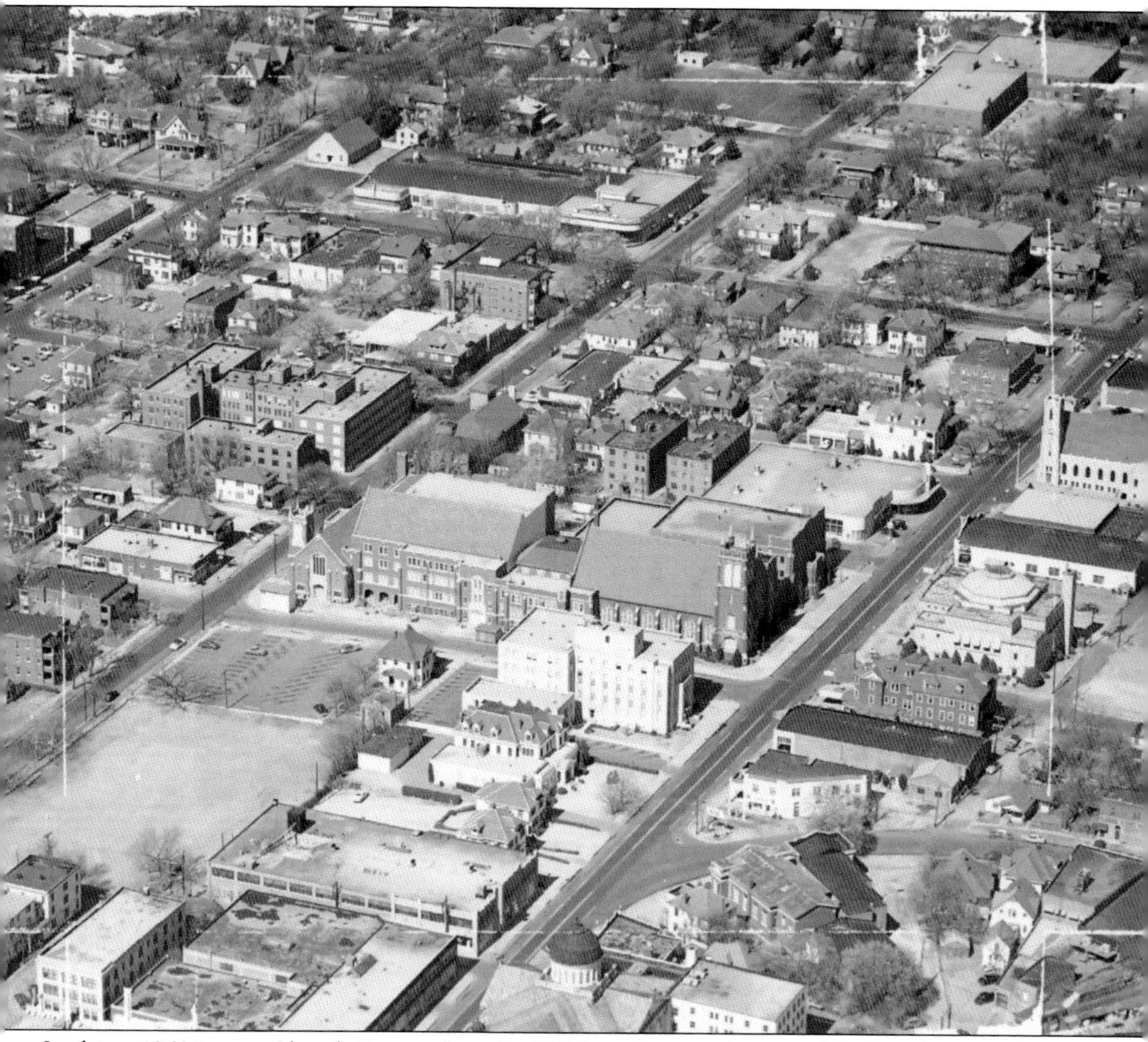

In this c. 1960 image, Church Row and much of Midtown's east side are visible. Broadway Circle is in the lower right with a parapet from First City Church just visible, and Temple B'nai Israel is just to its right with the dark roof. Across the street are the Packard and United Parts buildings. The Church of Christ, Scientist; First Baptist; Baptist building; and First Lutheran Church are also visible. The street running along the top of the image is Northwest Thirteenth Street, and to the far left is Hudson Avenue. Many of the buildings captured in this moment are missing from today's city skyline, especially the many residential homes seen here. (Courtesy of the Oklahoma Historical Society.)

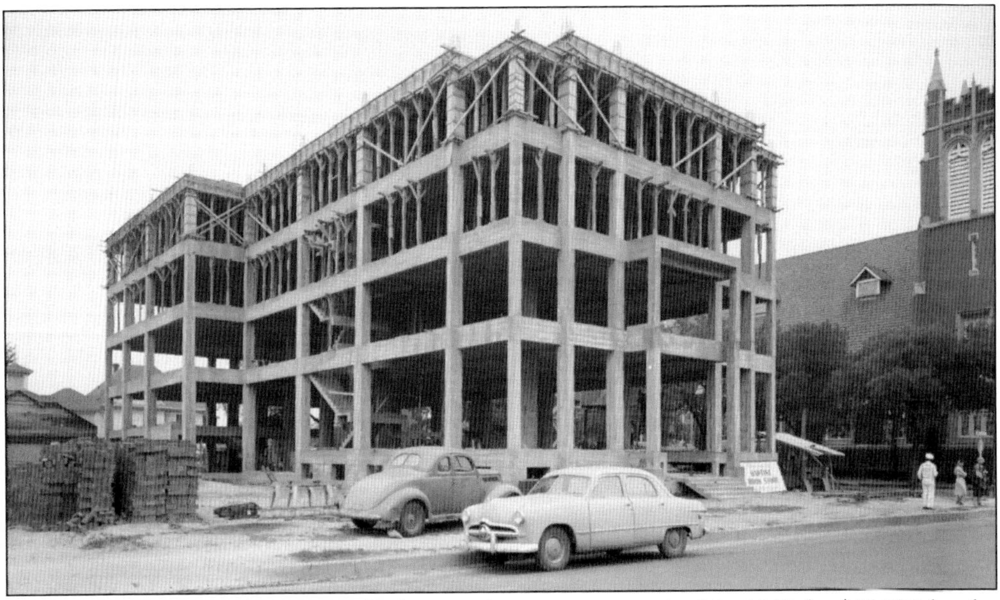

The Jack Jones Funeral Home on Robinson Avenue was acquired in 1945 for $45,000 by the First Baptist Church and then sold to the Baptist convention in 1948 to build a new general convention building at 1141 North Robinson Avenue. Ground-breaking occurred on June 7, 1948, with construction beginning the following Monday. Built at a cost of $700,000, the four-story Bedford limestone building was trimmed in granite with aluminum embellishments and featured corridors lined in Tennessee marble. The image below shows it nearing completion in May 1950; its dedication took place on June 29. The building also housed the Baptist Book Store. It was put up for sale in March 1990 and purchased that September by the Western Construction Company, who then invested $1 million in its renovation. Today, the property operates under the Lawyers Title Building LLC, whose exterior sign was replaced with new tenant Stryker Osteonics. (Both, courtesy of the Oklahoma Historical Society.)

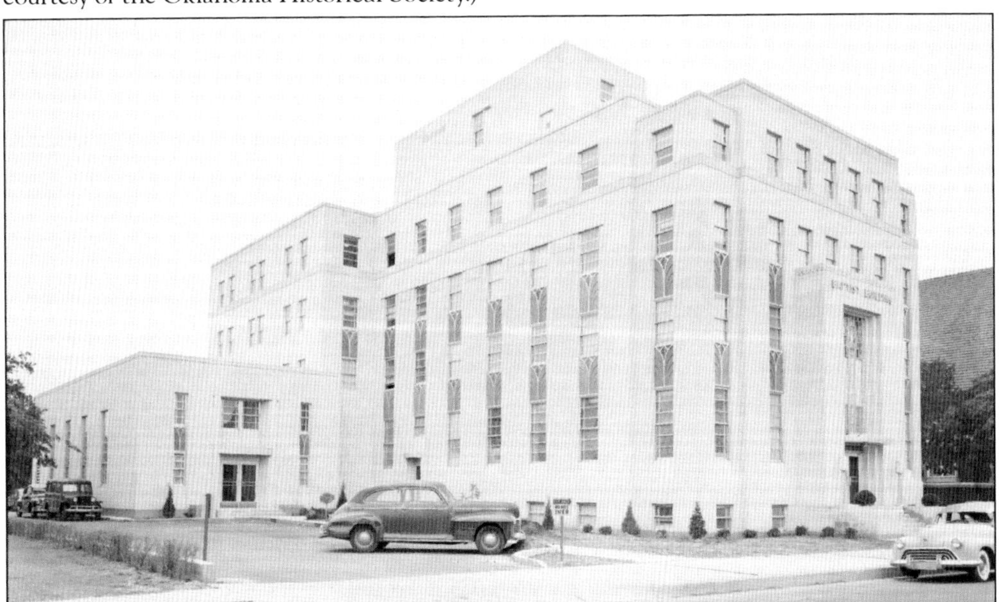

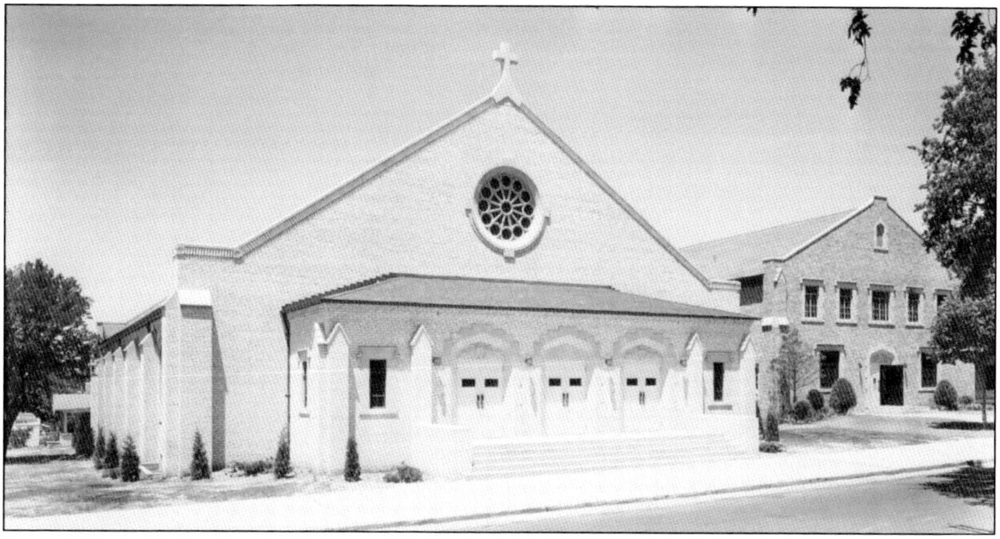

Formed around 1904, the original Church of Christ congregation met in the basement of the Adventist building at Northwest Seventh Street and Robinson Avenue. In 1914, the church raised funds for a new building and purchased lots at the corner of Northwest Tenth Street and Francis Avenue, which formerly hosted a five-room cottage. World War I postponed construction of their new home until 1918, but they met at the Oklahoma County Courthouse at Grand (Sheridan) and Dewey Avenues in the interim. A two-story bible school was added in 1929. Church expansion inspired a fundraising campaign for a new sanctuary with a pledge of $25,000 from its members in 1930. During construction, the bible school was moved to the west for Sunday school operations. The new sanctuary was built for approximately $60,000, opening in 1939. The facility included seating for 1,200 and a radio broadcasting station for its regular services. (Both, courtesy of the Oklahoma Historical Society.)

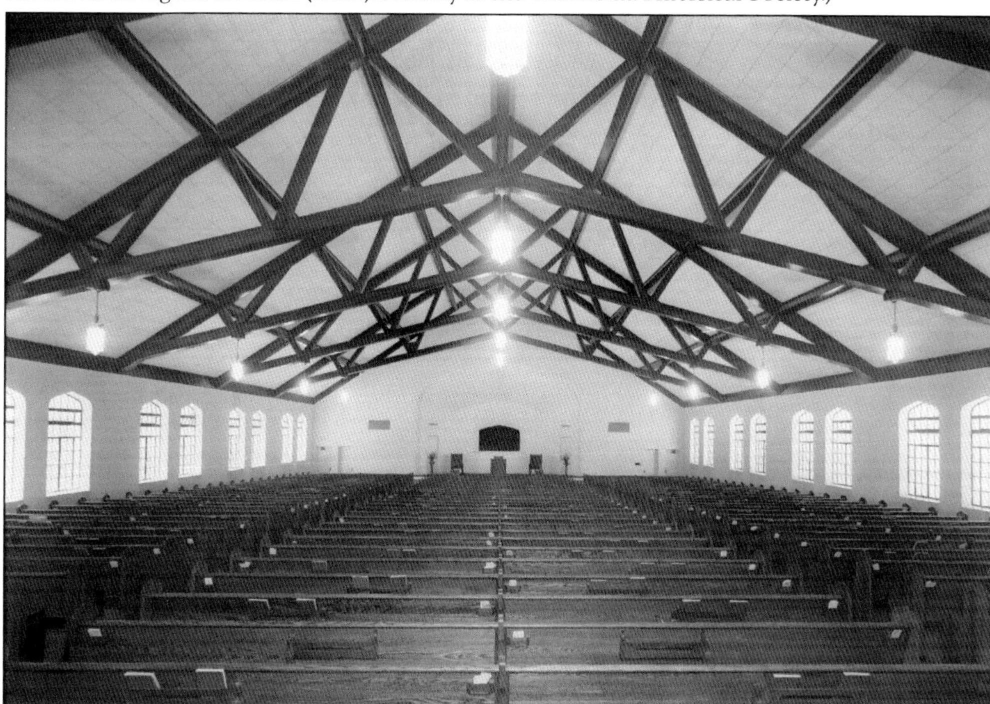

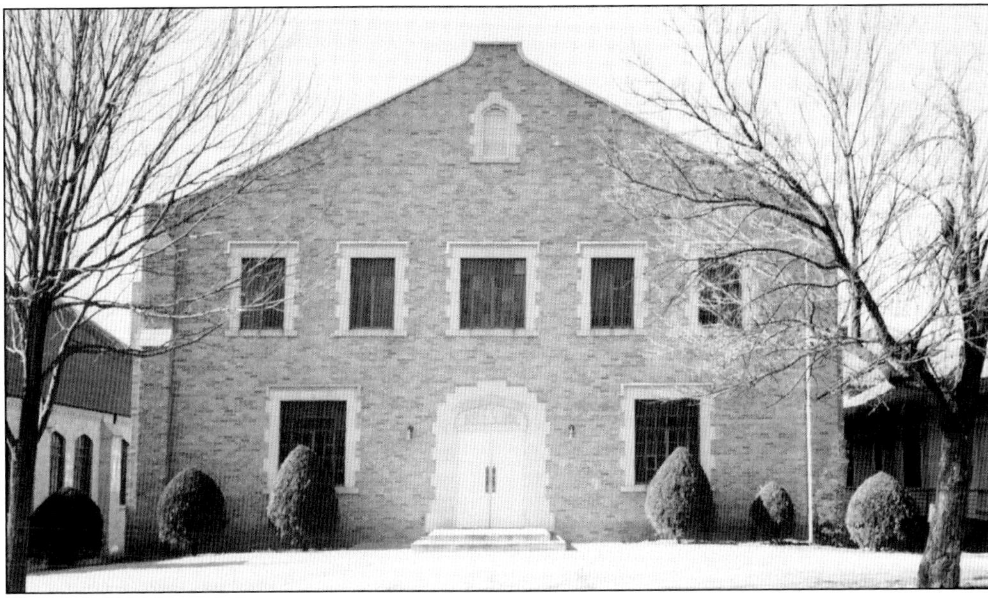

The church properties were sold to the Living Word Academy, a private religious school in 1975. The firm of Pierce, Couch, Hendrickson, Johnston & Baysinger, which began as a two-man partnership in 1923 in downtown's First National Bank building, acquired it in 1981 after the firm expanded beyond 60 attorneys and staff members. The former bible school that was used as the sanctuary had been converted into a gymnasium, complete with wood flooring, bleachers, and scoreboard. The original solid copper baptismal tub remained, and when a former partner suggested it be turned into a hot tub, the firm sold it for scrap. The gym continued being used for basketball and indoor soccer league play until expansion in the mid-1980s forced the firm to end the league's lease. Today, Pierce, Couch, Hendrickson, Baysinger & Green are Oklahoma's largest insurance defense law firm. (Both, courtesy of the Oklahoma Historical Society.)

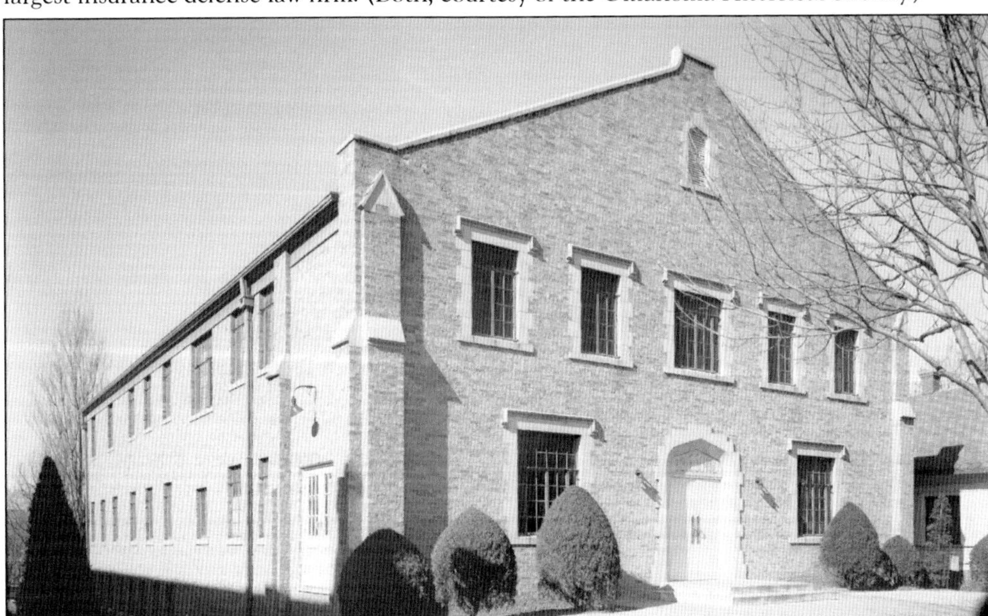

Five

Midtown Renaissance

It is hard to imagine how the near 400 acres called Midtown has evolved over the past 100 years. Yet, a drive or walk through this bustling community would show it is a living thing and the people are its heartbeat. Through both generosity and business savvy, developers have taken on many obstacles that were thought unreasonable or impossible and have transformed them into something that will continue the legacy that is Midtown.

Today, properties like Hadden Hall, the Marion, Mayfair, Osler, Packard, and Plaza Court have been restored and renewed, ready for a new generation of community and business to occupy and utilize them again. From machine shops and car lots to retail and lofty residential buildings, bold developers and the people of Midtown have overlooked nothing.

The Cottage District has been transformed into a mix of Territorial Victorian homes and Modern-style residential architecture. St. Anthony has grown from the small, simple hospital that became Oklahoma's first, into a modern caregiving complex with the latest advancements and prominent caregivers. The old Oklahoma General has also evolved into a massive facility named Mercy Hospital that is the only hospital serving the far Northwest portion of Oklahoma City and other communities—a complex where the Sisters of Mercy still serve. The former Central High School is now being transformed into an advanced Law Center for Oklahoma City University. The long-vacant Anderson Pritchard filling station is now a high-end Italian eatery. The list goes on and on.

Midtown is filled with people that roll with, or challenge, the times they live in. The community they have—and continue to develop—is a reflection of their mettle. It has become more than a legacy of change. It is a renaissance for the future.

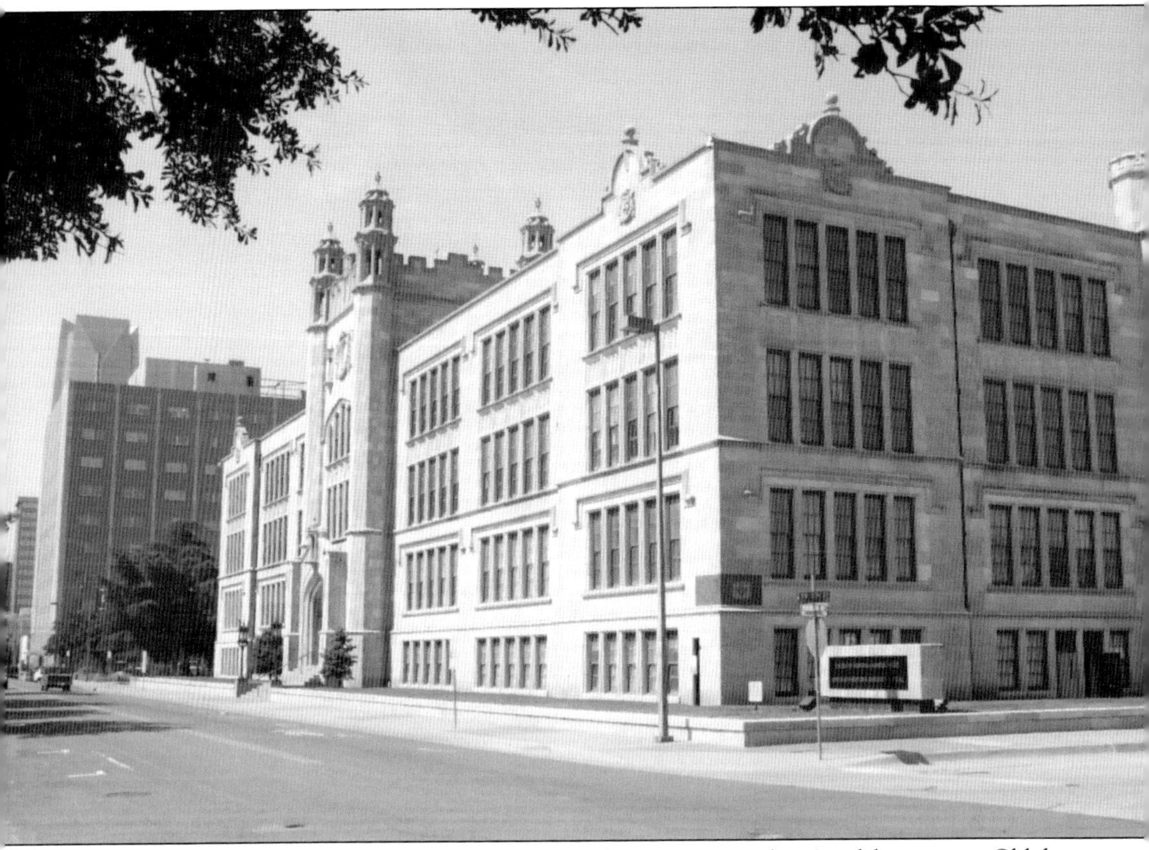

This image shows the former Central High School as it appears today. As of this writing, Oklahoma City University is preparing to renovate and recondition the building to accommodate their law school program. The law school's presence in the old high school will have a tremendous economic and social impact on the surrounding Midtown community for decades to come. (Photograph by William Hider.)

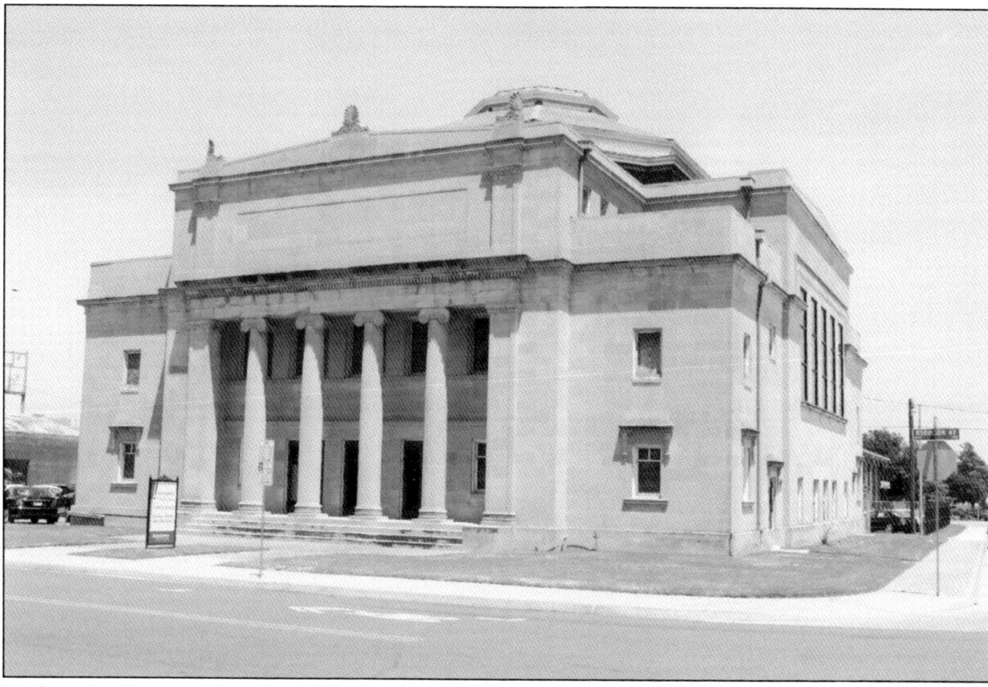

Today, the former Church of Christ, Scientist, property sits vacant and unused, as seen above. The former congregation relocated to 4700 North Portland Avenue in Oklahoma City. The property will need extensive restoration, as it still sustains damages like broken windows from the Alfred P. Murrah building blast. The former First Christian Church now operates as Frontline Church, whose congregation at the time of this writing continues drawing many people from the neighborhoods surrounding the downtown's core. (Both photographs by William Hider.)

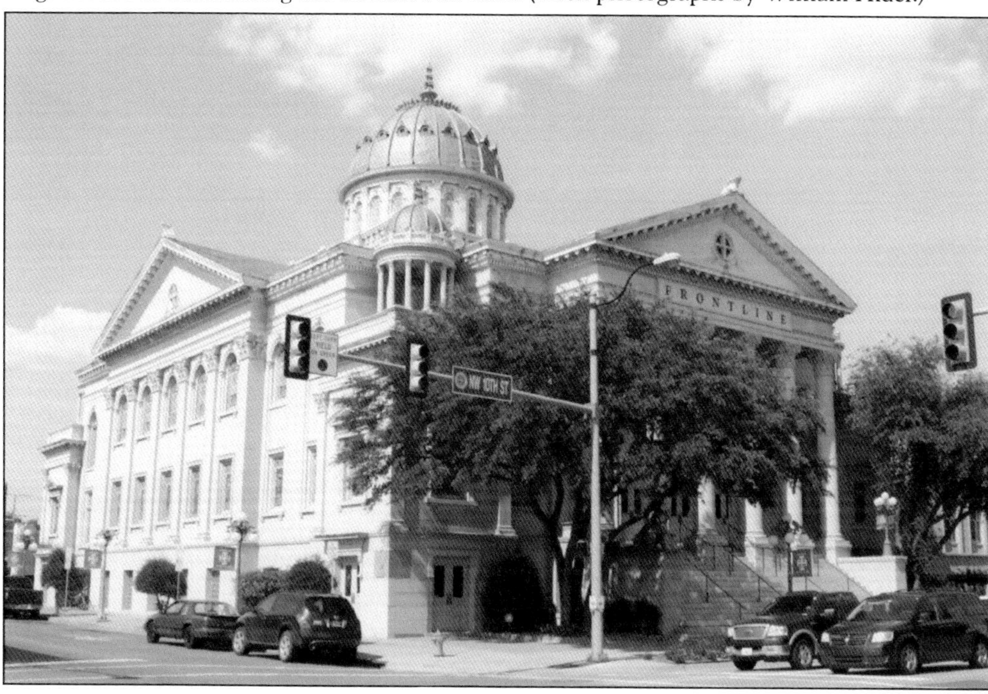

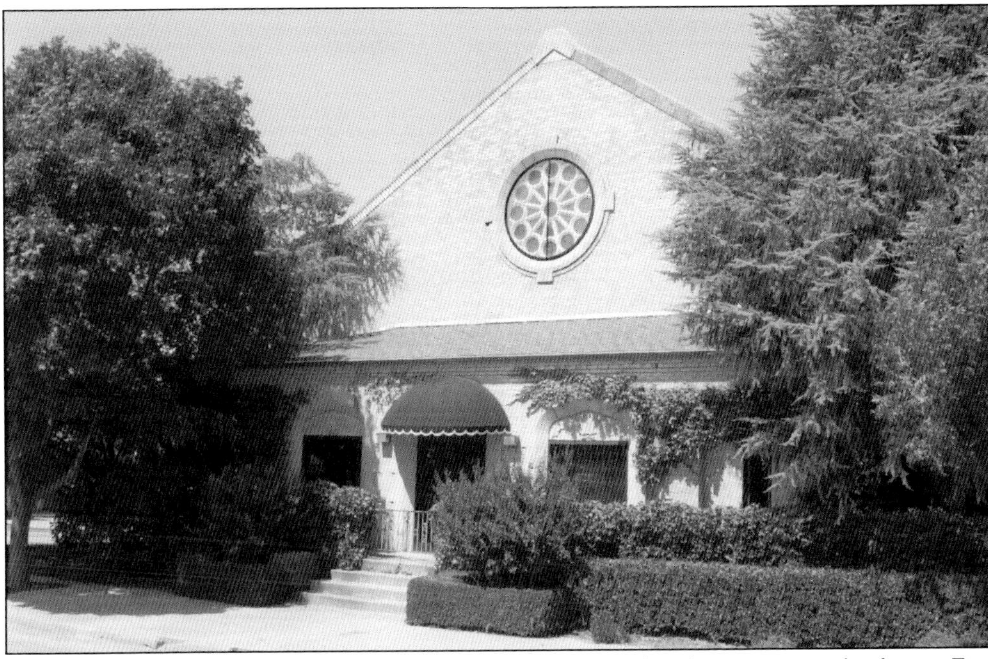

Today, the Pierce, Couch, Hendrickson, Baysinger & Green law firm occupies the former First Christian Church at Northwest Tenth Street and Francis Avenue. The renovation and reuse of the former church has received positive feedback, especially when its garden areas begin to fill in and give the illusion that the church has been there for decades longer. (Photograph by William Hider.)

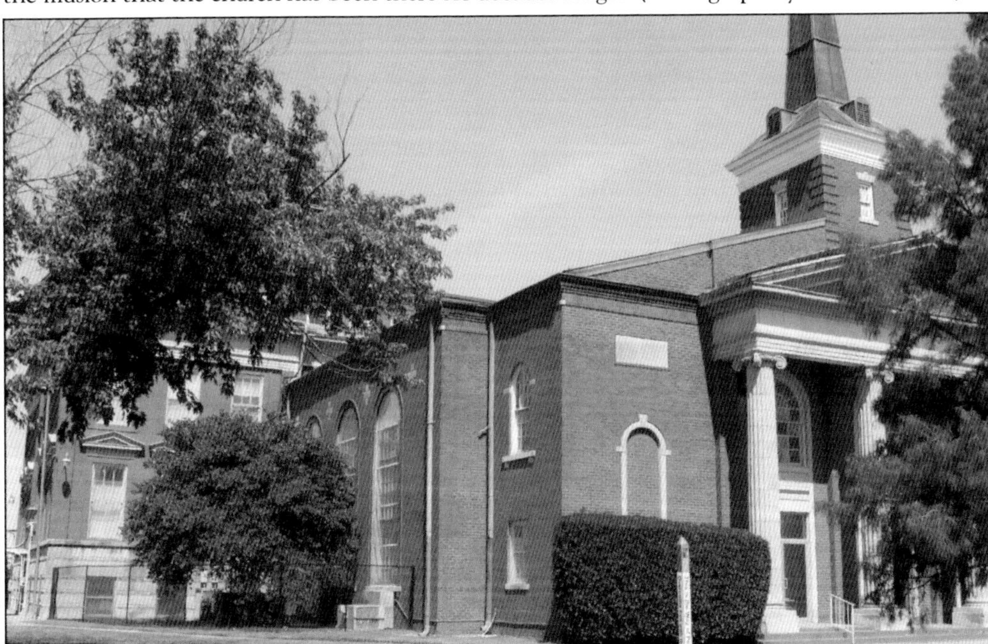

Funding for Epworth University ceased in 1911, forcing a declaration of bankruptcy. A portion of the university's land was transferred to the Methodist Episcopal Church, South, and a sanctuary was added to the university building in 1923. The original entry facade was reused, as seen in the image above. Now, it has become home to the Epworth United Methodist Church. (Photograph by William Hider.)

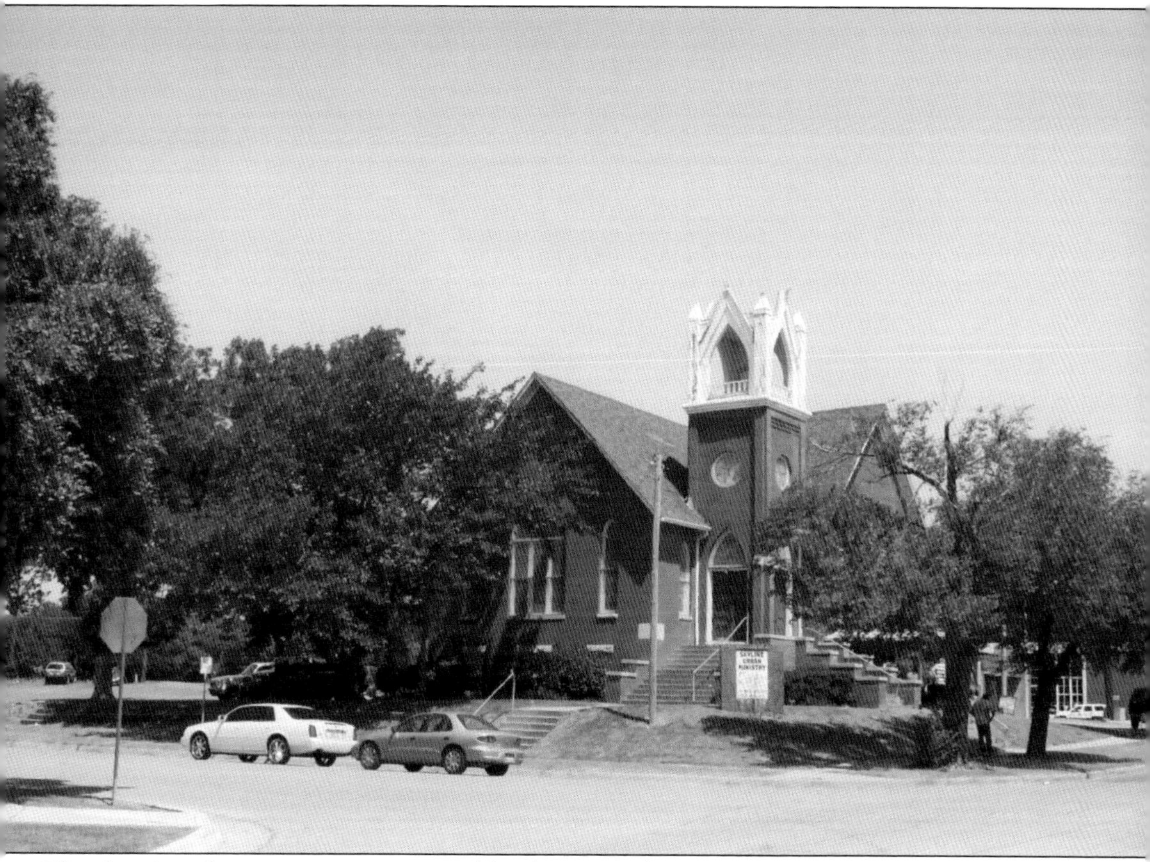

The church and its treasures, now owned by the St. Anthony Foundation, remain standing at the time of this writing, although the parsonage was razed long ago and the future of this historic structure is at risk. Today, the church is home to Skyline Ministries, an outreach center for the surrounding community. The steeple was removed in 2011, as the cost to replace it exceeded Skyline's budget. This left only the bell tower. Ms. Elliot, a nurse from St. Anthony Hospital, just one block away, stated in an issue of Skyline's newsletter that "anytime there was a difficult moment in a surgery or when they could not save someone's life, she would look through the window of the surgery room where she could see the steeple, perfectly framed with the cross on top, and she would pray. 'It was so beautiful and perfectly placed there in the window,' she said. 'It was like a piece of heaven on earth.' It got her through those moments as a young woman." (Photograph by William Hider.)

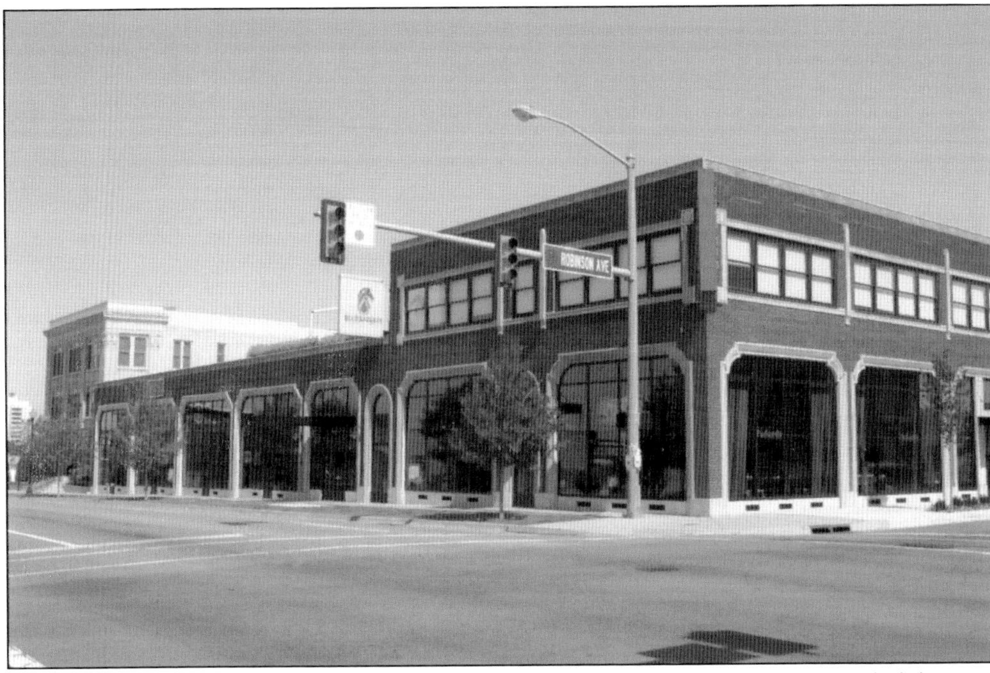

The Packard building, seen above, has come a long way in a short time in regards to rehabilitation. Today, the building is a mixed-use space catering to an exclusive restaurant and more. The former United Parts building is now referred to as the Guardian building, as it was used temporarily in the past as a parking venue for the Guardian Funeral Home next door. This space has also been refurbished and enhanced by the Midtown Renaissance group. Between the Packard and the Guardian is Park Place, a former city street that ran from east to west and is now a pedestrian crossway to other portions of Midtown. (Both photographs by William Hider.)

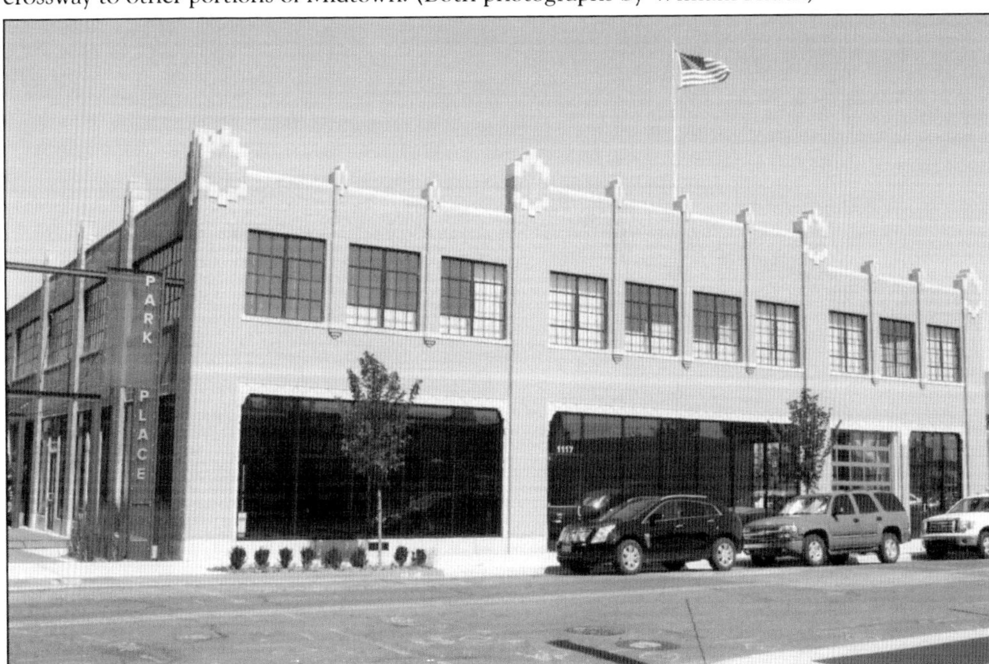

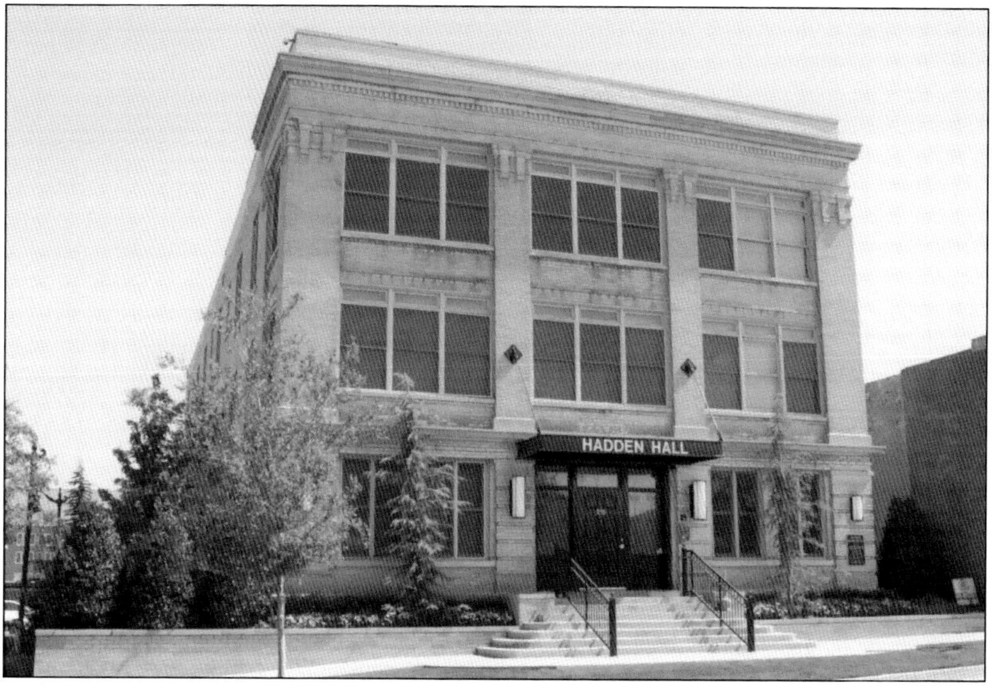

Today, Hadden Hall (above) at 215 Northwest Tenth Street and the Mayfair Apartments (below) at 1315 Broadway Place have come a long way from their early days. After complete renovations, they continue to serve as a residential buildings, a much-appreciated addition to the growing need for residential space near the downtown core. The Midtown Renaissance Group made the changes in 2010–2011 as an overall improvement to the Midtown area. (Both photographs by William Hider.)

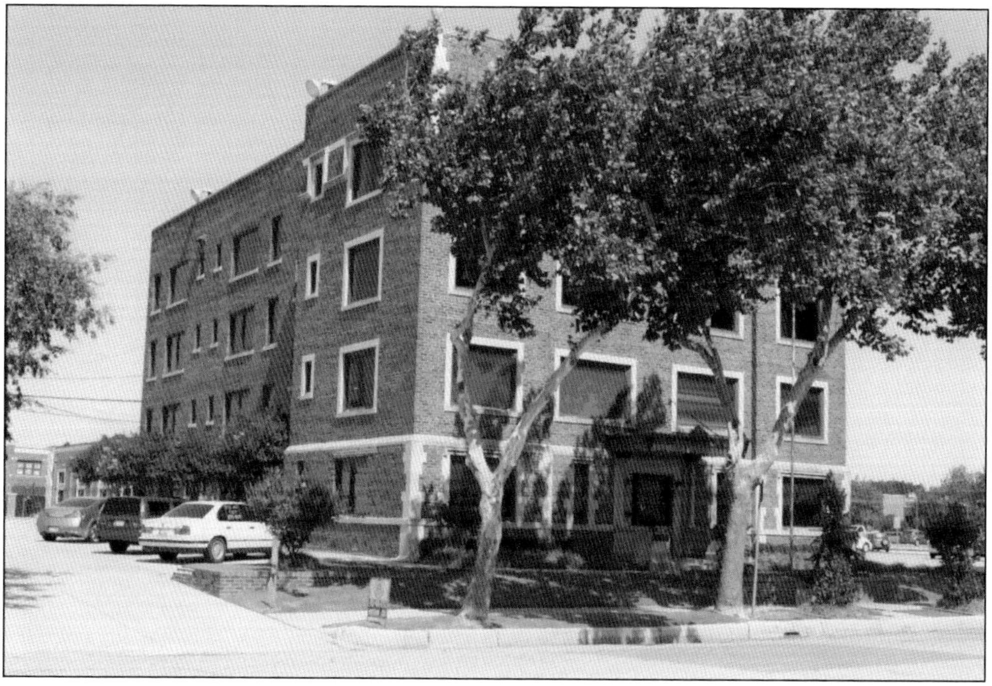

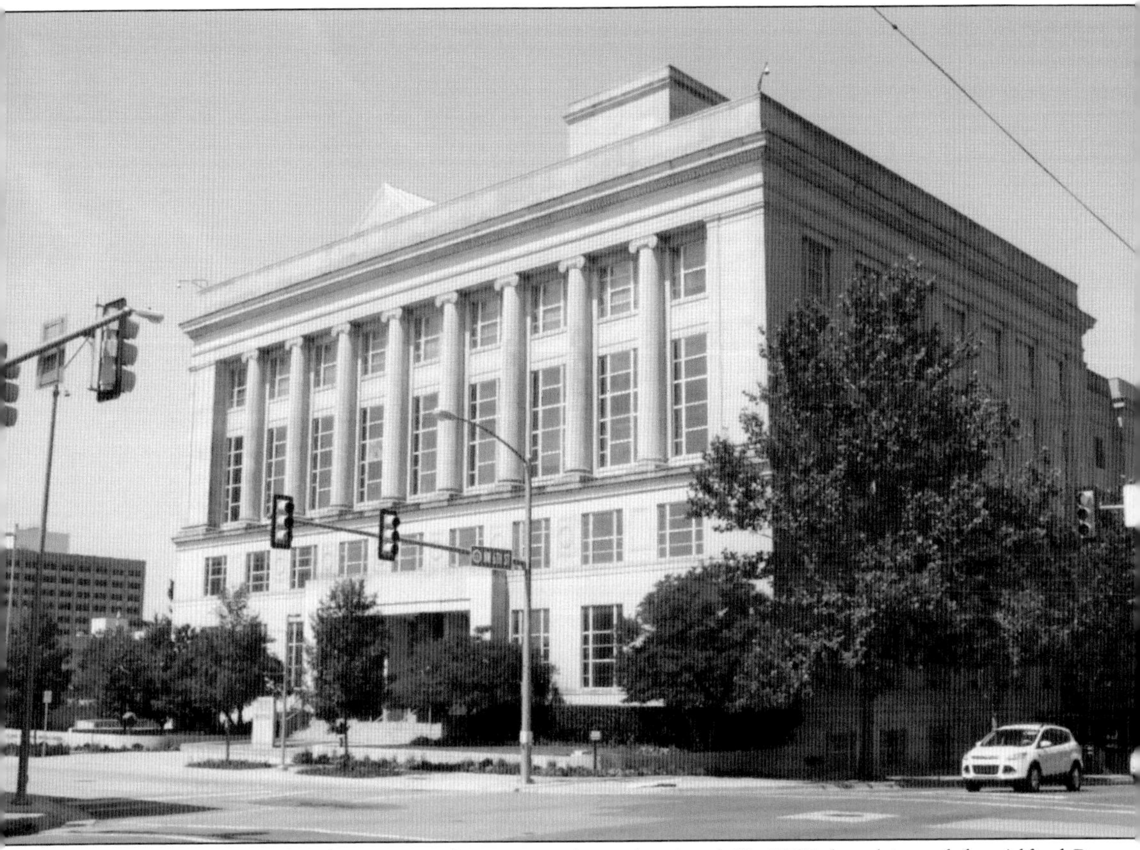

After surviving the devastating destruction from the April 19, 1995, bombing of the Alfred P. Murrah Federal Building, the former Temple and Journal Record newspaper building now houses the Oklahoma City Bombing Memorial's offices and museum at 621 North Robinson Avenue. The Journal Record was forced to relocate after the 1995 destruction of their offices. The building also houses the Memorial Institute for the Prevention of Terrorism, where training is offered to law enforcement agencies from around the nation about hate and extremist groups with the goal of preventing future events of terrorism. As of this writing, the museum and building are preparing to undergo a multimillion-dollar renovation and expansion. (Photograph by William Hider.)

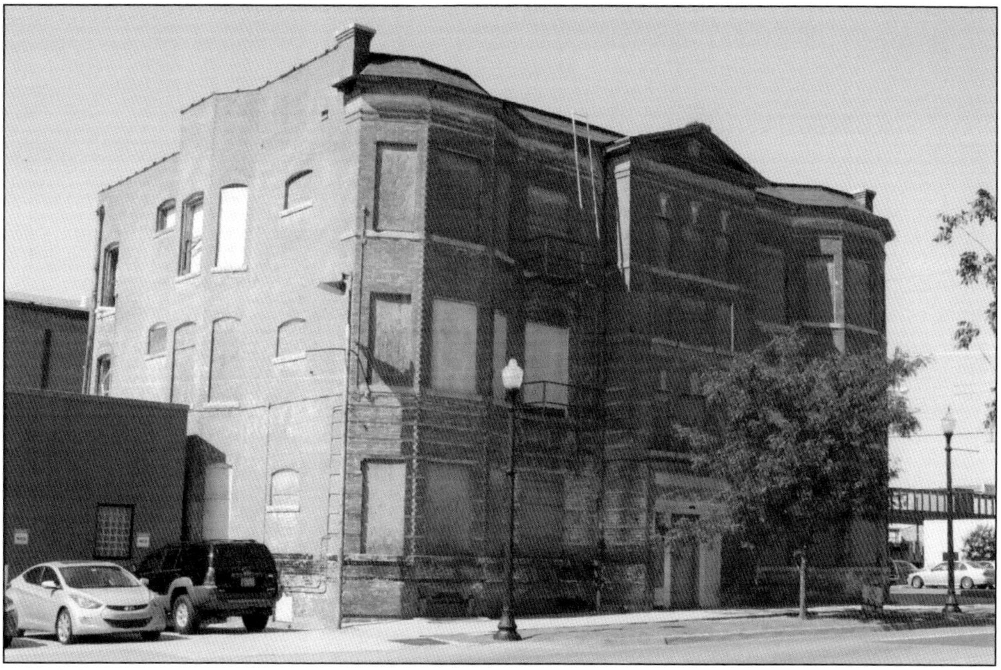

As of this writing, the former Marion Hotel at 110 Northwest Tenth Street is undergoing a complete renovation, after 110 years. Its spaces are being converted into 10 apartments ranging from approximately 1,250 square feet on the upper floors to about 600 feet in the basement. Project architect David Kraszewski states that restoration efforts will strip and renew the interior, while the exterior mostly retains its original look. After restoration, as seen in the rendering below, the Marion will be considered one of the oldest occupied structures in the city. (Above, photograph by William Hider; below, rendering courtesy of Midtown Renaissance.)

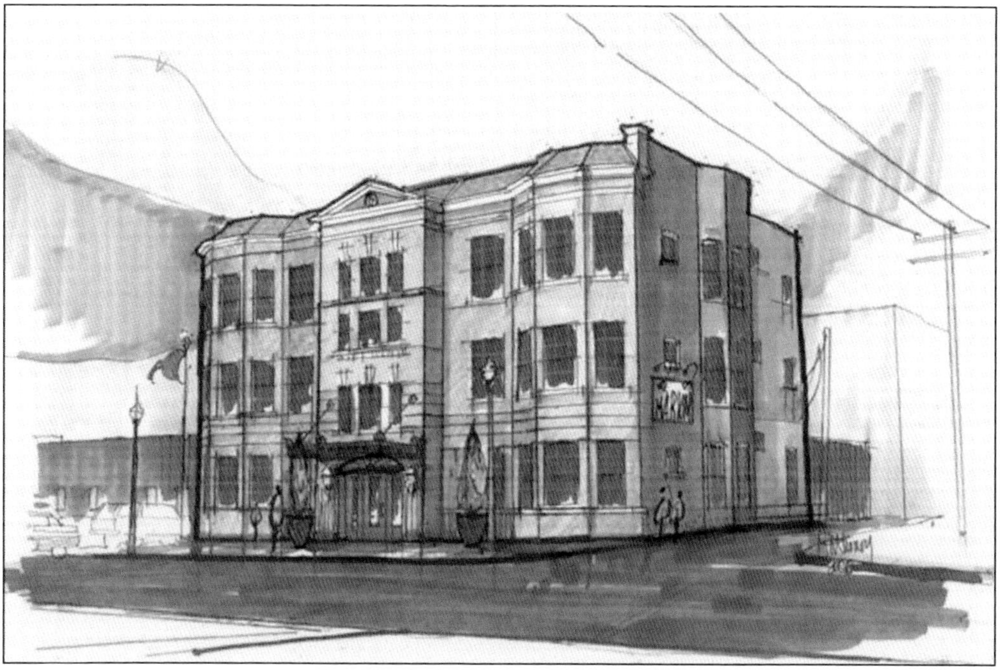

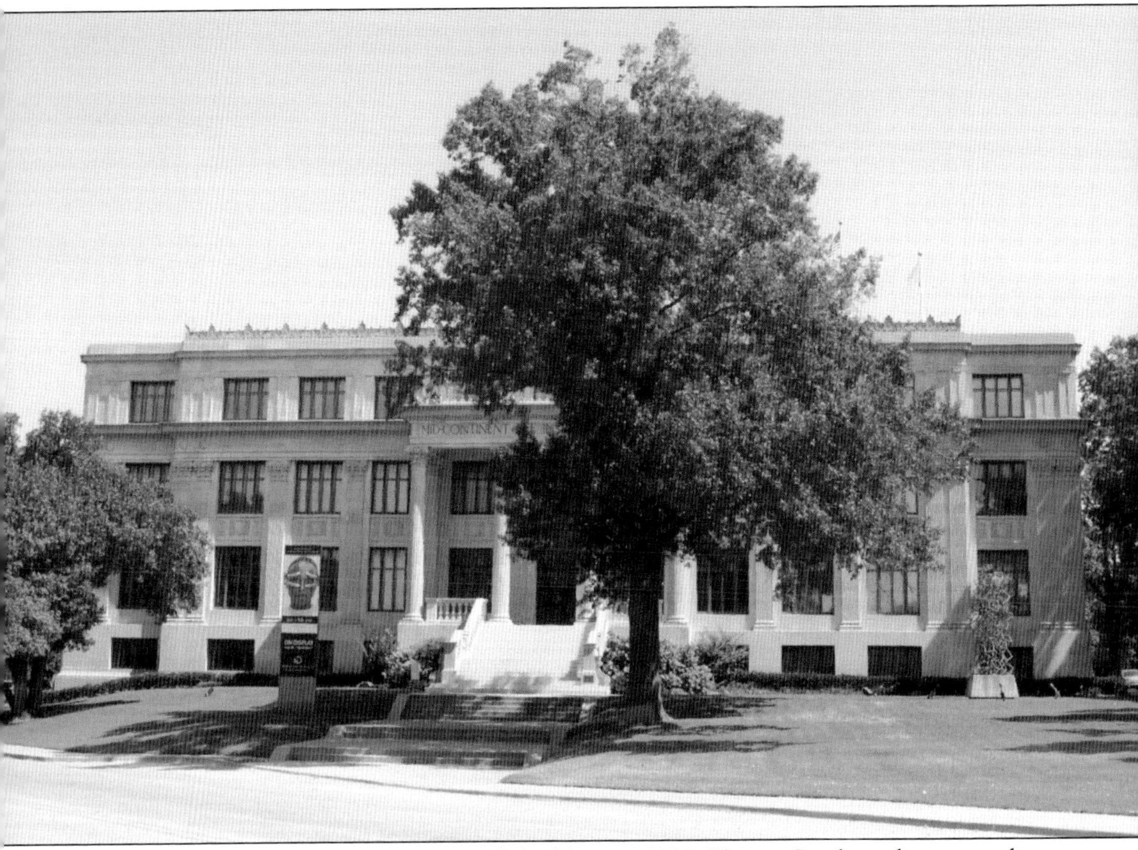

Today, the former Mid-Continent Life building at 1400 Classen Boulevard serves as home to the Oklahoma Heritage Association and the Gaylord Pickens Museum. The association was founded in 1927 by Anna B. Korn to recognize Oklahomans who have given outstanding service throughout their lifetime. The museum presents high-tech interactive exhibits that focus on telling Oklahoma's story through its people. The building was acquired by the association in 2001 from the American Fidelity Assurance Company with a gift from Oklahoma philanthropist E.K. Gaylord and has since received many awards. (Photograph by William Hider.)

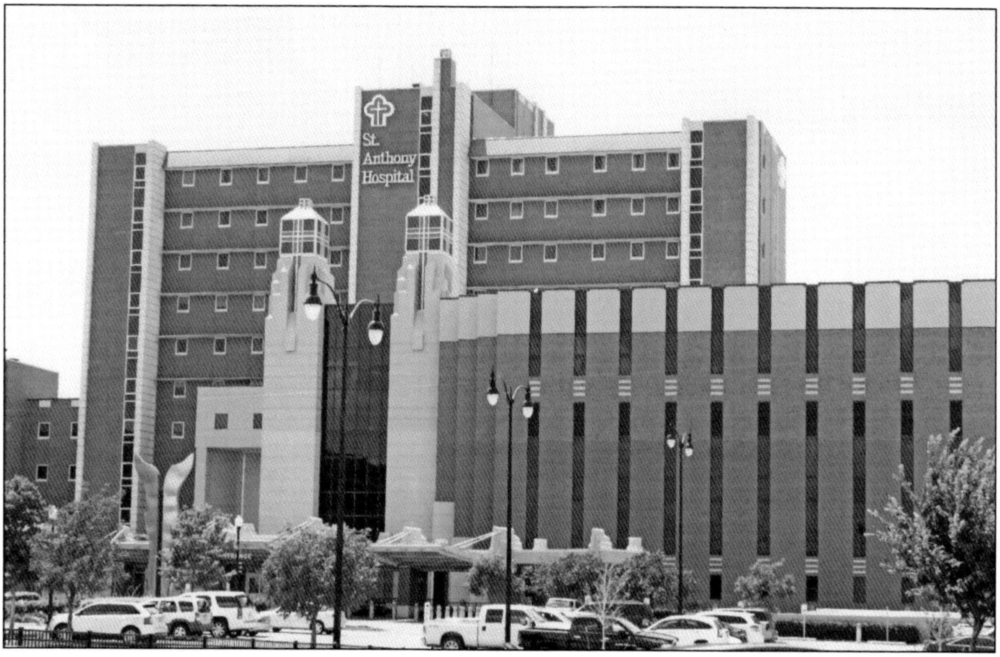

St. Anthony Hospital, pictured above, continues growing and as of this writing has begun construction near Northwest Eighth and Lee Avenue on another expansion, which includes additional beds, care facilities, and parking. The hospital continues to be ranked among one of Oklahoma's finest, which is an added bonus as it was also the state's first. Today, the Pasteur Medical Building at Northwest Tenth and Lee continues serving the health community and has changed very little on the exterior, as seen in the image below. It still houses clinics and doctor offices. (Both photographs by William Hider.)

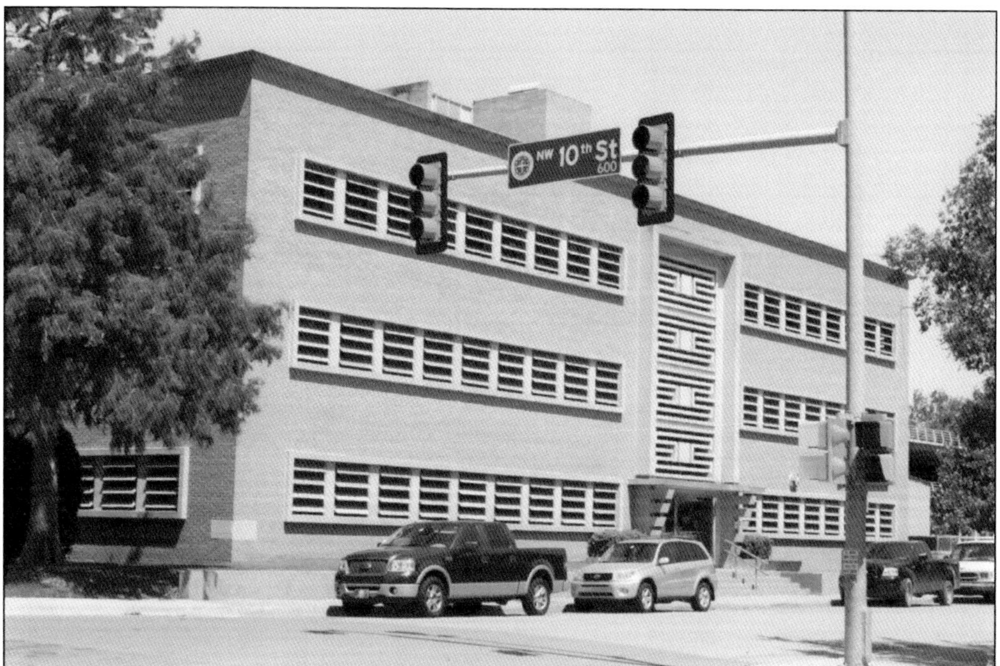

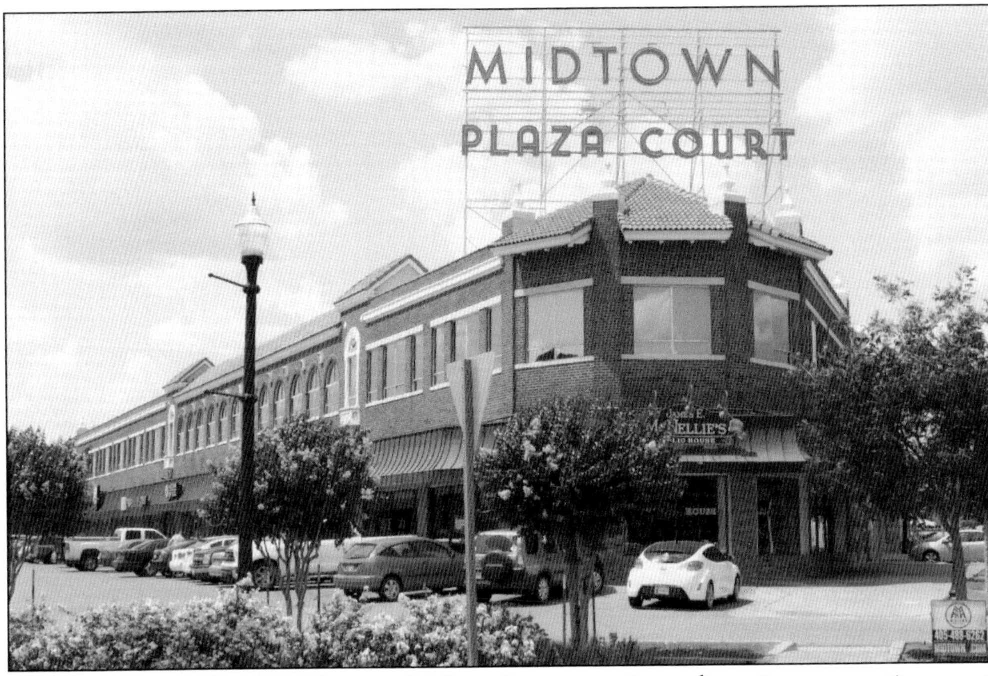

The Plaza Court (above) has become Midtown's center point and continues attracting guests to its many businesses, which includes a YMCA on the upper floor with cafés and retail below. The building's complete restoration has been a driving force that has inspired public support for the neighborhood. Just around the corner, the Ambassador Hotel (pictured below) is doing the same as it prepares to offer housing and office opportunities again. As of this writing, a complete exterior restoration and interior renovation is on track to be completed in 2014. (Both photographs by William Hider.)

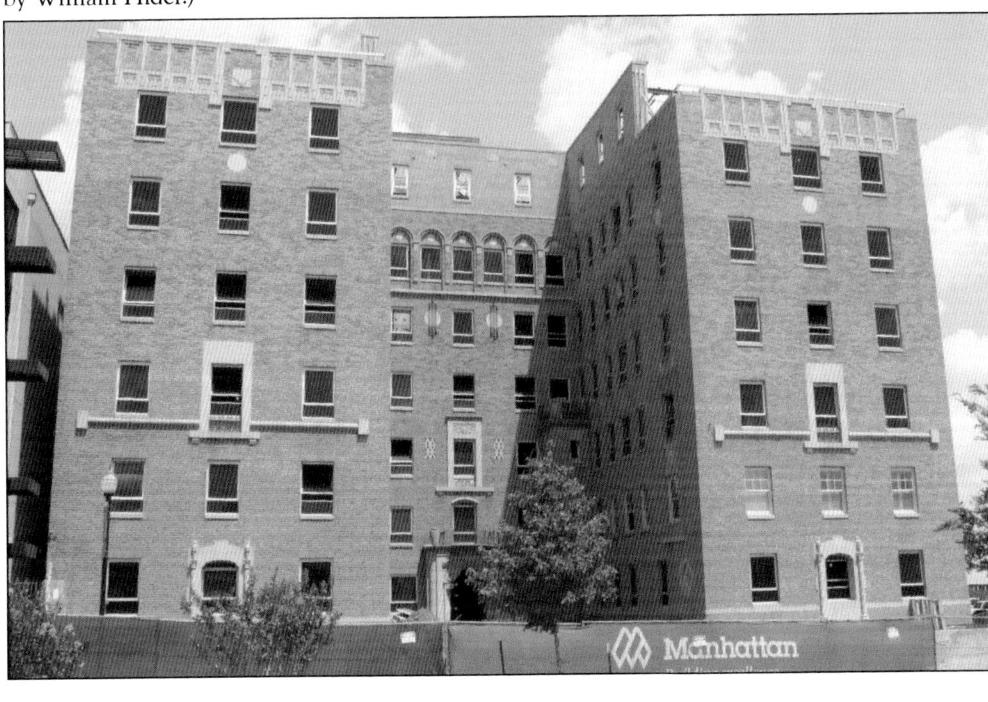

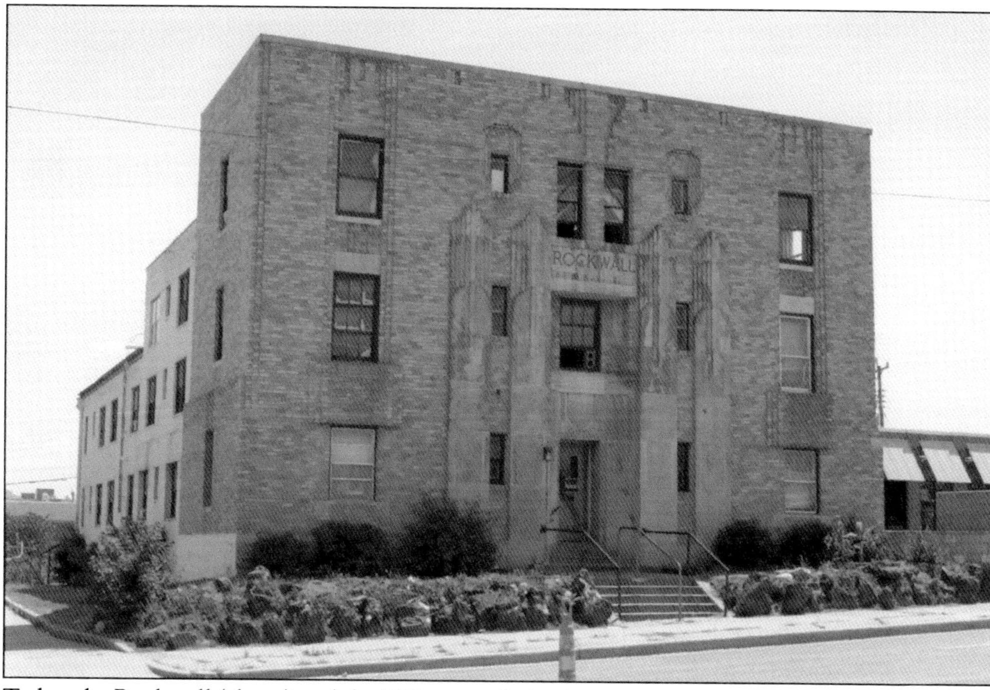

Today, the Rockwall (above) and the Hillerman (below) continue to serve as residential buildings, while the latter also hosts some businesses—including law firms. The Rockwall has often been overlooked in past years, but development and improvements in the area today have brought its unique facade back to life. The Hillerman building remains in the downtown corridor, surviving both Oklahoma City's Urban Renewal program from the 1970s to the 1980s and the terrorist attack on April 19, 1995. (Photograph by William Hider.)

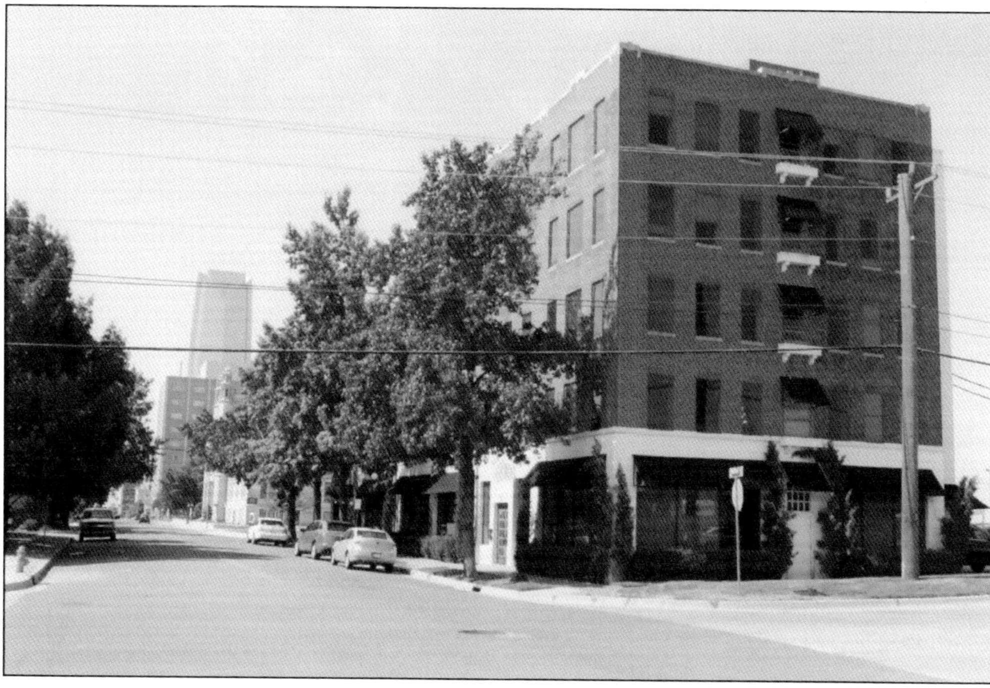

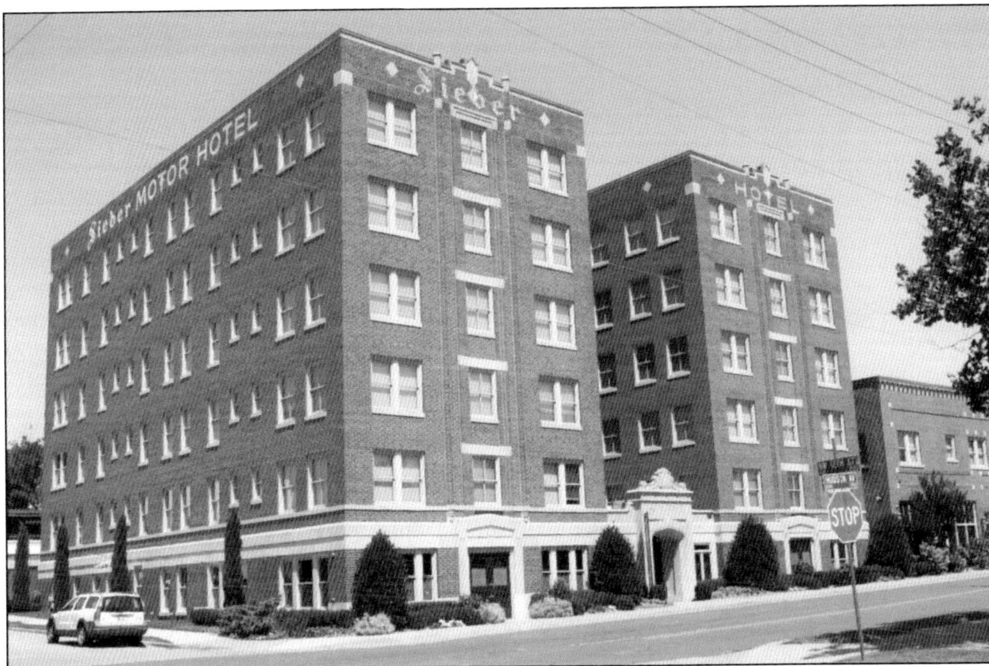

The former Sieber Hotel at 1305 North Hudson Avenue is now simply known as the Sieber and offers completely renovated rooms in impressive residential spaces. The neighborhood around it, once decimated with downtown exodus to the suburbs in the 1960s–1980s, is now becoming a solid anchor point for that portion of Midtown. (Photograph by William Hider.)

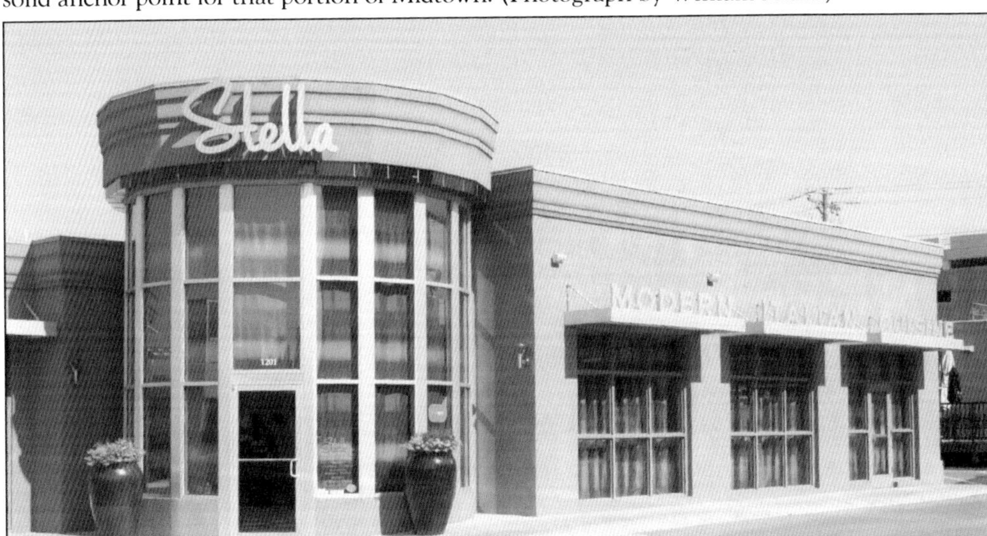

The former Anderson Pritchard service station has since been transformed into Stella, a modern Italian cuisine restaurant, which is across the street from the newly redeveloped Osler building. Stella's owners have enhanced the original design by adding their own embellishments, including flowerbeds filled with herbs for their signature dishes. The other most notable difference is the missing roof cupola. (Photograph by William Hider.)

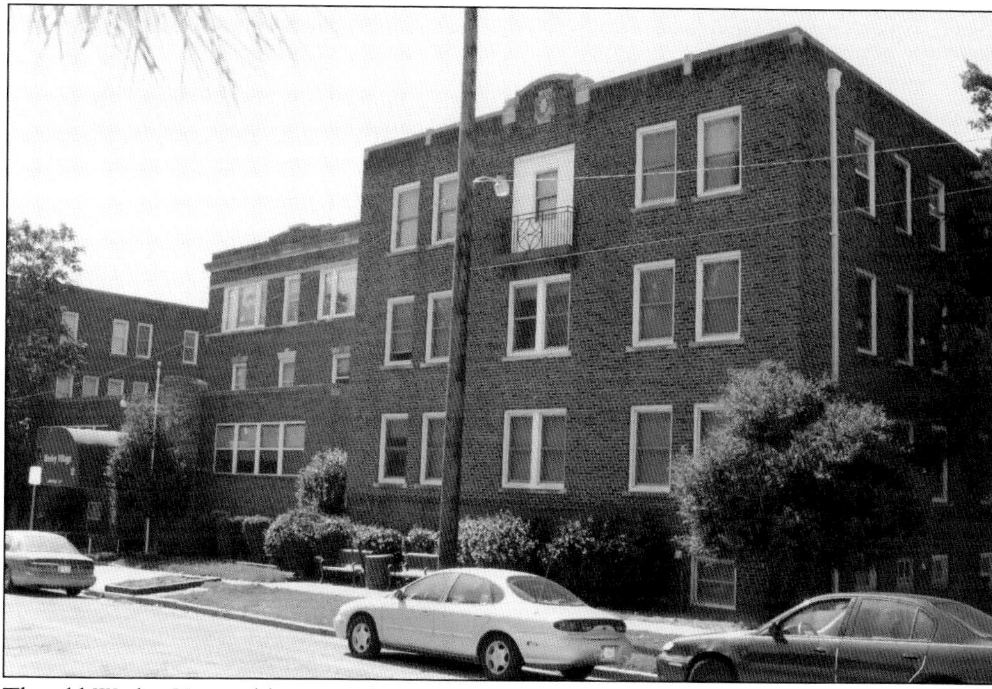

The old Wesley Hospital has since become the Wesley Village Retirement Community but was acquired by Midtown developers in 2005. At the time of this writing, the former hospital is being prepared for exterior renovation and will remain a senior center. The need for residential space in the Midtown area continues to grow. (Photograph by William Hider.)

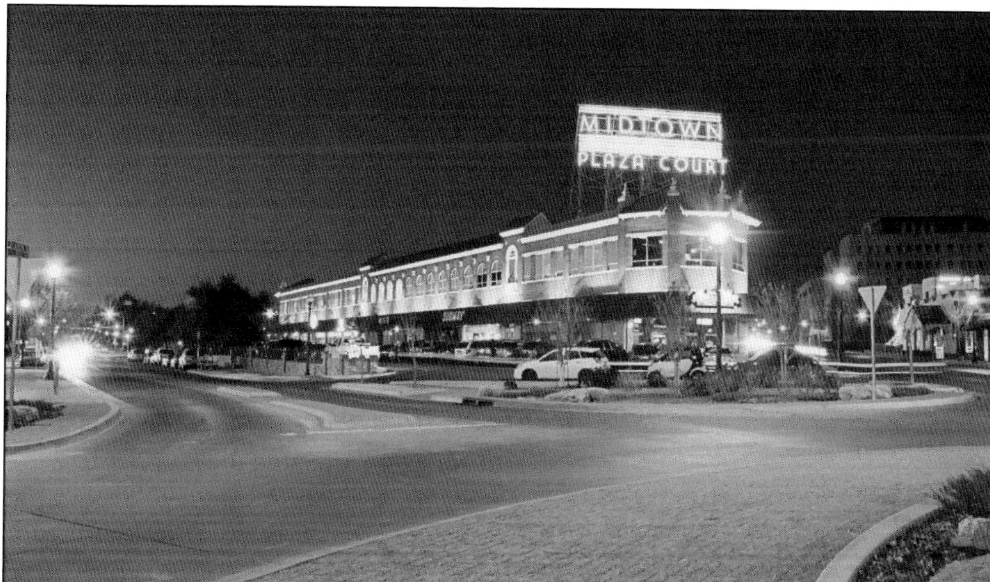

Midtown's most iconic and recognized structure, Plaza Court, now adorned with its restored neon crown, has reigned as queen over the Midtown community for nearly 90 years. The neighborhood surrounding her continues growing with numerous improvement projects that are either underway or forthcoming, all of them exciting and each of them filled with their own unique challenges. But what's a renaissance without a challenge or two? (Courtesy of the Midtown Renaissance Group.)